RENZO PIANO BUILDING WORKSHOP

Complete works

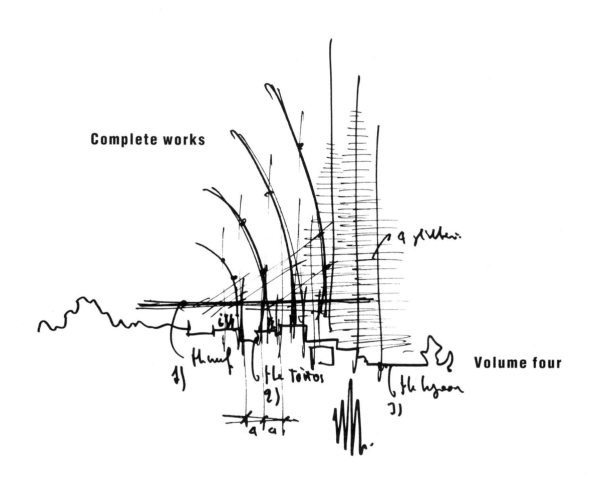

Volume four

Peter Buchanan

Contents

6

Gesturing to Context

The buildings and projects published in this volume confirm yet again the characteristic qualities of the works of the Renzo Piano Building Workshop as described in the introductory essays to the previous volumes in this series. Most immediately striking, as always, is the heterogeneity. The examples in this volume are utterly different from one another. The ship-like, green metal hull of the newMetropolis science and technology centre (pp36–55) floats above a transparent ground floor over the waters of Amsterdam's harbour, the sloping deck of its roof a public piazza offering a grandstand view of the old city. By contrast, the earth-bound walls of the Beyeler Foundation Museum (pp56–85) emerge gradually from the earth and water of a park near Basle to support an oversailing diaphanous steel and glass roof that settles as light as a butterfly on the dark stone walls. In a corner of a new vehicle development plant outside Stuttgart, the Mercedes-Benz Design Centre (pp124–35) has several oversailing roofs with smoothly silver curves that radiate horizontally to resemble a fragment of a gigantic turbine. By contrast, the curved and slatted wooden 'cases' of the Tjibaou Cultural Centre (pp86–117) reach skyward from the crest of a peninsula near Nouméa, New Caledonia. Almost as delicately filigreed as the cases, which establish such rapport with the surrounding vegetation, are the terracotta facades framing the public spaces of the vast and urban Potsdamer Platz scheme (pp156–213) in what had been a wasteland in central Berlin.

No other architect's œuvre exhibits anything like this diversity, which is not just of location, programme and materials, but of the architectural forms and details that are appropriate to all of these. Some schemes, such as the Beyeler Foundation Museum and Potsdamer Platz are recognizably by Piano. But even those familiar with his previous works were probably surprised on first encountering the project for the Tjibaou Cultural Centre. And, if not already tipped off, nobody would guess that the office towers now under construction, Aurora Place in Sydney (pp220–9) and the KPN-Telecom Tower in Rotterdam (pp214–19), are by the Building Workshop – nor indeed credit them as by the same architect. Crucially, there is nothing forced about this heterogeneity. It is not the result of spurious quests for novelty or demonstrating 'creativity'. Instead it arises from the goal that each design be right for the specifics of the situation from which it emerges, as if naturally and inevitably. Hence the diversity and perpetual freshness of designs which seem shaped less by the inevitable limits set by the personality, ambition and skills of the architect, than by an unprejudiced response to the world around and the pressures and potentials of our times.

Consequently the Building Workshop's architecture is consistently topical. Because architects work to commission to satisfy some current need or demand, their work is always in some way topical. But a lot of work by the Building Workshop seems exceptionally

1

Previous page Tjibaou Cultural Centre, Nouméa, New Caledonia, 1991–8: contemporary architecture with a resonant affinity with local vegetation and traditional buildings.

1 Ushibuka Bridge, Kumamoto, Japan, 1989–95. The simple, grand gesture of the horizontal sweep of the bridge is enlivened by repetitive smaller-scale incident.

2, **3** Atelier Brancusi, Paris, France, 1992–6: **2** view from courtyard; **3** inside reconstruction of studio.

timely and germane, both because of the kinds of projects undertaken and, more importantly, because of its particular approach to each project. Indeed the introductory essay to Volume three described how the projects included in it constitute almost a manual of exemplary contemporary practice, each showing an instructively pertinent approach to a crucial current architectural problem.

Yet there are also Piano projects that go beyond exemplifying the best of current thinking and practice, and instead are seminal in defining a paradigmatic new approach. The Pompidou Centre (Volume one pp52–63) encapsulated the emancipatory spirit of Paris in May 1968 by replacing cultural elitism and the isolation of the arts with an active and accessible machine in which the arts might interact with each other and all social strata. It profoundly altered the architecture of its time (though too often its legacy was manifested in countless exaggerated displays of structure and services). The UNESCO Neighbourhood Workshop, as used at Otranto, (Volume one pp68–77) deserved to be even more influential, as a brilliant strategy to regenerate rundown historic towns, by empowering rather than marginalizing or disrupting the local community. The Menil Collection (Volume one pp140–63) showed how a high-technology architecture as innovative as that of the Pompidou Centre could be a quiet backdrop for the contemplation of art and assimilated into a low-key neighbourhood setting.

These examples are from only the first volume of this series. In the preceding volume to this, the fourth, the most important seminal work is the Passenger Terminal of the Kansai International Airport (Volume three pp128–229). This shows how the computer can bring to architecture new geometric disciplines, with their own economies and efficiencies, as well as an unprecedented integration of the building's various systems. The terminal at last realizes and combines key ambitions that originally inspired, and ever since have underlain, the whole development of modern architecture (or at least what some have called its bio-technic strand): that of approximating the efficiency of a machine and the unity of an organism, as well as the tight fit between function and form that both exemplify.

In this volume the prime candidates for such seminal status are the Potsdamer Platz scheme and, perhaps more so, the Tjibaou Cultural Centre. Both are hybrids that look to the past and the future to draw on and fuse traditional and historical elements with contemporary technology and practice. Both are concerned with reconciliation after tragedy. Potsdamer Platz resurrects something of the spirit of what had been the liveliest part of Berlin, before being destroyed by Allied bombing and the division of the city into East and West. The cultural centre commemorates the Kanak people's murdered leader, Jean-Marie Tjibaou, as well as their culture that has been disrupted by colonialism. Both schemes play their parts in the larger projects

2

3

4

newMetropolis: Centre for Science and
Technology, Amsterdam, 1992–7. Views of
roof terrace during opening ceremony.
4 Looking westwards.
5 View to north-west and post office
sorting centre.
6 View from outside roof entrance towards
Maritime Museum.

5

of recovery and reintegration after the depre-
dations of the whole modern era, including
colonialism as well as the various forms of
'development' that have destroyed nature
and our cities. And they do so in their design
approaches as well as programmatically. The
issues addressed and the ways of addressing
them could hardly be more topical.

With the Potsdamer Platz scheme in Berlin,
Piano has created a 'piece of the city', complete, for once, with round-the-clock city life:
a vibrant urban quarter in which to live, work,
shop and be entertained. This resurrects the
city's historic street and block patterns and
reconnects what were East and West Berlin,
even connecting the lumpy anti-urban buildings of the Kulturforum into the reunified
German capital. It is, however, the handling of
the spaces of the public realm, and of the
facades of the buildings that frame these, that
are the most seminal aspects of the scheme,
even though there is precedent for both.

Here, the spaces that make up the public
realm are not merely residual, left over after
designing the buildings, nor do they merely
form a neat pattern which has been carefully
detailed with pavings, street furniture and so
on (which is about as far as most such
schemes tend to go nowadays). Instead the
spaces, and the network they form, are
carefully configured to achieve several crucial goals. Not least of these is that mere location within the network confers particular
characteristics to a specific place, even before
being elaborated formally. Together, the

9

6

1

10   Beyeler Foundation Museum, Basle, 1991–7.
1 View from path to entrance across pond in
front of south porch.
2 Looking past Monet's Water Lilies to lily
pond and garden.
3 At dusk both the inside and outside, and
the way these interpenetrate, can be seen.

2

configuration of the network, and the spaces forming it, bestow upon the whole area a richly articulated character and coherence, made up of a variety of hierarchically organized parts (from busy focal spaces to quiet backwaters) each with their own character. This same framework could in future permit, yet control, change by ensuring a certain continuity of character as well as undiminished coherence should any or all of the buildings be replaced. Hence it is the equivalent of what was known as a 'capital web', once a key concept in American urban design theory and a precedent which has been forgotten until unknowingly resurrected by Piano.

The nature of this urban space network (or capital web) and the design guidelines that conditioned the various architects' responses to it, have together ensured the urbane qualities of the area. Key guidelines are those insisting on recessed arcades to shelter pedestrians and a cladding material with the earthy colour and texture associated with brick or stone – yet which is also a repetitive industrial product (or family of such products) that can invest buildings with great vivacity and lightness. The precedent for this lies in Piano's own work, for this is yet another exercise in terracotta cladding. In this instance, the Building Workshop have worked up a whole vocabulary and syntax to clad different building types. Thus a thread of similarly clad buildings run right through the site, like the cello and harpsichord continuo in Baroque music, against which the other archi-

tects' buildings play in counterpoint. As with the public realm network, the theme is of unity in diversity. On the office towers at the extremities of the scheme, the terracotta is supplemented with an outer layer of glass louvres to achieve energy savings without sacrificing direct contact with the outdoors.

Yet the terracotta cladding, particularly of the Building Workshop designs, achieves something more difficult and rare today: the area would feel comfortable to stroll through even if empty. This is normal in an historic city, but virtually all modern buildings and urban areas tend to feel like dry and lifeless husks when deserted and not in use. But here the facades have a mellow warmth of colour and texture, an abundance of human-scale incident and a liveliness to the eye that help one to feel at home here. This is very different to the alienation instilled by frostily forbidding modern architecture, a feeling compounded by the undefined, and so essentially unvaried, outdoor spaces with which it is customarily surrounded.

The Tjibaou Cultural Centre is to play a crucial role in the conservation and continuing evolution of Kanak culture, helping to revitalize its roots while adapting to, and drawing on, new circumstances. Its architecture is sensitively attuned to the traditional buildings and culture of the indigenous people. Yet, despite unambiguously evoking traditional Kanak huts, the building treads nowhere near the pitfalls of kitsch or the overly imitative folkloric. Its forms also

3

4

Tjibaou Cultural Centre, Nouméa, New Caledonia, 1991–8.

4 The projecting ribs of the cases and the varied spacing of the slats establish a harmony with the surrounding vegetation.

5 Night view of a case.

6 Section and elevations of traditional Kanak huts.

7 For all the differences in form, the cases capture something of the spirit of the traditional huts under construction, and still unthatched, in the foreground.

5

6

7

suggest an exceptionally close harmony with the surrounding vegetation and its spirits that the Kanak worship, as well as with the trade winds on which they sailed and that now ventilate this building. Though built by the French government, the architects worked closely with representatives of the local people so that now the Kanaks and other peoples of this Pacific region claim the building as theirs: an evolution of, but still part of, their culture. Yet it is uncompromisingly contemporary. Here is an object lesson in fusing the local and the global, the traditional and the modern, a reverence for nature and up-to-the-minute technology.

Potsdamer Platz and the Nouméa cultural centre are architectural milestones that address very topical issues in ways that are immensely instructive, if properly engaged with and considered. Both schemes are deeply appealing: Potsdamer Platz for the vibrancy of urban life it shelters; Nouméa for evoking a dream of co-existing in harmony with nature in an Eden-like paradise. This, together with Piano's established position in the architectural firmament, are bringing them widespread but, so far, superficial attention. Many architects and critics seem unsure as quite what to make of these schemes, and their ambivalence tends to suspend, rather than spur, more inquisitive engagement.

There are those who claim that the Berlin buildings are too conventional – yet some of these then argue that if buildings are to be conventional, then these are not sufficiently

so. For them, the terracotta is too obviously just a thin facade and has none of the sense of depth and mass suggested by the stone and brick of 'the new heaviness' advocated by influential Berlin architects. Yet the latter buildings are as mute and creepily alienating as those in a de Chirico painting. By contrast, it is Piano's buildings that transcend this curse of so much modern architecture, to once again provide a warm and vivacious backdrop that is as comforting and comfortable as traditional architecture.

The 'cases' of the Nouméa cultural centre are strikingly strange: exotic, enigmatic and immensely evocative. Yet some have expressed unease simply because they were originally inspired by Kanak huts, no matter how different they are now. But what unsettles more people is how big and complex is each case in relation to the space enclosed and the climatic control achieved. The largest cases reach up 28 metres, as high as the tallest naves of Gothic cathedrals, yet enclose only comparatively modest single-storey spaces. This is fair criticism, especially from the rational and utilitarian perspective that dominated much modernism.

Yet the precise relevance of this building could be that it transcends the modern paradigm and belongs to a new era. Here the cathedral analogy is telling, for a Gothic cathedral is also hugely tall and complex for a single-storey meeting hall. Perhaps the Nouméa cultural centre is best seen as a semi-sacred building, a secular temple of a new era

11

1, **2** Ferrari Wind Tunnel, Maranello
(Modena), Italy, 1996–8. The tunnel is raised
at an angle for increased formal impact.
3 Mercedes-Benz Design Centre,
Sindelfingen (Stuttgart), Germany 1993–8.
The studio bays are flooded with light from the
clerestoreys and fully glazed ends.

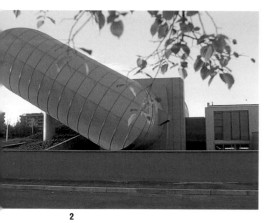

in which nature is not merely a resource to be exploited. The building suggests a reverence for the plants it establishes such affinities with, the winds that whisper in its slats and the sun which casts the slatted patterns that enliven all its parts. Even the insistence of the Kanak clients that the building's elements be immediately legible in terms of their interrelationships and structural functions corresponds with the vision that everything in the world carries a narrative and so is invested with human meaning. This is not superstition but the only way we will once more feel fully at home in the world.

A building such as this challenges peoples' expectations and intellectual 'comfort zones'. Belonging to an emerging era that we are enticed by, but not yet ready for, it is, like the Kansai terminal, far more significant than any work by those still considered avantgarde – a modernist notion that is now very tired. But with the widespread confusions that limit the critical appreciation of architecture today, Nouméa might be hailed as merely another formal extravaganza establishing some place, and its architect, on the map – what is now widely called (after Frank Gehry's Guggenheim) the 'Bilbao effect'.

A curse of our pluralist times is a lack of discernment. The tolerant label of pluralism suggests that the plethora of current design approaches all have value; but it really conceals a crucial inability to discriminate between what is frivolous and fashionable and what is of both topical and lasting value. This

is certainly a time of great vitality in architecture. Much good work is being produced. But there is even more dross, and much of this is acclaimed too. That architects and critics disagree as to what is of value and what is merely dross, confirms the confusions that underlie pluralism. Yet the confusions within architecture are largely a reflection, or intensification, of those pervading all of contemporary culture. This is a subject worth dwelling on briefly because to do so throws more light on the topicality of Piano's architecture.

The current confusions in our culture result from this being a period of major transition. As numerous pundits claim, we are witnessing the breakdown of the cultural paradigm of the modern era which had started to emerge along with science 400 years ago and was consolidated during the Enlightenment. Today's confusions are compounded because the nature of the new cultural paradigm is still far from clear, but two conflicting models seem to be emerging. The crucial distinguishing feature of the three paradigms (the modern and those competing to replace it) are their views of reality – or what constitutes for each its touchstone of truth.

The modern paradigm has been characterized many ways, as scientific, mechanistic, reductionist, rationalist, progressivist, utilitarian, all of which apply. But behind these and other characterizations lies a single idea: that there is an objective reality, external to, and quite independent of each of us. To

4

5

Banco Popolare di Lodi, Lodi, Italy 1991–8.

4 Central precinct sheltered by suspended glass canopy.

5 Portion of west facade facing broad new street.

6 Above the roof seen in **4** which is supported by cables radiating from drum of auditorium on left.

people in other cultures, or prior to the Enlightenment, this would have been a strange idea: reality for them lay in the interplay between the observed and the observer who could influence the gods and even the largest and most distant of natural phenomena through ritual, sacrifice and so on – all the things the modern view rejects as superstition.

Though now much criticized for its failings, it is as well to remember that modernity has been stupendously successful: it has brought immense benefits in material wealth, knowledge, medicine, communications and all other forms of technology. It also seems to be an inevitable and necessary phase to pass through before reaching the next long-term paradigm that will replace it. But, with its emphasis on the objective observer and rational method, it has also been profoundly alienating, discounting and so severing us from so many of our reciprocal interactions with others and the world – and even from much of our own psyche beyond the rational mind. This is the desensitized mind-set that has led to social, psychological, urban and ecological breakdown.

Freud at the turn of the century, and then especially quantum mechanics in the 1920s, initiated the erosion of the modern paradigm. This has gathered increasing momentum since the 1960s, as the negative consequences and internal contradictions of modernity have become increasingly apparent. We are thus in the age of postmodernism. But the postmodernism now dominant and so much

debated might prove to be merely a transitional phase.

To distinguish it from what might be the longer-term paradigm, this transitional phase has been called Deconstructionist Postmodernism (in particular by cultural critic Charlene Spretnak in the *Resurgence of the Real*, Addison-Wesley 1997). In it, the pendulum of what is deemed to be reality has swung to the opposite extreme. The notion of an objective reality has been replaced by one in which what is taken for reality is merely an arbitrary social construct or a consensual hallucination. Yet this idea challenges common sense, particularly of the scientific among us; and a paradigm, by definition, should be in such accord with current common sense as to be unquestionable. Moreover, this transitional postmodernism shares and even intensifies many of the modernity's most problematic aspects, not least those that result in its hyperindividualism and its abstractions from physical reality. Besides, replacing the modern era's central legitimizing narrative of progress with the rejection of all such 'grand narratives' is not only equally alienating but compounds this with a strong streak of nihilism.

Fortunately, another paradigm has been emerging which is much more likely to prevail over the long term: this corresponds with what Spretnak calls Ecological Postmodernism. It is predicated on a larger reality, which also furnishes its 'grand narratives': the unfolding cosmological processes

13

6

1

2

Potsdamer Platz, Berlin, Germany, 1992–9.

1 Portion of terracotta facade showing range of elements used.

2 Top of southern elevation of Debis tower.

3 Looking south along top of shopping arcade towards Debis tower. The buildings to the right, of which the facades are visible, are by the Building Workshop.

that science is revealing to us, and the biological and social evolution which extend these processes, and which we have been affecting with increasing potency. It is neither the objective reality of modernism, external to and untouched by us, nor the mere mental projection of conventional postmodernism. Instead it is a complexly unfolding, multifaceted process in which mankind plays a creative and participative role. This much expanded, more integrative view of reality, made up of complex webs of interacting and interactive enmeshments, is the antithesis of alienating reductionism, mechanicism and rationalism. Engaged through more than the mind, this reality is also experiential; and all experience is shaped by context, as well as enhanced by an awareness of how it is embedded in multiple contexts.

Most of today's architecture conforms to either the crumbling modern or the transitional postmodern perspectives. Some of the most highly regarded of current approaches, such as high-tech and minimalism, might be best understood as attempts to stake out a very narrow, and so critically safe, territory within the ruins of modernity. And the spuriousness of much current theorizing and form-making could be explained as consistent with the Deconstructionist view of reality as merely an arbitrary human construct, and any creative endeavour as little more than a game. However, just as the greatest of the early twentieth-century architects transcended modernity, so there are architects

today whose work points towards aspects of this emerging paradigm.

What then are likely to be the characteristics of this new architecture? For a start, design would involve much more than serving function, organizing and expressing construction and services, and responding to context. Instead, it would involve analysing and intuiting all the forces that might impact in any way on the place or programme, and then guiding these forces to ends best suited to not just the client and user but also to the larger world around: the city, its citizens and nature with all its ambient forces and creatures. Design of this sort is an art not of imposition, but of detecting and bringing into play latent potentials, of helping these all to flower into form. Rather than being a constraint, it involves a vastly expanded kind of creativity, one less egotistical than in the former paradigms. The results would be regenerative, reintegrative and reconciliatory, not just helping the new to be born but also to heal the modern era's assaults on the city and the psyche, on community, nature and the particularities of place. As an ideal, design is a mode of participating in as much as possible in as many ways as possible.

Perhaps the most immediately graspable idea already emerging in architecture is that it should be conceived and appraised in all its multiple contexts. Today a new building must be considered in terms of both its local context (of neighbouring buildings, history, traditional materials and constructional

3

4

5

6

methods, micro-climate and eco-niches, etc.) and a global context (of universally available technologies, international media and common critical debates, etc.).

The architectural practice whose work (certainly in sympathies and instincts) tends closest to this characterization is the Renzo Piano Building Workshop. This is ultimately what makes Piano's architecture so topical, and also why in these pluralist times it has yet to be widely recognized that his approach is more than merely yet another amongst many. This may also be because it is not an approach that was immediately or consciously arrived at, nor theorized about in lecture halls and publications. Instead Piano has been evolving slowly towards such an approach as guided by his instincts and openness to the contributions of his collaborating clients, colleagues and consultants. His is an architecture that aims to engage, in a spirit of participation rather than imposition, with all its multiple contexts. In particular, with each project Piano always seeks the balance that is appropriate to the specifics of programme, place and time, between responding to and using what is available in the local context (in terms of materials, craft skills, etc.), and what is imported from the global context in which he also operates.

Kenneth Frampton recognizes this when he says that in Piano's work the implicit opposition between 'placeform' and 'produktform' has been resolved. Yet most architects today combine forms and materials that are taken from, or respond to, the place with those that are standard industrial products. What is different about Piano is that the prime repetitive components, what he calls the 'pieces', are unique to project and place. The 'piece', which (with one or two recent exceptions) is always utterly intrinsic to the identity of a Piano building, is both the 'produktform' and inextricably part of the 'placeform'. Perhaps it is Frampton's emphasis on form that confuses. Piano is concerned more fundamentally with process and equilibrium. For instance, with deciding what ways of doing things (uses of materials, technology, craft and form) should be local in source and/or associations, and what ways of doing things should be drawn from those universally available; and what should be the balance between these, as well as between what is conventional and what is innovative.

However, Piano's approach to design is continually evolving. The work in this volume, particularly the newest projects, suggests that there has been a change in the degree and the way in which the buildings respond to context. Some threshold has been crossed and the gestural response to context is increasingly taking precedence over rigorous piece-by-piece assembly. The introductory essay to Volume three charts the evolution of Piano's design approach until just prior to this new phase. The earliest projects were very narrowly focused on the shaping of lightweight components and their assembly – design in this phase tended to progress from

15

7

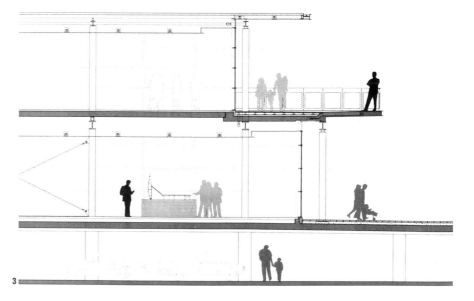

1

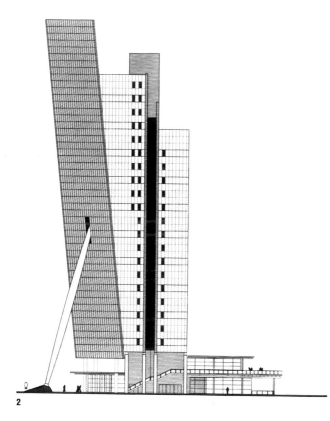

16

2

KPN-Tower, Rotterdam, 1997–9.
1 Model shows how towers by Building
Workshop and Foster and Partners, to the
left and right respectively of mast of Erasmus
Bridge, form 'book ends' to future
development of wharf.
2 Elevation from river Maas with main,
electronic billboard facade angled to be seen
from river and leaning forward at same angle
as stays of bridge.
3 Part section through podium that
accommodates public uses.

the particular to the general. Over the years,
and with each project, the range of Piano's
design concerns expanded and design has
proceeded by working both from particulars
upwards and from the general downwards.

Ever since The Menil Collection (Volume
one pp140–63) the Building Workshop's
designs have been shaped by context. But it is
as if the contextual pressures focused pre-
dominantly inwards on the building, which
was shaped also by the pieces and their assembly. Hence The Menil roof and plan were conceived as microcosms of the urban grid in
which the museum is situated, and it is clad in
the same clapboarding as the surrounding
bungalows. Yet, the building is also dominated by the roof canopy that is assembled
from purpose-designed pieces to create ideal
light conditions throughout the gallery level.

The Beyeler Foundation Museum is clearly
a very similar sort of building. The parallel
walls which dominate its plan are almost like
a 'standing' wave pattern formed by the
'interference' of the rippling influence of the
boundary walls on the two long sides of the
narrow site. The stone with which these walls
are faced was chosen to resemble the local
sandstone with which the boundary walls and
Basle cathedral are built. The oversailing roof,
however, is shaped only according to its own
rigorous disciplines to create ideal, control-
lable light conditions. Even the very suggestive and temple-like portico ends, which add
such symbolic resonances, are in large part
merely the fortuitous by-product of the need

to have external columns to support the projecting roof without deep cantilever beams.
The rhetorical dimension might be mostly
unintentional, but it projects the building's
presence outwards to address the garden and
approaching visitors. Hence the Beyeler can
be seen as a near perfect summation of the
now familiar Piano approach, which, in retro-
spect, also hints at what is to come.

Some more recent designs are shaped
explicitly as a response to context, and are
much less a product of the pieces and their
assembly. The clearest example is new-
Metropolis which is a very direct, graphically
gestural response to the harbour context and
the road diving below it, and in which nothing could be called a piece. Architecturally,
the triumph of this design is that though the
external form clearly came first, a processional interior has been created which is so
convincing that it seems this could also have
initiated the design concept and generated its
final form.

Other new designs follow this trend to be
shaped even more so by context. They too are
shaped from outside inwards, with any
equivalent to a piece restricted to cladding
elements rather than distinctive structural
elements. But there is also a new dimension to
the way they respond to context which goes
beyond being shaped by inward pressures
from the context. Their forms seem to gesture
outwards to create their own selective connection with elements in the context. If previously there was something shyly passive

3

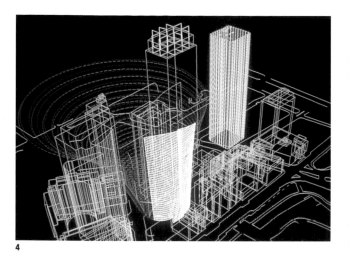

4

Aurora Place, Sydney, Australia, 1996–2000.
4, 6 Computer aerial perspectives showing
how shape of facade of office tower was
generated: **4** facade in its immediate context,
and **6** as abstracted from context.
5 Elevation from Royal Botanic Garden with
apartment block to left and taller office
tower behind.

about the way Piano's buildings were shaped by context, they are becoming more assertive, even brash, as they both reach out to their context and draw attention to themselves.

This trend is clearly illustrated by the two office towers now under construction. These both seemingly reach out to make explicit connection with the structures with which their respective cities are most closely identified. The gleaming white curves of the sculptural Aurora Place in Sydney will quite clearly dissociate it from its immediate company while gesturing to, and implying its relationship with, the Sydney Opera House some 700 metres away. The KPN-Telecom Tower in Rotterdam will fraternize with its neighbours, but these are the handsome new Erasmus Bridge in front of it and the as yet undesigned buildings behind it which will have to follow the conditions it dictates, such as extending a common plinth. The tower's leaning form and electronic billboard facade are contextual gestures unrelated to its internal workings; they gesticulate outwards to context rather that only reflecting internal function.

These two towers are the most extreme manifestations of a trend. But other designs, such as newMetropolis, Tjibaou Cultural Centre and the Ferrari Wind Tunnel (pp118–23) point in a similar direction. These are all buildings that are deliberately expressive in their forms – some might say expressionist. But though this trend is obvious, it is difficult, or might be too early, to decide definitively on what to make of it. For Piano,

it could represent a freeing-up, due perhaps to a greater confidence gained in his own design powers, and so less concerned with conceptual and aesthetic safety nets such as structural rigour or the assembly from, and maximum use of, repetitive components. On the other hand, these same characteristics might represent the absence of Peter Rice's structural and critical contribution. (Indeed it is interesting to speculate on what Rice might have thought about a building like the Sydney office tower, which in its way pays homage to the Sydney Opera House on which he started his professional career.)

All this may lead to yet greater heterogeneity in Piano's output, while the designs will become more personal – which will be paradoxical because to date the heterogeneity has arisen from the absence of a constraining personal idiom. Certainly, the new designs seem more overtly wilful in form than those in the earlier of these volumes. But need this threaten the participative ethos – whereby design proceeded by quietly divining and registering the inward ripples of the various forces in the building's multiple contexts – rather than brashly gesticulating and sending ripples back? Or, perhaps it is that to truly participate in the unfolding of our world it is actually necessary to enter into an even more active dialogue with context than Piano has pursued to date. We cannot yet know for certain the answers to such questions; but it is part of the continuing topicality of Piano's architecture that it provokes us to ponder them.

17

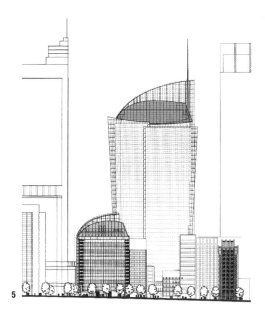

5

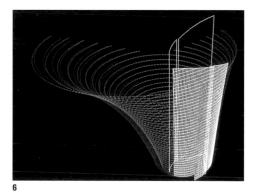

6

18

Ushibuka Bridge Kumamoto, Japan 1989–96

Just as context can provoke an increasingly expressive response from Piano, as several designs in this volume testify, so it might also elicit understatement. This is true even of the design of a bridge, currently a chic commission among architects from whom it tends to provoke virtuoso exhibitionism. Hence the beautiful and varied backdrops of the Ushibuka Bridge led to a design that, instead of competing for attention with the setting, impinges on it as little as possible visually and physically. The bridge has been reduced to the barest of statements: just a horizontal girder of constant cross section sweeping in a broad horizontal curve over a few equally reticent piers. Yet for all this simplicity, a closer view, or the experience of actually crossing the bridge, reveals it to be enlivened by smaller-scale incident.

Ushibuka, on the south-western tip of the Amakusa Peninsula, is in the Kumamoto prefecture on the west coast of Japan's southern island of Kyushu. The Building Workshop's commission – to design a bridge across the mouth of Ushibuka's busy fishing harbour – was awarded as part of the Kumamoto Artpolis project. Initiated by the then governor of the prefecture, Morihiro Hosokawa, the project sought to raise the prefecture's profile and add another dimension to its identity by erecting innovative buildings and other structures in the city of Kumamoto and the towns and countryside surrounding it. To this end, Arata Isozaki and Hajime Yatsuka were appointed as commissioners responsible for the selection, appointment and briefing of architects. As well as choosing established (and for the most part Japanese) architects – such as the Building Workshop, Martinez-Lapeña & Torres, Tadao Ando, Toyo Ito and Kazuo Shinohara – most of the projects were given to young up-and-coming or as yet unknown architects.

As usual, Piano chose to design the bridge in collaboration with the late Peter Rice, the structural engineer from Ove Arup & Partners; it is one of their last joint designs. The architect in charge was Noriaki Okabe, then an associate of the Building Workshop who had moved back to Japan to supervise the design and construction of the Kansai International Airport Passenger Terminal (Volume three pp128–229). Hence both the Genoa and Osaka offices were involved in developing the

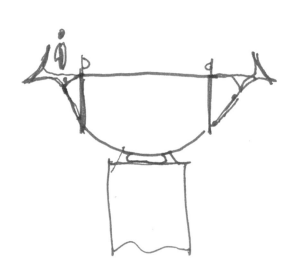

1

Ushibuka Bridge

Previous page Night view shows how bridge is illuminated to great effect, accentuating the contrast between simple big gestures and insistently repetitive smaller-scale articulations.

Preliminary studies.
1 Peter Rice viewing the site.
2 Aerial photograph shows buildings squeezed between mountains and sea and curving arc of bridge across mouth of fishing harbour.
3 Model of portion of bridge and supporting pier.
4 Location plan of bridge with unbuilt helical ramp connection to island.

2

design. The local collaborating engineer was the Maeda Engineering Corporation.

Piano visited the site with Rice and Okabe. On seeing the lushly vegetated, bumpy hills of the peninsula, the intricate scale of the fishermen's houses crowded between the hills and the water's edge, as well as the nearby islands arising from the Ariake Sea, they decided that the bridge should be quietly unobtrusive – or as much as is possible for a bridge 900 metres long and elevated above the sea by 19 metres. It was also

apparent that another crucial consideration would be the wind and its impact on the safety of users, especially pedestrians and cyclists. Thus the bridge is designed to be unobtrusive in another way, causing minimal air turbulence while also deflecting wind high above the road bed and the pavements on either side.

To keep the bridge as restrained and recessive as possible, all notions of suspension structures, or other visually complex solutions, were dismissed in favour of the simplest of forms. A 4.8 metre-deep steel box-girder structure was chosen to curve across the water in a single clean arc, supported by simple rectangular concrete piers set as much as 150 metres apart. To visually soften the form of the girder, as well as to smooth the air flow below it, the girder's underside is curved and its internal structural framing is enveloped in a sheath of flush-jointed welded steel plate.

Providing a shadowy, rhythmic articulation to the curving girder are triangular steel brackets reaching out along either side. Spaced at regular 2.5 metre intervals, these support 2.5 metre-wide pedestrian pavements made up of precast concrete units. The

pavements are set below the road deck so that people in cars can see over the baffles that protect the pedestrians from the wind. These baffles, the design and placing of which had been refined in wind tunnel tests, are rectangular panels that are dished in section and made of glass reinforced cement (grc). They are placed and angled to deflect strong winds over the vehicles as well as the pedestrians; yet the baffles also admit enough slow-moving air, between their backs and the pavement edge, to maintain sufficient air pressure above the pavement and road deck to prevent wind eddies gusting down onto them.

Cast steel elements secure the grc baffles to the ends of the large brackets supporting the pavements. Viewed close to, the shape of these castings, like that of the baffles, gives the huge structure the sense of tactility, at the human scale, that usually

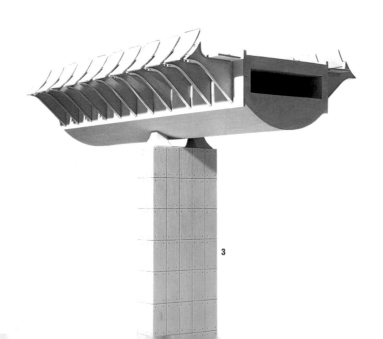

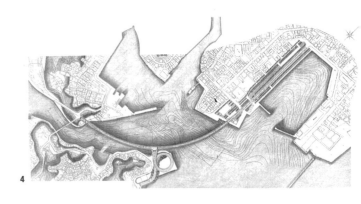

3

4

5

6

7

8

Ushibuka Bridge

Construction.

5 Cantilevered end of box girder awaits next portion.

6–8 Portions of bridge being lifted into place by floating crane.

9 Section through sea with bridge in elevation.

characterizes Piano's work. Behind the baffles and edging the pavements are steel balustrades detailed with the delicacy typical of the Building Workshop. These provide further small-scale incident to accompany the pedestrians. They are mostly concealed from distant views by the baffles, as they would have seemed too spindly and insubstantial in comparison with the huge scale of the whole bridge.

The six rectangular hollow concrete piers that support the box girder are not evenly spaced. They were instead erected where most convenient: for ease of constructing the foundations and so as not to obstruct the movement of boats. Each span of the bridge was fabricated on-shore and floated on barges to be lifted into position by gigantic floating cranes. The box girder is fixed directly to the central pier only. Sliding joints on top of the other piers and expansion joints at both ends of the girder (where it meets the hillsides) absorb all the considerable movements caused by thermal expansion and contraction and seismic activity, as well as the lesser deflections from wind and heavy trucks. Planting around the base of those piers that arise from land further diminishes their visual impact.

The curved underside of the box girder and the raised sliding joints give the impression that the graceful bridge floats freely above the piers, thus satisfying Piano's perpetual quest for lightness, both perceived and actual. The rhythmic shadows of the brackets and the views up beneath the baffles and the pavement heighten this sense of lightness. The bridge also cleverly combines a whole hierarchy of scales, so as to be aptly scaled to the landscape, as well as to being seen from fast-moving cars and by ambling pedestrians. Hence it is the most modest and simple of statements within the larger landscape and seascape, yet it becomes ever more richly articulated as one approaches and looks more closely. If the Ushibuka Bridge seems rather ordinary at first glance, closer inspection reveals just how subtle and successful is its design.

9

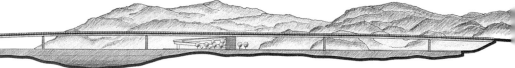

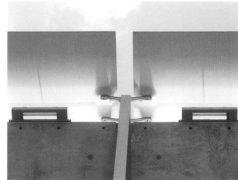

1

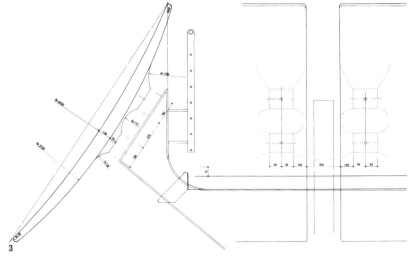

2

22 **Ushibuka Bridge**

1 View down between two grc wind baffles showing cast-steel elements that support them.

2 View up of baffles and supporting elements.

3 Section and part rear elevation of baffles showing how balustrade is secured to steel bracket that supports footpath and baffles.

4 Night view of precast concrete footpath edged by balustrade and baffles.

5 View down on sweeping arc of bridge with backdrop of mountains and villages.

6 Balustrade, baffles, footpath and supporting brackets.

7 The simple sweep and repetitive elements of the bridge contrast with the visual busyness of the natural and man-made elements of its backdrop.

8 Cross section showing box girder and projecting brackets supporting footpaths.

9 Portion of bridge over pier and sliding bearing.

4

3

5

6

7

8

9

Ushibuka Bridge

Client Kumamoto Prefecture

Architect Renzo Piano Building
Workshop in association with Maeda
Engineering Co.

Design team R Piano, N Okabe (senior
partner in charge), M Yamada (architect
in charge), S Ishida (senior partner)

Assisted by J Lelay, T Ueno

Modelmaker D Cavagna

Structural engineering advice Ove
Arup & Partners

24

Atelier Brancusi Paris, France **1992–6**

The reconstruction of the studio of the sculptor, Constantin Brancusi, presented Piano for the third time with the daunting challenge of building in the shadow of his early masterpiece, the Pompidou Centre (Volume one pp52–63). With the original IRCAM (Volume one pp202–6), Piano + Rogers avoided all confrontation with the Pompidou and buried the music and acoustic research centre in a deep pit under a new piazza. The Place Stravinsky now shows off the end elevation of the Pompidou and side elevation of the church of Saint-Merri. But then, later, when providing an extension to the subterranean building, Piano designed a tower (Volume one pp202–13), an early exercize in terracotta cladding. This blends seamlessly with the adjacent old brick buildings now converted into a library and offices for IRCAM. Yet the tower also steps forward and up from its neighbours to become a visual pivot between the Place Beaubourg and the Place Stravinsky, and to imply a connection with the Pompidou.

The Atelier Brancusi (project design, Volume three pp36–7), set at the other (northern) end of the Place Beaubourg, presents quite different contextual challenges. It is a free-standing pavilion, although it has been so skilfully embedded in place that it hardly seems to be. Moreover it is dwarfed by the Pompidou which looms above it, and looked down upon by the thousands of visitors who daily ride the Pompidou's external escalators. A small building had to be created that not only sat comfortably and looked right from very different perspectives, but would be an oasis of calm against the vast animated bulk of the Pompidou and directly adjacent to the hubbub of the Place Beaubourg. There was yet another great design challenge: how to honour the bequest of Brancusi, who stipulated that his works be displayed precisely as he had left them in his original studio (thus implying an exact reconstruction), while also meeting contemporary curatorial concerns with protecting the works from both deterioration and the crowds of visitors, which the original studio could never have accommodated.

Brancusi had moved into a studio in the Impasse Ronsin in Paris' 15th arrondissement in 1916. The Impasse was a mews of thirty wooden shack-like studios, with shed roofs reaching up to northlight clerestorey windows, all arranged along pedestrian lanes with trees and flower beds,

1

Atelier Brancusi

Previous page At dusk the transparent layers of the building become evident in this view over the courtyard wall.

1 A leafy lane in the Impasse Ronsin, location of Brancusi's original studio.
2 View from the top south-west corner of the Pompidou Centre showing the Atelier Brancusi in context at northern end of the Place Beaubourg.
3 Location plan: **a** Atelier Brancusi
b Pompidou Centre **c** Place Beaubourg
d Place Stravinsky **e** rue Renard
f rue Rambuteau

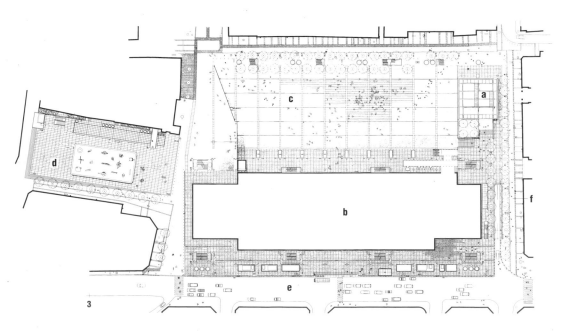

2

giving the whole a charmingly rustic air. Max Ernst and the young Jean Tinguely were among the other famous artists with studios there. Over the years Brancusi expanded into adjacent studios, knocking holes in the walls between them until by 1941 he occupied what had been originally five studio units facing onto two of the parallel lanes.

Initially Brancusi had thought of the sculptures in his studio primarily as models for gigantic outdoor works. But he gradually came to see all the sculptures – those that were finished, were taking shape or were still just raw material, as well as the relationships between these and the studio they were set in – as constituting a single artwork, his magnum opus. He constantly refined this work in progress, placing most sculptures on rough-hewn bases and a few against draped backdrops, and clustering the taller works like trees beneath the peak of the shed roofs. From 1951 onwards, this was the only way Brancusi exhibited his work, personally guiding visitors around in a similarly much-rehearsed ritual. Yet the painstaking arrangement of his work was also for his benefit. He would spend hours quietly contemplating the whole, detecting latent themes in the works and new relationships between them, thus sparking ideas for new works. To help him see things constantly afresh, some works rotated almost imperceptibly slowly on turntables.

Brancusi realized that the Impasse Ronsin might be demolished one day and was dismayed at the prospect of his works being removed from their setting and dispersed. So, in 1956, the year prior to his death, he bequeathed the whole collection – sculptures, drawings, paintings, photographs, tools – to the French nation with the stipulation that they be kept and displayed exactly where and as they were. This did not save his studio: in the early 1960s the Impasse Ronsin was destroyed to make way for an extension of the adjacent Necker Hospital.

In 1962, Brancusi's studio was rebuilt inside the Palais de Tokyo which then housed the National Museum of Modern Art. Here the studio was not only wrenched from context but deprived of the natural light that was so essential to the display and its atmosphere. Then, in 1977, the studio was once again rebuilt, this time outside and in front of the north-west corner of the Pompidou Centre. Besides looking scruffily and forlornly out of place, perched above the northern retaining wall of the Place Beaubourg, neither security or suitable access for large numbers of the public could be properly arranged. Finally, in 1990, following damage inflicted by a storm, the studio was closed to the public. It has now been rebuilt as part of the refurbishment of the Pompidou Centre.

The new studio is built in much the same place as in its previous incarnation. But it is set lower, between the street level (the rue Rambuteau) where it was, and the sunken piazza. It is also wrapped in a protective

3

4

Atelier Brancusi

Studio in context:

4 Looking north up length of Place Beaubourg to atelier dwarfed by Pompidou Centre to right.

5 Looking west along rue Rambuteau with corner of Pompidou Centre to left and walls reaching forward from atelier.

6 View down on atelier from above shows how it defines its own sanctuary-like precinct.

7 Portion of west elevation with Pompidou Centre behind.

8 Portion of south elevation.

5

6

precinct defined by an outer wall which encloses a covered ambulatory around the studio as well as a cobbled courtyard. The ambulatory and tree-shaded courtyard could be seen perhaps as recalling something of the lanes of the Impasse Ronsin.

Lowering the studio 1.5 metres below street level has brought two seemingly contradictory benefits. Having to descend external stairs to the entrance emphasizes the precinct as different in character to, and separate from, the bustle of its surroundings. (The walls, one of them enclosing the courtyard, reach out to flank the approach route and reinforce this effect.) Yet the lowered precinct also invites views from street level, right through the entrance and ambulatory and into the studio. This transparency, as well as the materials and immaculate construction, emphasizes the contrast between the suavely urbane new building and the original building, and indeed the shabby and uninviting eyesore it replaces. No doubt there are pedants who object to this because, though the new studio itself is identical in shape and dimensions to the original, its character is so dissimilar.

There are further reasons the construction of an exact replica of the original studio was unfeasible. The new building had to be a complex hybrid: both an evocation of the original studio and a museum for displaying and preserving important artworks. Brancusi's works are now immensely valuable and need the protection against theft, fire and fluctuations in temperature and humidity that the original timber shack could never offer. An exact replica could never accommodate the concealed mechanical plant and ducting required for ensuring carefully controlled and stable environmental conditions. The exhibits also need protection from visitors, and in Brancusi's arrangement the works are too exposed and closely packed to allow large numbers to move freely among them. Inevitably, visitors can no longer enter the studio and its contents must now be viewed from outside.

Also, the previous reconstruction not only looked absurdly misplaced and evoked nothing of its original setting, but most people would now deem anything similar to be too undignified to display such important artworks. Furthermore, replicating a historic original raises further issues today, such as authenticity. Neither a spanking clean reconstruction nor an attempt to recreate ramshackle conditions with cracks in walls and draughty glazing, as well as stains, wear and other signs of prolonged occupancy, can be convincing. Indeed, in the age of Disneyfication, replicas seem more preposterously phoney the closer they replicate the original.

Instead, Piano has replicated only the layout, volumes and light of the original studio, and framed these with construction that has a quiet and timeless dignity of its own. A simple timber structural frame infilled with plaster walls, the whole minimally articulated and painted white, creates a background that is in no way scenographic but provides a serenely disciplined constructional order to the complex form of the studio. The studio is then set within a larger pavilion that is square in plan and has a flat roof. The north-

27

7

8

2

Atelier Brancusi

1 Studio-gallery with sculptures laid out in a manner similar to their arrangement in the original studio. Visible through the glass and across the ambulatory is the courtyard. The cotton ceiling has yet to be installed in the ambulatory.

Photographs by Brancusi of the original studio:

2 Self-portrait.

3, **4**, **5** Show careful arrangement of sculptures within the space of the studio, as well as the latter's dilapidated state.

3

4

5

light shed roofs projecting above this announce the presence of the studio, as do the views into it from outside.

The residual space between the outer walls of the pavilion and the studio is the ambulatory, which serves as a viewing gallery from which to look into the studio. It is wider on the east side, part of which is an entrance lobby, while the rest overlooks the courtyard. In the north-west corner, the ambulatory widens into a re-entrant corner into the studio to form a room for an explanatory exhibit about the original studio. And just as the ambulatory's southern arm opens at its east end into the courtyard, so windows at either end of the northern arm offer views in from, and out to, the street which, eerily, is elevated by half a level and can be seen but not heard. These variations to the arms of the ambulatory may seem minor, but immeasurably enrich the experience of visiting the building.

When shown as a project in Volume three, it was intended that the studio's contents be viewed through openings corresponding to the original doors and windows. But these openings would have been insufficient for easy viewing of all the works, as well as impractical, especially if several visitors were to crowd an opening; they also complicated the provision of stable environmental conditions in the studio. Now, more and larger openings have been created; but these are sealed with sheets of glass so that the studio is separate as an environmentally controlled volume. To draw the eye through the glass and minimize reflection on it, the ambulatory, though naturally lit through a fully glazed roof, is illuminated more softly than the studio. The only place where reflections on the glass are sometimes irksome is where the large panes face those along the courtyard.

The clerestoreys were initially clear-glazed. But because the buildings on the other side of rue Rambuteau that were visible through them proved distracting, a frosted translucent film was added inside. All flat parts of the pavilion roof are covered in curved panes of insulating glass, with a frosted internal laminate, supported by small arches of bent T-sectioned steel. These span between a grid of horizontal steel channels that form a secondary structure on top of the timber beams, as well as serving as gutters draining to a large steel cornice-gutter around the roof's perimeter.

Above the glass, protective stainless-steel panels perforated with slots limit the light

admitted. In the ambulatory a cotton ceiling is stretched between the bottoms of the timber beams which further diminishes and diffuses the light from both the roof and a strip of horizontal windows at the head of the perimeter wall; it also hides all such distracting elements above it. This is consistent with the detailing throughout, which is kept sparse and simple to distract as little as possible from the flow of space between studio and ambulatory, as well as from the artworks. The large panes of glass separating the spaces are set directly into beams, columns and floor; and the same floated concrete floor finish extends throughout the building. But despite all this, the glass as usual betrays the promise of its transparency and seems to distance the artworks as much as render them visible.

The perimeter wall around the courtyard and ambulatory, which along the southern edge of the building rises from a plinth of granite facing the Place Beaubourg retaining wall, is of fair face limestone and has the same finish inside and out. This is the same stone comprising much of historic Paris, including the old buildings edging the Place Beaubourg, and so helps nestle the building into place.

29

1

2

30   **Atelier Brancusi**

Interiors.

1 Exhibition area where ambulatory
widens in north-east corner.
2 View into studio and along southern arm
of ambulatory towards courtyard.
3 Plan: **a** studio-gallery; **b** ambulatory;
c entrance; **d** exhibition area; **e** courtyard;
f steps down to atelier.
4 Brancusi's tools as he arranged them.
5 Various versions of Bird in Flight.
6 South-east corner of ambulatory and
studio-gallery.

3

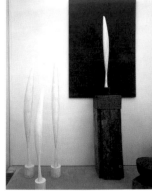

4

5

6

7

Atelier Brancusi

Interiors.

7 Looking east through southern bays of gallery towards courtyard.

8, **9** Views of studios with heating stoves and tools on walls.

10 North-western bay of studio with stair to small balcony.

8

9

10

1

Atelier Brancusi

1 Studio is set back beyond walls that extend forward from it, and down half a level from rue Rambuteau, to the right. This emphasizes that it is a separate precinct, yet also invites views into it.

2 Construction view shows how cast-steel element at end of wood beams sits on concrete post and supports steel cornice-gutter.

3 North–south section looking eastwards through widening of ambulatory into exhibition area in north-east corner and single bay of atelier. Also visible are the complex concrete substructures the atelier had to sit on.

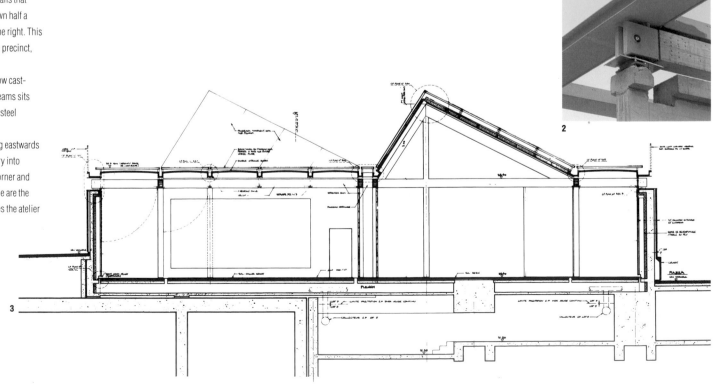

2

3

4

Atelier Brancusi
Construction views.
4 Still unclad concrete walls carry timber and steel beams.
5–7 Construction of roof: **6** steel secondary structure being laid on timber primary structure; **7** decking being laid on sloping roofs; **5** curved panes of glass roof being laid in place.

6

7

But as with the Cy Twombly Gallery and Beyeler Museum, this thick and seemingly solid wall is not loadbearing. It is hollow and conceals concrete columns capped by a visible cast-steel element. These support, via an expressed pin-joint, the cast-steel reinforced ends of the timber beams of the internal structural frame.

Spanning across the ends of these primary beams, and edged with a channel to stiffen it and give a crisp profile, is a rectangular-sectioned steel gutter. This is the cornice gutter

6

that also serves as a beam supporting the ends of the steel secondary beams. Between the primary beams, and set along the inner edge of the wall so as to be in deep shadow beneath the gutter-beam, are the horizontal windows above the ambulatory's cotton ceiling. These windows are here for formal reasons rather than for the light they admit (indeed, those facing west are problematic in admitting low evening sun). As at the Beyeler museum (p56–84), these strip windows separate and emphasize the contrast between the earth-bound wall and the floating roof. Together, the gutter beam, the cast-steel, pin-jointed ends of the primary beams and the windows between them create a richly articulated cornice, very different to the roof-concealing parapet of the project shown in Volume three, and better suited to the aerial views from the Pompidou.

Above the cornice gutter-beam can be seen the edges of the slotted steel panels further enriching the roofline. The whole roof, except for the studio's clerestorey windows, is covered with brushed stainless-steel panels, which are unperforated on the sloping shed roofs. This solution had already been used on the Bercy 2 Shopping Centre (Volume two pp16–33) and the Kansai International Airport Terminal (Volume three pp128–229). Here it both protects the inner water-excluding roof and

presents a neat aspect to the Pompidou. Moreover, just as the hollow limestone wall relates the Atelier Brancusi both to recent museums by the Building Workshop and the facing historic buildings, so these shiny steel panels also relate the new building to milestones in Piano's œuvre and claim an association, in their material and spirit, to the Pompidou.

Only 450 square meters in area, the Atelier Brancusi is, by Piano's standards, a tiny work. Yet its responses to precedent, context and function are complex and highly nuanced. It is also, as described in Volume three, a work with which Piano identified strongly during design. When speaking about Brancusi to curators and art historians, he realized that he too saw his designs, the studio spaces in which they are developed and the models and photographs of earlier works on display, as constantly cross-fertilizing parts of a single whole. Hence the Atelier Brancusi is not just another museum, but commemorates something very dear to Piano. It displays not only artworks but an essential aspect of the creative process, while also fusing an intimate relationship between art and its architectural container.

33

1

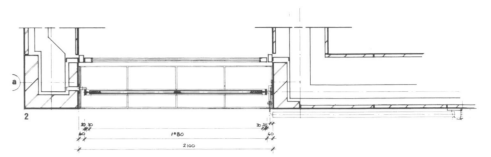

2

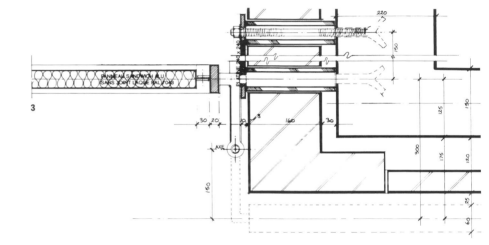

3

34   **Atelier Brancusi**

Constructional detail and context.

1 Detail view up from courtyard of roof structure and curved glass panes of roof.

2 Plan of window with external blind in corner of ambulatory.

3 Plan detail of anchorage of external blind.

4 Close-up view of strip window and cornice-gutter with Pompidou Centre behind.

5 View from north-west with Pompidou Centre behind.

6 Looking west across courtyard and ambulatory, and into studio-gallery.

7 Detail elevation of northern end of west facade.

4

5

6

Atelier Brancusi

Client Centre Georges Pompidou

Design team R Piano, B Plattner
(senior partner in charge), R Self
(architect in charge), R Phelan

Assisted by J L Dupanloup, A Gallisian
with C Aasgaard, Z Berrio, C Catino,
P Chappell, J Darling, P Satchell

**Structural and electrical
engineering, cost control** GEC
Ingénierie

Air conditioning design INEX

Car parking Isis

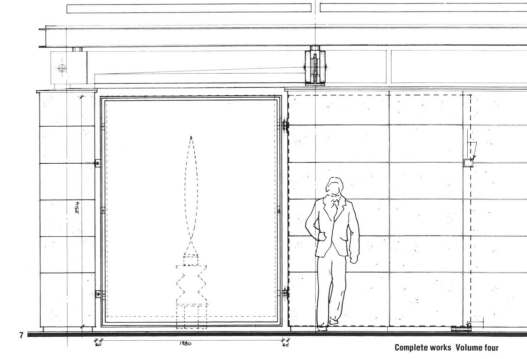

7

Where a major road projects into and dives below the waters of Amsterdam harbour's Oosterdok, a pedestrian ramp leads up to a roof so that together ramp and roof swoosh up to form in section a mirror-image counterpoint to the descending road bed. The space below the roof is then wrapped in walls that lean out to stress the dynamism of the gesture and, following the geometry of the tapering, curving site, sweep around and under the roof's highest point as a curved, ship-like prow. Such was Renzo Piano's spontaneous sketched response to the challenge of building a museum of science and technology straddling the entrance of the tunnel beneath Het IJ, the harbour's broad channel to the sea.

The final building, clad in green pre-oxidized copper and somewhat resembling a sinking ship (hence the local nickname, Titanic), retains all the immediacy and freshness of the generative sketch. It is possibly the most extreme built example of the recent trend for Piano's designs to be shaped as graphically gestural responses to context rather than elaborated from a study of programme and structure. It is also a milestone in his œuvre because it is the first major building in which there is nothing that could be convincingly argued to be a 'piece' – the repetitive constructional elements that the Building Workshop usually develops for a particular building and which become intrinsic to its very identity.

At newMetropolis the external form clearly came first, prior to the interior layout which is not even hinted at on the outside. Yet inside, Piano and his team (Shunji Ishida and the architect in charge, Olaf de Nooyer) have contrived such an exciting and functionally convincing spatial sequence – which entices visitors through all the exhibition areas that step up diagonally through the building to connect its ground-level and roof-top entrances – that it now seems that this could just have easily been the initial impulse that generated the external form. To climb through the building, experience all this and exit onto the sloping roof to note the strong visual

newMetropolis (National Centre for Science and Technology) Amsterdam, The Netherlands 1992–7

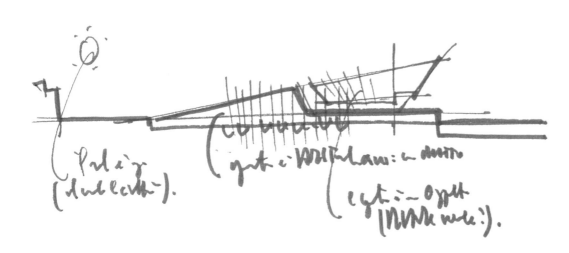

1

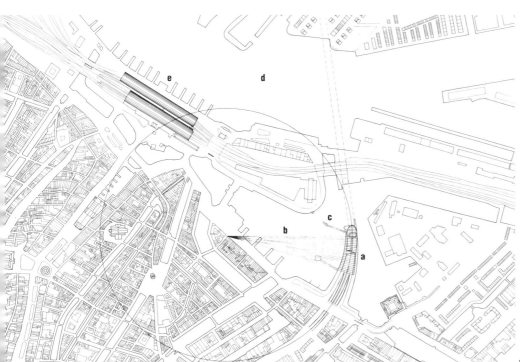

2

38 **newMetropolis**

Previous page Aerial view of museum in
context, straddling a road diving under the
waters of Amsterdam harbour, with a
pedestrian ramp leading to its upward-
sweeping roof. In the right foreground is
the Maritime Museum, and between this
and the new building float some of its
exhibits. The grey triangle over nearest end
of nearside quay is the roof of new pavilion
by the Building Workshop.

connection cemented with the
old city could clinch the
conviction that this
functional–spatial sequence
came first, and the external
form is only its by-product. The
seamless synthesis of vividly
legible gestural response to
context with immediately
intelligible spatial sequence,
both of which seem almost
inevitable and utterly
uncompromised, is a major
triumph of the design.

The evolution of the design
was charted in Volume two of
this series (pp132–9). Its basic

organization remains
unchanged. But the tight
budget led to some
compromises, such as less
wood and a less ambitiously
detailed copper cladding than
originally envisaged, as well as,
in places, less precise
construction than expected of
the Building Workshop. Also, at
the client's insistence the central
strip of roof lights was omitted.
This had been part of the
original concept of a naturally-lit
route that climbed through wells
that not only allowed views up
through the length and height of
the building, but also brought
natural light down to all the
exhibition floors. But, to the
disappointment of the
architectural team, the client
decided not to include any of the
authentic historic exhibits that
were available and to use instead
only purpose-built interactive
displays. Many of these have
self-illuminated electronic
screens best viewed in dim light,
hence the exclusion of natural
light. The client has even blocked
up windows that were built in
the prow, which were intended
to light and give outlook to the
uppermost exhibition space.

newMetropolis is the latest
manifestation of what had
started, at the beginning of the
century, as a Museum of
Labour. This had a collection

centred on machines of the
period and paintings by the
industrialist-founder, Herman
Heijenbroeck. Over the decades
the museum had moved
periodically and come into
public ownership, in its fourth
and penultimate phase
occupying an old school
building. Sadly, apart from a
few of Heijenbroeck's paintings
now adorning a boardroom, ties
with the past have been cut.
Instead of exhibiting a rich mix
of beautiful old machines and
contemporary interactive
exhibits, all the former have
been discarded. Director Joost
Douma did not want to create a
traditional museum or scientific
institution but a 'knowledge
centre' where, he envisioned,
'people can see things and try
them out for themselves, get
informed and talk freely as they
would in an urban forum'.

Some of these changes,
and more, are signalled in
the institution's name,
newMetropolis. This was chosen
to convey its intended role in
regenerating the surrounding
area – newMetropolis and the
adjacent Maritime Museum are
together a major tourist draw,
and client and city have claimed
that the accessible rooftop might
serve both as a public piazza
for visitors and tourists and
as a social focus for the
neighbourhood. The new
name also puts a twist on that
of Fritz Lang's famous film,
Metropolis, to now signal a
positive view of technology. But
ironically a contrast, similar to
that shown in the film, persists
between the gloomy, artificially-
lit world of machines and the
sunny world of play on the
rooftop piazza above.

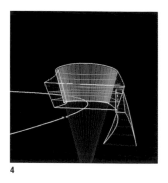

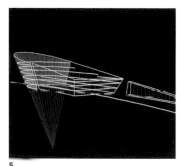

4

5

newMetropolis

Location.

1, **2** Aerial views of site over mouth of tunnel diving into Amsterdam harbour before and after the construction of newMetropolis.

3 Location plan: **a** newMetropolis; **b** Oosterdok; **c** pedestrian bridge; **d** Het IJ; **e** Central Station.

4, **5** Computer projections of geometry generating external form of building.

6 Aerial view from north-east with edge of old city at top of photograph. The ramp and roof sweep up in counterpoint to the road that dives below the building.

7 Sunken road emerging from under museum and its entry forecourt.

8 Longitudinal section of museum and road tunnel.

6

7

Whether or not the building helps regenerate its immediate surroundings, and its roof serves as a social focus for them, it certainly adds new dimensions to Amsterdam. Huge and enigmatic in form (both despite and because of its obvious nautical affinities) it is conspicuous from much of Amsterdam's main waterfront, while the tall prow is prominently visible from trains as they slowly pull into and depart from Amsterdam's Central Station. And, once on the rooftop piazza, there is an elevated view of the old city. Such a view might be commonplace in other countries, but is new to Holland's flat landscape.

newMetropolis's construction and operation is funded by both the city and central governments. The extraordinary location was chosen as the only way of creating economically within the old city a site large enough for the 12,000 square-metre building. Besides, it has the crucial added advantages of being close to the adjacent Maritime Museum and the Central Station, which is only ten minutes walk to the north-west. Because the foundations of the existing tunnel approach had been designed to take the loadings incurred during construction (when it was flooded), since completion these foundations were no longer loaded to full capacity. The original idea was that the new building exploit this spare loading capacity by simply sitting on the walls which flank and divide the sunken road, thus obviating the need for, and cost of, further foundations.

Only as design advanced was it remembered that the foundations still must cope with possible flooding of the sunken approach road. (Huge steel doors housed under the prow of the new building can be lowered to protect the tunnel itself from flooding.) Thus a structural raft now spans across the heads of the walls to rest partially on the approach road's foundations and partially on new piles driven down just outside of these. Such complexities have led to a pragmatically impure superstructure. The bulk of the building has a concrete structure, with beamless slabs on cylindrical columns rising from the raft, all stabilized by four cores containing escape stairs and air-handling plant. Yet to both lighten the tall prow, and because its upper parts project so far beyond the ground floor, it has a steel structure; its steel floors supported by a steel perimeter cage.

Pragmatism and economics have also led to the cladding system and roof being less ambitious than initially envisaged. When presented in Volume two, the cladding was to be some evolution of that of the Bercy 2 Shopping Centre

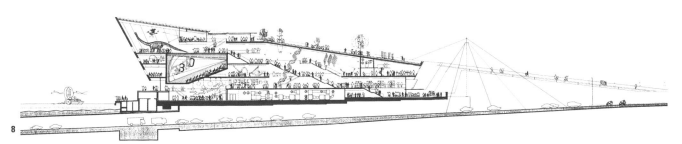

8

1

newMetropolis

Construction of prow.

1 Looking out through unclad structural steel cage.

2 Structural steel cage prior to cladding.

3, 5 Erecting cladding of insulating sandwich panels.

4 Isometric view of structural steel cage.

2

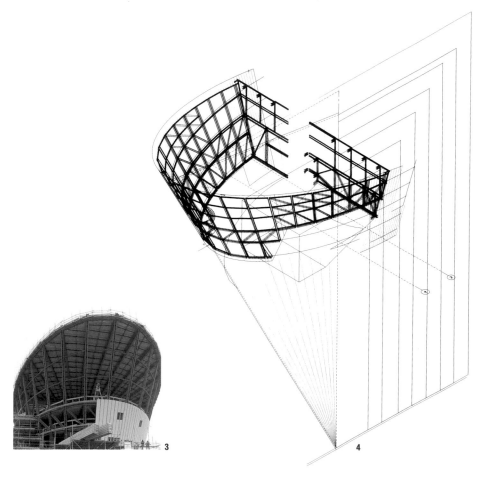

3

4

5

(Volume two, pp16–33) and the Kansai International Airport terminal (Volume three, pp128–229): repetitive panels that might even form a membrane which could open and breathe. The roof was to have been stepping precast concrete beams. Now, however, the outer walls are enclosed by sandwich panels over which the copper is dressed in a fairly conventional manner, and the roof is a sloping slab on which rest precast units that form the stepped surface.

From a distance, the building's sloping roof line and lack of conventional windows compound its enigmatic quality by giving little sense of scale or of the spaces and functions within. Access from the Central Station is by a waterside road and then footbridges across Oosterdok to land beneath the prow that looms 32 metres high overhead. From the old city, it is reached by the quays edging both sides of the sunken road to extend right around the site. These quays thus lead up to, and beyond, the main entrance in the building's lower, southern end. From the eastern quay the ramp rises to the rooftop piazza and the secondary entrance at its upper end. Also along the eastern quay are moored sailing vessels of varying type and age (exhibits of the nearby Maritime Museum) which make a very apt connection between the two museums. Hence, newMetropolis' location literally conjoins the two technologies on which historically the Dutch have been dependent as well as expert in: water craft and water-related civil engineering. The location is also poignantly appropriate to a country wrested from the sea and constantly battling its encroachment.

On approaching newMetropolis, it becomes apparent that the hull-like volume, with its curving

outward-sloping green metal walls, floats not on but above the water and the quayside, over a transparent ground floor enclosed almost entirely in glass. Only the bottoms of the escape-stair shafts are not transparent, but faced in the same brick as the base of the ramp and the lift shaft that projects from, and above, the south elevation. The standing seams and slightly pillowing bulges in the green metal reveal it to be only thin copper sheathing. Windows, and grilles of slotted openings, align with the seams and joints in this sheathing and so not only depart from the horizontal and vertical norm but also follow the geometry of the hull.

Those who look up to inspect such details, or the subtle difference between the cornice/coping which edges the roof-top piazza and that which edges the prow, might find that the sloping walls and roofline have a momentary dizzying effect. This slightly disconcerting effect disappears within a few seconds. Though a rare occurrence, this unsettling moment confirms the astuteness of Piano's design instincts which led to pulling the lift shaft forward of the low southern facade, to stabilize perceptually the whole composition, and extending forward from the same elevation a canopy as a reassuring horizontal

6

datum. Together lift shaft and canopy affirm the conventional coordinates.

The canopy announces, and leads visitors to, the main entrance, which is oriented towards the old city and cars passing below. The entrance doors open off a forecourt, which connects the west and east quays and is raised a few steps above them. The splayed triangular form of the forecourt complements the asymmetrical placings of the single ramp to the roof, the external lift shaft and the canopy. Like the rest of

the floor-to-ceiling glazed ground floor, the entrance lobby is paved with the same brick-like paviour as the forecourt and quay outside so as to appear to be an inward extension of them. Beyond the lobby, opening off the western quay, is an office offering guidance in careers in science and technology. Opposite, on the east, is the workshop where the preparation of exhibits can be glimpsed by the public. This reworks a similar device Piano had already used at The Menil Collection (Volume one pp140–63), putting normally behind-the-scenes activities on educational display. To the north, below the prow, is a double-height space for temporary exhibitions which provides tempting glimpses for those outside.

Once inside the double-height entrance lobby, the arrangement of much of the building's public space is on immediate display. To the left is a café, its tables and chairs occupying the lobby's sunny southwest corner, and on warm, still days spilling onto a terrace outside. To the right is a reception and information counter, and open to the lobby on the floor above this is the museum shop. Attention, however, is commanded mainly by the vista which extends straight ahead and diagonally upwards through the full length

and height of the building, an effect contrived by the way the stairs, and the wells that they climb through, are aligned and staggered along the building's slightly curving axis. Without natural light, whether flooding down through the wells as originally intended or from the windows in the prow beyond the head of the stairs as eventually provided, the intended effect has been compromised. Nevertheless, the result is still a dramatic processional that compels visitors onwards and upwards through all four above-ground exhibition levels that also step up diagonally under the roof.

This sectional arrangement not only creates a dramatic vista and a compelling, immediately-grasped processional route (as well as the now-unrealized potential for all exhibition levels to receive natural light), but it also leaves space at either end of the building for ancillary accommodation. For instance, on the first floor the shop can be seen from below. This is reached by turning right at the head of the stairs up from the lobby, before entering the control gates into the museum proper. From the northern end of the same floor, stairs descend into the double-height temporary exhibition area to which visitors are drawn by the light entering its tall glass walls (and very

41

newMetroplis

6 Close-up view of bottom of south-east corner of glazing of entrance lobby.
7 Approaching from south along western quay.
8 Section detail through edge of roof terrace; **a** concrete roof slab; **b** concrete upstand; **c** copper-sheathed coping; **d** copper sheathing; **e** insulated sandwich panel; **f** precast concrete stepped paving element; **g** steel balustrade; **h** steel grille; **k** rain water outlet; **m** insulation; **n** waterproof membrane; **p** recessed light fitting.
9 Close-up view of balustrade on ramp up to roof.
10 Close-up view of water cascade on roof.

7

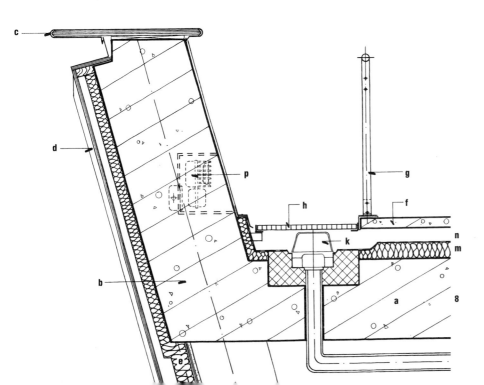

8

9

10

1

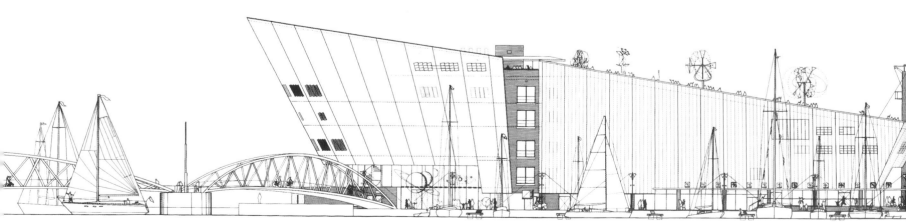

newMetropolis

1 View from west with ramp reaching up to roof. Windows in grey wall in recessed slot open to admit large objects hoisted up the slot.

2 West elevation with pedestrian footbridge on left.

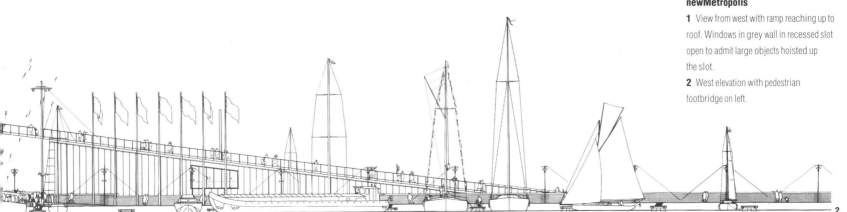

1

newMetropolis

Copper sheathing.

1 Canopy projecting forward from main entrance in south-east corner provides a horizontal datum below the leaning, curving wall above with its angled sheathing.

2, **3**, **4** Portions of the copper sheathing with openings and grilles aligned to fit the same geometry.

5 Plan of windows in uppermost exhibition area in prow.

2

3

4

5

6

likely by the memory of what they might have glimpsed from outside). At the second floor's southern end, and on a mezzanine above this, are the museum's offices reached by the lift in the exposed shaft. (This lift also provides a shortcut between lobby and roof.) At this floor's northern end is a 'black box' flexible theatre, for performances with scientific themes, and a 200-seat cinema/lecture theatre. (The latter partially projects out from the sloping, curving prow as the most prominent of the elements which deliberately interrupt the schematic purity of the original design gesture.) In the prow is the boardroom. Above the auditoria and boardroom is the

top-most exhibition space. As with the offices and boardroom, the windows in this (when not blocked and concealed) are jauntily angled within the sloping walls, because they are aligned with the sheets of copper cladding outside.

Other exhibition floors have only a single window each positioned near the internal lifts. Tucked into a corner, these windows are not intended to light the exhibition areas. Instead they offer some visual 'release' in the form of a view westward back to the old city through a vertical slot up which, in traditional Dutch fashion, large exhibits are hoisted up and admitted through the opening window. The gloom that pervades everywhere else may not show the splendid spatial sequence to best effect. But the compensation is that the fragmenting emphasis on spot-lit displays and axial vistas draws attention away from the starkly rudimentary and cavernous quality of the spaces. This is the best that could be

achieved on the construction budget of 28 million guilders (excluding professional fees), out of a total budget, including exhibits and fees, of 80 million guilders.

To make the most of the enforced frugality of material and finish, Piano conceived the interior as 'the noble factory', where elements are revealed as unfusslly as possible, simply for what they are. Except for the plasterboard and painted walls, all materials are unfinished and construction is expressed straightforwardly: off-shutter concrete columns and ceilings, grey linoleum floors, perforated galvanized sheet-steel balustrades and wooden handrails. Yet even such a pragmatic and tolerant strategy has stretched the local construction industry: galvanizing is uneven in colour and reflectivity; and the casting of the few concrete stairs (most are steel with open risers) is far from pristine. (The imperfections of those welcoming visitors up from the lobby and into the exhibition areas are particularly distracting.)

Furthermore, the exhibits are designed (by an in-house museum department) in an exaggerated caricature of the sort of high-tech to which the Building Workshop's approach is a deliberate antithesis. The result is a little too like a video games arcade. No doubt with time a better feeling will develop

45

newMetropolis

6 View out through office windows on southern end of second floor. Windows are aligned with the sheathing outside.

7 Copper sheathing of facades as it would look if spread out flat.

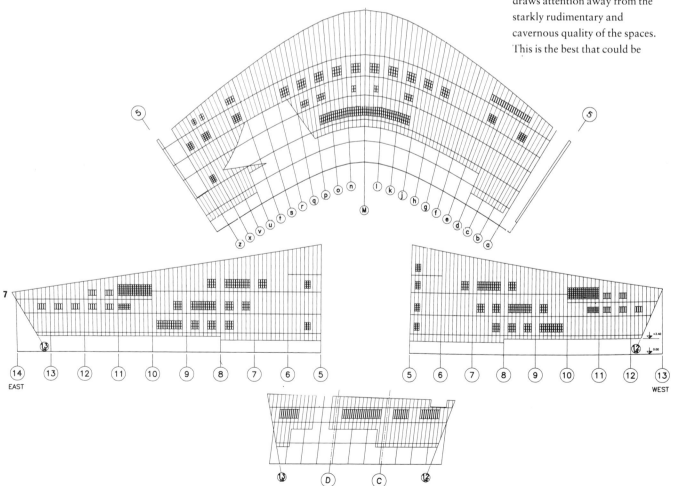

7

1

2

3

newMetropolis 47

1 View from north-east across Oosterdok. Projecting through sloping wall is corner of cinema/lecture theatre.

2 Sectional detail of office window in south elevation.

3 Sectional detail of cladding extending down past top of double-height glazing of ground floor temporary exhibition gallery.

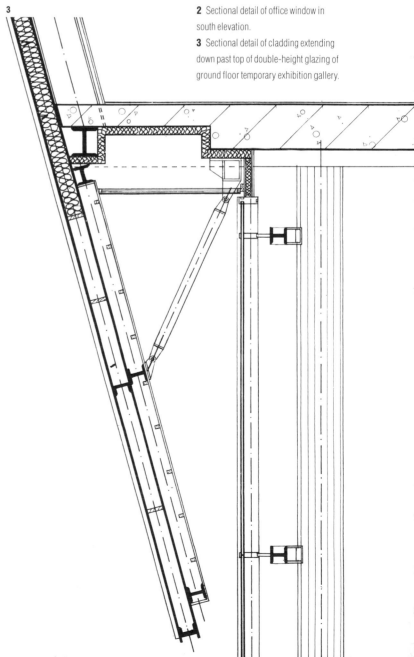

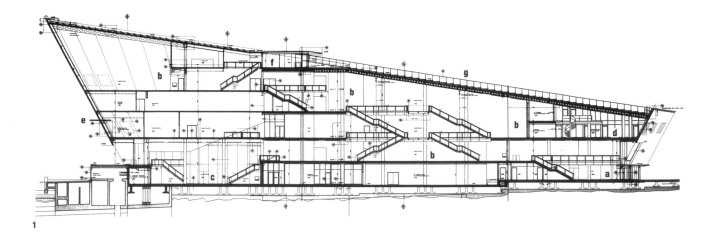

1

48

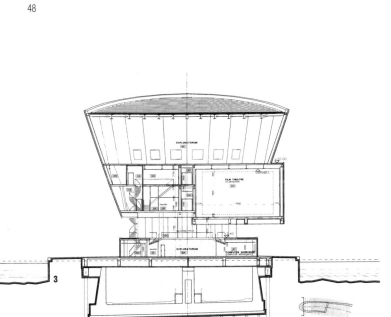

2

3

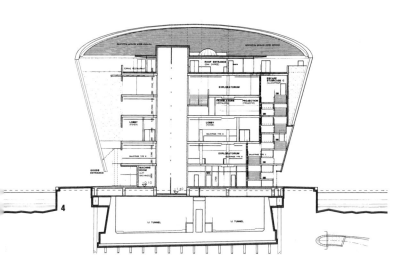

4

newMetropolis

1 Longitudinal section: **a** main entrance;
b exhibition space; **c** temporary
exhibitions; **d** offices; **e** board room;
f cafeteria; **g** roof terrace.

2 View from south shows how ramp
sweeps up to roof terrace overlooked by
cafeteria at its head.

3 Cross section through exhibition area in
prow and cinema/lecture theatre with road
tunnel below.

4 Cross section through vertical slot for
hoisting, elevator shaft and escape stair.

5 Head of ramp, looking west along
balustrade at bottom edge of roof terrace.

5

6

newMetropolis

6 East elevation seen beyond bow of
floating exhibit of Maritime Museum.

7 South elevation with road in section
descending to mouth of tunnel.

7

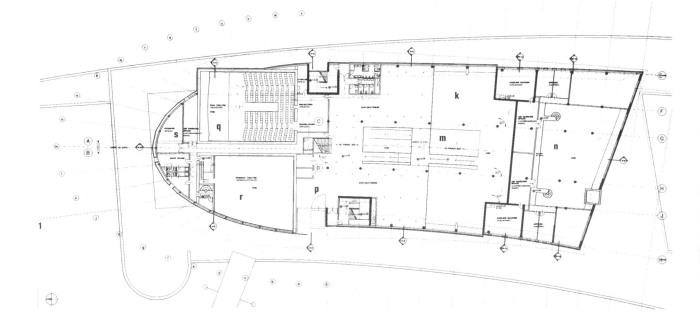

50   **newMetropolis**
      1 Second floor plan.
      2 First floor plan.
      3 Ground floor plan.
      4 Looking west across stair well
      from third floor.

Key
a forecourt; **b** pedestrian bridge; **c** housing
for tunnel flood gates; **d** main entrance
e careers office; **f** workshop; **g** temporary
exhibitions; **h** shop **k** exhibition area;
m void; **n** offices; **p** loading window
q cinema/lecture theatre; **r** 'black-box'
theatre; **s** board room; **t** quayside;
u elevator.

1

newMetropolis

1–5 Exhibits in use.
1, 2 Exploring the difficulties in steering and docking remote-controlled model ships.
3, 4 Children playing with interactive exhibits.
5 Exhibits include a huge turbine.
6 Cinema-lecture theatre.

2

3

4

5

for the spirit of the building and the potential of its spaces; the exhibits might then be designed and placed with greater sensitivity, perhaps with banners and other eye-catching devices fluttering down the stair wells, stressing the spatial continuities and drawing attention away from constructional imperfections.

From the prow-peak exhibition space that terminates the vista from the ground-floor entrance (which would offer a 120-degree panoramic view through its three-metre tall

windows, if these were not blocked), the route folds back up a final stair to the rooftop entrance from which the building can be explored from the top downwards. Up here too is a restaurant, with a sideways (westward) view of the old city, which opens onto a small terrace at the head of the stepping rooftop piazza. The panoramic view southwards from the piazza contrasts with the introversion of the exhibition spaces and reconnects newMetropolis with the city. Animating the expanse of the piazza is a water cascade. It was intended that this be joined by mobile sculptures by Shingu (the Japanese sculptor whose specially-commissioned works adorn several Piano buildings), the ensemble demonstrating in an educative as well as aesthetic manner the interactions of sun, wind and water. However, the commission has yet to be confirmed by the client, and there is now a danger that artists who are less appropriate but better-known locally might be commissioned. Furthermore, until sculptures or some other eye-catching and space-delineating elements are installed the view down the piazza from the top is rather foreshortened – which robs it somewhat of visual impact and so renders it rather less enticing to explore.

The roof is dished deliberately in a shallow catenary curve. There are three visual reasons

for this: to offset the foreshortening effect already noted (although Piano now concedes that the curve is too shallow to fully achieve this); to prevent the head of the side walls appearing to bulge outwards when viewed from below; and, most particularly, to give the roofline a certain visual tension and elegance when seen in elevation – like the sheerline of a ship.

On sunny days this canted piazza is sometimes crowded with people. But the idea touted by some of the city planners (though emphatically not by the Building Workshop) that so isolated, elevated and exposed a space might become a social focus for the neighbourhood is wildly optimistic. Otherwise, newMetropolis has been an immediate, immense public and critical success. However, a few local architects have whispered that because of the tight budget Amsterdam has only got 'half a Piano'. Such a comment is understandable to a degree. Yet it misses the point in failing to recognize some of the key strengths of the Building Workshop's approach.

Certainly newMetropolis's interior is spartan and lacks the zenithal natural light that so enlivens most Building Workshop design. The structure

6

is also a bastardized composite of concrete and steel, lacking the rigour and refinement as well as the exposed and empathy-inducing elements that are so memorably characteristic of Piano's buildings. Related to this, and most telling of all, is the lack of any unique and innovative 'piece' as the focus of crafted refinement and technical virtuosity. The resultant building retains the spontaneous, diagrammatic immediacy of the original sketch and the spatial fluidity that came with the design development

newMetropolis

Pavilion.

7 In context: as seen from main harbour edging road with Maritime Museum to the left.

8 Looking north past east elevation.

9 View from interior towards newMetropolis.

10 Section through dock, quay, pavilion and road down to quay.

7

8

9

charted in Volume two (qualities that together are reminiscent of architects like Oscar Niemeyer). But inevitably cost and constructional restraints have led to it lacking somewhat in the intensity and refinement of its working-through, especially perhaps because there is no piece, or its equivalent, as a focus for crafting and evolution.

Yet all of the above limiting qualifications are also part of what is so admirable about the design: this is the degree to which it is entirely a product of, and capitalizes upon, circumstance without the gratuitous imposition of a standard design approach or vocabulary; and the willingness to accept – within reason – constraint and compromise (or what Piano calls 'contamination'). One of Piano's greatest design virtues is that there is no such thing as a 'typical' Building Workshop design. Instead each is shaped by programme, place and the technologies and standards obtainable – whether from local industry, global marketplace or (more usually) a judicious mix of these – within the available budget. newMetropolis is yet another demonstration of this virtue.

With the universal enthusiasm that greeted newMetropolis, Amsterdam's city fathers commissioned the Building Workshop to build a separate small pavilion nearby, where a service road drops from

the main waterside road onto the eastern quay leading to the museum. The existing rubble-stone retaining wall between the pavement along the main road and the lower quayside has been extended upwards to create the side of the pavilion facing the road. Behind this, a triangular flat concrete slab extends the pavement level out over the quay to a row of columns that continue up, so that together with the wall they support the roof. Folded around the edge of this slab to meet either end of the stone wall is the glazed screen of the external wall which rises to the flat soffit of the oversailing roof. This latter terminates in a fascia formed by a galvanized steel channel. Together with the most conspicuously acute of the glazed corners, this is perhaps the most eye-catching aspect of the quietly detailed, recessively coloured building. Although completed, the pavilion has yet to open. Originally commissioned to be a bar-café (but probably a bit isolated for such a function), the city is now contemplating its use for exhibitions. Perhaps the best measure of the success of this design is that many in Amsterdam, including even architects, have yet to notice the presence of the new pavilion.

53

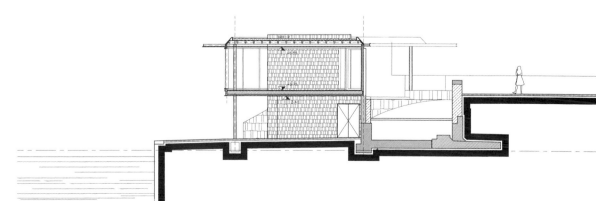

10

1

2

newMetropolis

1 View north from third floor across stairwell. Stair leading upwards on other side of well leads to uppermost exhibition area in prow. Circular tables with white cloths are only installed for opening party.
2 Looking south, across and down stairwell from third floor, towards main entrance to exhibition areas with its bright natural light from the entrance lobby just visible beyond.

Client NINT

Preliminary phase, 1992
Design team R Piano, O de Nooyer (partner in charge), S Ishida (senior partner)
Assisted by H Yamaguchi, J Fujita, A Gallo, M Alvisi with Y Yamaoka, E Piazze, A Recagno, K Shannon, F Wenz
CAD operators I Corte, D Guerrisi
Modelmaker D Cavagna
Structural engineers Ove Arup & Partners, D3BN
Services engineers Ove Arup & Partners, Huisman en Van Muijen BV
Acoustics Peutz & Associés
Local support Bureau voor Bouwkunde

Design development and construction phase, 1994–7
Design team R Piano, O de Nooyer, S Ishida
Assisted by J Backus, A Hayes, H Peñaranda, H Van Der Meyn, J Woltier
Structural and services engineers D3BN, Huisman en Van Muijen BV
Acoustics Peutz & Associés
Local support Bureau voor Bouwkunde

The Beyeler Foundation Museum is the most recently completed of an ever-increasing number of art museums by Renzo Piano and the Building Workshop. This series began with the Pompidou Centre by Piano + Rogers (Volume one pp52–63). It continues with various projects on the drawing board, such as the reorganization of, and extensions to, the Fogg Museum at Harvard University, the Art Institute of Chicago and the High Museum in Atlanta, all still too premature to illustrate.

It is a cliché and a truism to claim art museums as the temples of our times, and viewing art as the spiritual activity of our secular age. Art museums are thus the most prestigious of architectural commissions; and many of their architects feel they should express themselves as artists too. But since the seminal Menil Collection (Volume one pp140–63), Piano's museums are exceptional in foregoing self-expression to concentrate on humbly establishing the conditions in which best to see and contemplate art, and on relating the building and its contents to their setting and nature. Hence, when the Beyeler was finished it was hailed by critics and curators as a salutary

antithesis to the other, more high-profile museums designed mainly as virtuoso displays of their architect's artistic aspirations and expressed in their trademark style.

By contrast, the Beyeler is rigorous, reticent and serenely settled in place, rather than showing off and seeking attention. But though distinctly different from other Piano projects, it returns to themes elaborated in earlier projects. It is clearly a descendant of The Menil Collection: both are evenly lit through flat glass roofs oversailing outer walls clad in a material that relates the museum to its context (the clapboarding at The Menil, and a stone resembling the local sandstone at Beyeler). Nature, too, is intimately present in both buildings.

But the differences are just as marked, including the manner in which nature is present in both museums, and the organization of, and routes through, the gallery spaces. At The Menil large, fixed ferro-cement 'leaves' exclude direct sun, diffuse the incoming light and form a highly visible ceiling. But at Beyeler the sunshades are above the roof with adjustable louvres below it, all largely obscured from view by a perforated metal ceiling. In these respects, the Beyeler is

56

Beyeler Foundation Museum Riehen, Basle, Switzerland 1992–7

1

58　**Beyeler Foundation Museum**
Previous page Southern porch where
pond extends under oversailing roof to
meet floor of end galleries.

Relationship to villa and garden.
1 Aerial view of site as it was with historic
villa in foreground and demolished villa in
middle of garden.
2 Aerial view of museum squeezed
between boundary wall to west and main
road to Germany on east with Villa Berower
to south in bottom left corner.
3 Section through southern end of
museum, pond and garden with Villa
Berower in elevation.

related to the Cy Twombly
Gallery (Volume three pp56–73)
and the Atelier Brancusi
(pp24–35). Also like them, it
contrasts a floating steel and
glass roof with earthbound
masonry external walls – which
also, for all their seeming
solidity, conceal the real
structure of concrete columns.
But here the roof is yet more
diaphanously dematerialized
than those of the earlier
buildings.

Like The Menil, the Beyeler
was built for a demanding
private client to put his collection
on permanent public view. Ernst
Beyeler is an art dealer in Basle.
Like Madame de Menil and her
husband, Beyeler and his wife,
Hildy, have amassed over fifty
years one of the great collections
of Modern art, in their case by
retaining those works with
which they could not bear to
part. The 180 works range from
French Impressionism to
contemporary German art and
include Monet, Rousseau, van
Gogh, Cézanne, Braque,
Rauschenberg, Lichtenstein and
Kiefer with Picasso, Matisse and
Klee each represented by several
works. There are also sculptures
by Rodin, Giacometti and
Miró, and from West Africa
and Oceania.

The museum is a joint
undertaking between public
bodies and private interest.
The site was donated by Riehen,
a village five kilometres to the
north of Basle and close to
Germany. A portion of the
running costs is paid for by the
city of Basle. The rest is paid for
by a foundation set up by the
Beyelers, which also paid for the
$40 million building. Besides
choosing the architect (after
visiting The Menil and other
buildings by Piano) and
overseeing the design, Ernst
Beyeler determines curatorial
policy and all matters
concerning the use of
the building.

The site stretches along the
western edge of the main road to
Germany, with its tram
connections to Basle and the
nearby border, and slopes down
to agricultural fields that extend
to low hills rising steeply from
the far side of the flat-bottomed

valley. The park-like grounds
punctuated by large trees were
those of the eighteenth-century
Villa Berower, which remains at
their southern end as a historic
monument. Just as some
departments of The Menil
Foundation occupy bungalows
around the museum, the Villa
Berower houses the Beyeler
restaurant and its administrative
and curatorial offices.

The full glory of Beyeler's
collection was first widely
appreciated when exhibited at
the Centro de Arte Reina Sofia
in Madrid in 1992. Bernard
Plattner and Loïc Couton (the
associate and architect in charge
respectively) first saw it there in
this converted eighteenth-
century hospital with long
barrel-vaulted galleries ranged
side by side with few openings
between them. In these simply
whitewashed, austerely plain
and generously proportioned
spaces the paintings looked
stupendous.

The Reina Sofia's galleries
inspired the initial conceptual
plan of the Beyeler: four
110-metre-long parallel walls,
oriented roughly north–south,
defining three elongated
galleries. The dimensions (walls
7.5 metres apart, 70 cm wide
and some 5 metres high) were
copied from Madrid. The
Spanish galleries, however,

2

3

depend on artificial light, and, from the beginning, Beyeler and Piano were convinced that the paintings should be viewed, as much as possible, in natural light alone, and that the whole gallery space – not just the walls – should be evenly lit. Arups advised them that in Basle this would require an almost entirely glazed roof, allowing for light lost in transmission through the layers of glass and the devices for diffusing and controlling the light. So instead of vaults between the tops of the parallel walls, a glass roof was now to

Beyeler Foundation Museum
4 Renzo Piano and Ernst Beyeler in conversation on steps in winter garden.
5 Sectional sketch by Renzo Piano.
6 Site plan.

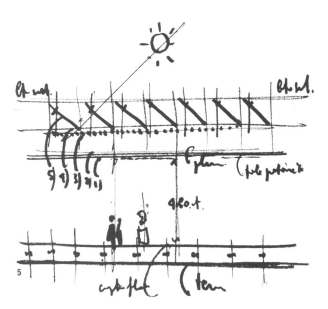

float over them and the solid end walls were to be replaced with glass. In contrast to the introverted, artificially-lit galleries of the Reina Sofia, these galleries would enjoy the benefits of transparency: be flooded with natural light that changes with the external conditions and open up to extrovert views of nature. Instead of sub-dividable, flexible space or fixed rooms, the initial concept was an updated version of the classic gallery form, the long yet broad, corridor-like spaces found in old museums such as the Louvre.

The purity of this original concept inevitably became simultaneously compromised and enriched. Cross walls were inserted to create more hanging surface and distinct rooms, each for a different period, style or painter; and gaps were created in the long main walls, not just for circulation between the structural bays but also to create some rooms two bays wide. At one stage, planted courts were inserted, interrupting the long spaces and bringing nature right into the building as at The Menil. But this was rejected very soon as inappropriate.

Much better is the adopted solution. This provides a finely judged balance in the contrast between the majority of rooms closed in the middle of the building and those that open up, through the glazed screens between the ends of the main walls, to the garden (which has been relandscaped as an intrinsic part of the total scheme by local landscape architect Jochen Wiede). There is an

equally finely judged contrast between the framed and intimate engagement with the landscaped nature of the garden, as viewed from these end galleries, and the more elevated and expansive view over agricultural fields offered by the addition of a glazed winter garden stretched along the museum's western front.

The winter garden forms a longer, narrower and transparent counterpart to the elongated entrance lobby and adjacent bar of service spaces which are squeezed between the easternmost long wall and the main road. The lobby (which further inverts the winter garden in having glazed end walls precisely where the winter garden is solidly enclosed) expands into the first of the top-lit gallery bays and the bookshop directly opposite, to imply an asymmetrically-placed cross axis to the whole building. The meandering route through the museum starts from this lobby-gallery to proceed southwards at first. It eventually returns to the northern arm of the lobby through openings from the galleries usually used for temporary exhibitions. (There is another temporary exhibition gallery in the basement, reached by stairs and an all-glass lift in the winter

59

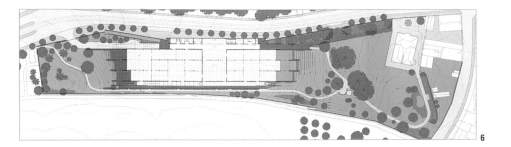

1

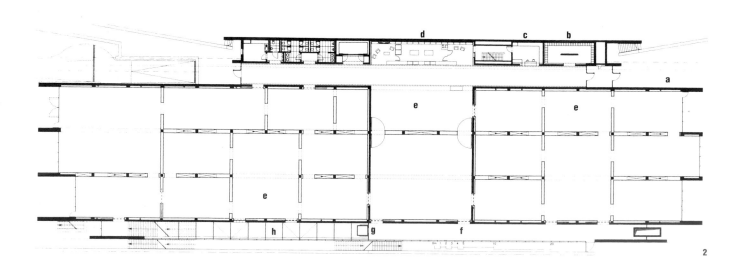

2

Beyeler Foundation Museum

1 West elevation seen from fields overlooked by glass-sided winter garden nestled below oversailing glass roof.

2 Ground floor plan: **a** approach path; **b** cloaks; **c** tickets; **d** bookshop, **e** gallery; **f** winter garden; **g** elevator; **h** sunken portion of winter garden.

3 Basement plan: **a** temporary exhibition gallery; **b** loading bay; **c** plant room.

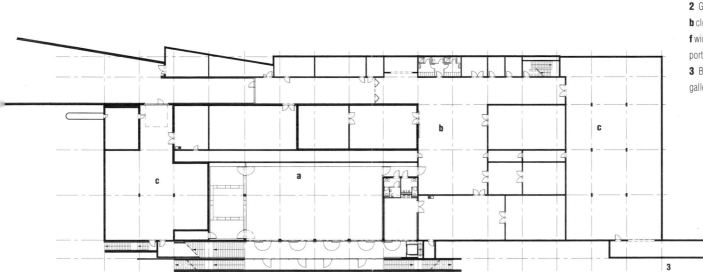

1

Beyeler Foundation Museum

1 Construction view shows grid of steel roof structure raised above unclad concrete structure of walls.

2 Main road to Germany is edged by stone wall which will soon be festooned with creepers.

3 Rebuilt boundary wall on west and northern corner of museum.

2

3

garden. Also in the basement is staff car parking, a loading bay and space for packing and unpacking art, a workshop and storage space.)

As the plan became more elaborate so too did the walls, in part to engage with the site and nature. Inside, the walls remained thick and abstractly white. But in reality they are hollow, merely plasterboard on metal studs, and conceal concrete columns and air-conditioning ducts. Those parts of the walls that extend out beyond the glazing are of solid concrete, although faced in stone. They also step down in height and extend out to embrace the earth and garden as low retaining walls. The easternmost of these guides visitors, who enter the site by a gate near the Villa Berower, towards the entrance. As design proceeded, the glazed roof also became more complex and multi-layered as it acquired elements to exclude direct sunlight and a loft space below it to improve insulation and house further controls of natural light as well as the artificial lighting.

This was the state of the design when published as a project in Volume two (pp170–9) when two different solutions for the roof were being investigated, both using glass structurally to span the full width between the main walls. The then-preferred solution, had v-shaped troughs of glass that spanned as beams over a supporting structure of laminated wood beams and shapely v-props.

A full-size mock-up of the preferred solution was erected on site. But the large glass troughs could not cope with the thermal movement and shattered with the rapid contraction after sunset. Such a result constitutes feedback rather than failure. Architects who challenge the limits of technology and materials inevitably enter the realms of the unpredictable. Hence the necessity of testing and full-size prototyping. Thus the roof has been rethought; the glass is no longer structural, yet the result is more elegant conceptually and visually. Independent glass sunshades enclosing nothing might seem a little weird at first, but are not uncommon on elevations. Besides the advantages of relatively straightforward construction, exposed sunshades dissipate heat outside rather than transmit it into the interior.

The 4,000-square-metre glazed roof is supported by a horizontal grid of 250 x 140 millimetre welded steel box beams with horizontally projecting flanges. (Where these oversail the interior they become the exposed I-beams of the eaves.) Off this grid are propped large sheets of clear double glazing (coated to exclude ultra-violet light) that slope slightly to drain to gutters over the heads of the main walls. Cast-steel elements rise from these same props to support the sunshades, which consist of inclined sheets of tempered 12 millimetre glass that are entirely fritted with two white coats of enamel to exclude 50 per cent of direct sunlight (and its heat energy). To separate roof and wall, the steel grid does not sit on the head of the external walls. Instead the columns, and their stone cladding, extend up by one course to support a cast steel piece, to which are pin-jointed lugs projecting down from the structural grid. A strip of glazing then fills the space

4

between the underside of the gutter and the head of the wall. Inside, the heads of the walls are hidden by the ceiling. Here too the roof grid is attached to the same steel element that caps the heads of the columns or sits on the welded steel box beams spanning the openings in the main walls.

Further dramatizing the contrast between hovering glass and earth-bound masonry, the roof also oversails the long facades to shade the strip of glazing at the head of the walls from low east and west sun –

hence the white dashes of fritting on the projecting glass. The roof also projects beyond the short ends of the building, thus shading the fully-glazed southern ends of the galleries. The fritting eliminates the need for sunshades above the oversailing parts of the roofs, creating a satisfying formal distinction between the different parts of the roof, the presence of the sunshades outside also indicating that of the loft below. This is very different to the two rejected proposals where the projecting roof would have been, as at The Menil, the same as that over the body of the building. The white fritting also makes the projecting glass seem paradoxically more present and yet more diaphanous, and helps unify the glass and white steel grid of the roof as a single floating element.

To keep the purity of the structural steel grid that supports the glass, and avoid the need for larger beams below it, external freestanding columns have been added beyond the ends of the walls. Again, these columns do not compromise but enrich the design, making it more suggestive and revealing of the building's true nature. The columns elevate the porch into a form of pronaos or temple front, thus alluding to the museum's role as a quasi-sacred sanctuary for art. The exposed columns (along with the cast-steel elements visible along the tops of the external walls) also make it clear the walls are not structural and that the roof is carried by more columns hidden within them. Like the external walls, these freestanding columns are clad in stone. The original intention had been to

use the local red sandstone of which Basle Cathedral is built. But this is not durable. Several substitutes were found, but eventually a more durable porphyry from Patagonia in Argentina was chosen.

The water- and sun-excluding upper layers of the roof, described so far, are part of a deeper, multi-layered mechanism designed to further control and modulate light, and to achieve maximum energy efficiency. Over the gallery spaces is the loft enclosed at its bottom by a ceiling of clear glass. This sits in a steel frame suspended from the same steel grid from which the upper glass layers are propped. During maintenance, workmen walk and kneel on this laminated glass, crouching in the 1.2 metre headroom below the horizontal, motorized adjustable louvres set between the beams of the structural grid. The louvres, oriented parallel to the building's longitudinal axis, control the amount of light admitted, and exclude it altogether when the museum is closed. The museum takes its alignment from site constraints and the road it abuts, and is oriented 14 degrees off due north–south. So in mid-summer, early morning sun steals behind the sunshades to fall directly on the clear glass

Beyeler Foundation Museum

4 North porch of museum.
5 Glass of oversailing roof is propped from structural steel grid. Along side eaves, the glass extends beyond the frames it sits in, while end sheets of glass are supported only by being clamped at one edge by small circular plates.
6 Study of earlier version of structure of oversailing eaves. The truss of tubular elements has now been replaced by the grid seen in **5**.

5

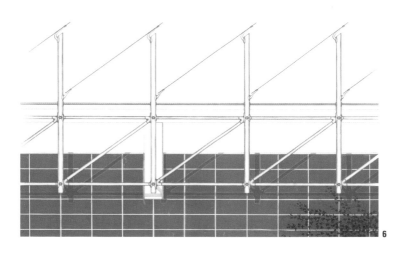

6

1

Beyeler Foundation Museum

1 Temporary exhibition gallery
in basement with show of works by
Richard Long.

2, **3**, **4** Computer simulations of varying
temperatures in section of gallery and loft.
2 shows stratification of air temperatures,
which are hot in the loft, and warm directly
below it, yet temperate throughout most of
the volume of the gallery.

roof. This is one reason the museum does not open until 11 am, by which time the sunshades block all direct sunlight and the adjustable louvres can be opened. The lowest layer of the roof, which further reduces the incoming light, is suspended below the glass bottom of the loft. It is a ceiling of steel panels perforated by rows of rectangular slots – which echo the pattern on the fritted glass on the oversailing eaves.

The numerous layers of roof, loft, ceiling and mechanisms to shade, diffuse and control the

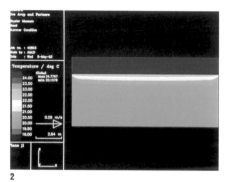

2

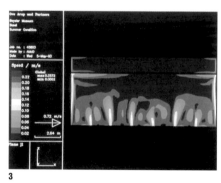

3

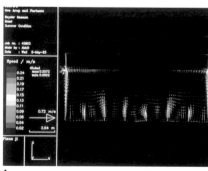

4

light, each transmit only a portion of the light that falls upon them. The glass sunshades reduce the incoming light by 50 per cent, of which 70 per cent is transmitted through the glass of the main roof, which is not only uv-coated but has to be thick enough to provide security. The layer of structure and horizontal louvres admit up to 60 per cent of light falling on it, of which 75 per cent reaches the glazed bottom of the loft. This transmits 85.5 per cent of the light falling on it, of which 52 per cent passes through the perforated metal ceiling. In turn, 57 per cent of this light then falls on the walls at the height of the paintings. Thus, only 4 per cent of the light hitting the roof actually reaches the paintings – the target figure recommended by Arups.

All these arrangements to exclude sun and control natural light, as well as the artificial lighting and air-conditioning, and the energy-saving strategy these are all part of, were devised in consultation with Tom Barker and Andy Sedgewick of Ove Arup & Partners. The museum, and in particular its roof and loft, was to a degree conceived of as a mechanism that is self-adjusting and tuneable. Sensors measure the light and adjust the louvres to exclude excessive natural light and, if this falls too low, progressively activate the artificial lighting. Moreover, the thresholds at which natural light is excluded or artificially supplemented can be reprogrammed. And, as well as such fine-tuning of environmental conditions, the column and hollow wall construction allows easy

adjustment of the openings between galleries, and so for future variations to the route through them. Provision has also been made to adjust the amount of openness between the winter garden and its adjacent galleries.

During design it was agreed that the normal illumination of the galleries would be about 280 lux, though both natural and artificial illumination could exceed or be less than this. This is considered safe for oil paintings, though not for more fragile water colours, drawings and other works on paper. Such vulnerable pieces can be provided for at the Beyeler in three different ways. Most straight-forwardly, they can be shown in the basement gallery that is artificially lit, except for the natural light admitted from the sunken portion of the winter garden from which it is entered. However, this gallery might often be used for visiting exhibitions. In the upper galleries, large light-vulnerable works, such as the Matisse paper cut-outs, are protected by adjusting the louvres to keep light levels low. (The lighting in adjacent galleries must also be lowered somewhat to avoid too abrupt a contrast with the dimly lit space.) But most of the vulnerable works in the

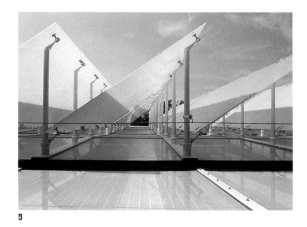

9

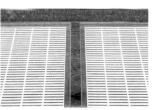

6

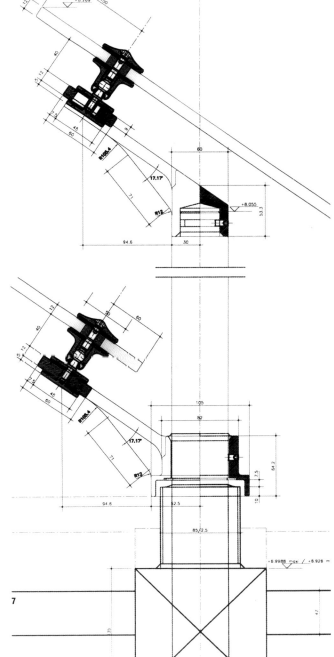

7

permanent collection are small. When best shown in the same gallery as larger paintings, as in this collection with Picasso's drawings and paintings, they are hung in a small independent structure placed inside the gallery. The ceilings of these structures shade the works inside so that the light on them is of acceptably low levels even when the surrounding paintings are well lit.

Although all this works well, there were some teething troubles – none of them of the architect's making. The system to monitor and adjust light levels recommended by Arups was quite straightforward: it depended only on sensors measuring light levels in the galleries and adjusting the louvres and artificial lighting accordingly. But installed instead was a very complex and sophisticated system that measured a range of external factors, recalled from memory the adjustments it had made previously in similar conditions, and then responded. It never performed properly. Compounding this problem, Ernst Beyeler, influenced by the most cautious of art conservationists, kept light levels very low, between 100 and 140 lux. So some visitors, particularly those familiar with The Menil, were disappointed with the lighting. However, the control systems have now been revised and Beyeler has agreed to let the light approximate the original design levels.

Ecology- and energy-conscious Switzerland's stringent regulations prohibit air-conditioning, unless it can be proven essential and as efficient as is currently possible. Air-conditioning is unavoidable for fragile works of art requiring stable temperatures and humidity. Although an all-glass roof inevitably allows thermal transmission through it, the Beyeler achieves exceptional energy efficiency. It consumes only 155 kilowatt hours per square metre (in contrast to 800 kWh/square metre at The Menil Collection and 250 kWh/square metre at the Cy Twombly Gallery, both in the hot Houston climate that requires considerable energy-intensive cooling).

The Beyeler achieves this energy efficiency, as well as by making maximum use of natural light, by exploiting the tall volume of the galleries and using the loft as a thermal buffer between inside and outside. Thus freshly conditioned air is admitted through the floors to rise slowly as it increases in temperature before being extracted at the heads of the walls. Because this air stratifies in layers of differing temperature, conditions remain equable and stable in the bottom 2.5 metres or so of the room, occupied by people and paintings, while temperatures directly under the 5.25-metre-high ceiling vary quite considerably. Temperatures in the void fluctuate even more, rising to 32 degrees Centigrade in summer and falling to 20 degrees in winter, when the loft will be heated occasionally to prevent temperatures dropping any further. The winter garden is also a thermal buffer, though to be comfortably habitable the temperatures fluctuate less, from 20 to 26 degrees Centigrade.

However, the success of a museum lies not only in its technical solutions but also in the experiences it offers, both of itself and of viewing the art it houses. A visit to the Beyeler is a revelation as to how richly

65

1

2

66

3

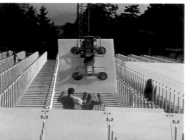

4

5

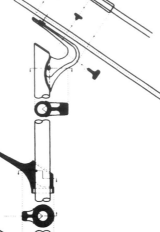

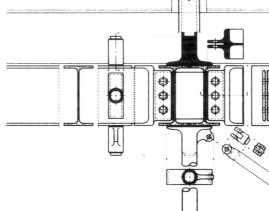

6

Beyeler Foundation Museum

Fitting the sunshades:

1, **2** Fixing the supports for the sunshades on top of the glass roof.

3, **4**, **5** Manoeuvering the sunshades into position.

6 Study of earlier system of roof structure and support of sunshades above roof, and glass ceiling enclosing loft below it.

7, **8**, **9** Fixing the sunshades to their supports.

10 Banks of angled sunshades supported on tubular- and cast-steel elements shade the clear glass roof.

7

8

9

1

Beyeler Foundation Museum
Architecture and nature.
1 Southern porch end seen from garden
west of Villa Berower.
2 Vaguely temple-like south elevation
rising from pond.
3 View across pond and garden from
gallery in south-west corner of museum.
4 East elevation from road to Germany
showing Villa Berower, entry gate and
museum. In the final building, the sloping
sunshades underneath the roof at the
porch ends are replaced by the perforated
steel ceiling .

3

2

satisfying such a rigorous and
relatively understated building
can be. Photographs cannot
capture fully the elusive magic
added by the generosity, as well
as the precision, of its
proportions, nor the vivacity of
its soft and subtly changing
light. Another triumph of the
design is how the different views
the building offers of itself to
those passing-by, approaching
and moving around and through
it are so precisely apt to where it
is viewed from. Even close to,
the detailing, for instance, is
seen to be understated yet

flawless, with no elements overly
elaborated or too reduced in
scale or material, as has
sometimes been the case with
the Building Workshop.

Though the museum edges
the main road, its presence
barely registers on passers-by.
The straight stretches of wall
edging the pavement are clad in
the recessive dark-red porphyry;
part of the wall is screened by
gingko trees, while elsewhere
creepers climb up or tumble
over it. What arrests the eye is
not the wall but the roof floating
enigmatically above and beyond
it. This combines the
mechanical repetitive rhythms
of projecting steel beams,
glazing bars and angled
sunshades with the unassertive,
diaphanous delicacy of the
frosty fritted glass. It can be
particularly eye-catching in the
early morning and towards
sunset when the walls sleep in
shadow and the roof blazes
brightly in the low-slanted
shafts of sun.

Entering the grounds, visitors
are greeted by a view of the
gardens, with the Villa Berower
to the left and the restaurant
terrace ahead. To the right is the
museum. Set somewhat lower
and seen end-on, it seems
smaller than it really is, just a
pavilion rising from the pond
before it. Yet this transparent
end reveals, in immediate x-ray
view, the fundamental design
concept which, as usual with the
Building Workshop, is
manifested largely in the
organization and details of the
section. Here Piano's obsession
with transparency transcends
mere views in and out to offer

direct perception of the
essentials of concept and
construction. The effect is
magically pronounced at dusk
when artificial light fully reveals
the spaces and works inside
while all external materials and
detail remain visible. The
visitors inside are also put on
show, inviting others to join
them as well as to anticipate,
and be aware of, how special is
the activity of viewing art.

As you come closer, this porch
end progressively reveals more
and asserts something of the
building's atmosphere on the
surroundings as well as on those
approaching; also the museum's
real size and generosity of
dimensions become apparent.
Above, you see the oversailing
roof float out to embrace its
surroundings, supported on the
crisp white steel grid and the
glazing bars propped from this
and stopping short of the ends
of the glass sheets which reach
out unconstrained by frames.
You notice that the white
fritting not only helps unify the
glass and steel, but also that its
pattern and the slight slopes of
the glass add a visual rhythmic
energy that helps the roof fly
free of the earthbound walls.
Visible too are the steel column
heads that support the roof grid,

4

5

both those that read as capitals to the freestanding columns – so reinforcing the porch's vaguely temple-like aspect – and those rising from the long walls behind.

Both the exposure of the building's organization and construction, and the projection of its potent atmosphere gain immensely from the complex overlapping of the building's various elements in a way that also blurs distinctions between where it begins and ends. There is far more to this than just the way the roof and columns

project forward of the ends of the walls and galleries. Crucial also is the counterthrust of the pond extending inwards under the roof so that the columns rise from it. This interlocks museum and garden and seems to project the calm serenity of the still pond into the galleries. This effect is intensified by the meticulous attention to detail: the pond's surface is at exactly the same level as the gallery floor into which the window frames are sunk so as not to disrupt this sense of continuity through the glass. After dark, this illusion is aided by the underwater lights illuminating the pond from under these windows.

The loft stopping short of the end of the building makes clear the difference between the size of the overall building and that of the inner galleries. The glazing that both closes the end of the loft and reveals its presence is set back above low roofs over the ends of the galleries. Outside the loft-end glazing, the perforated panels of the internal ceilings step up and are fixed directly under the steel structural grid to deepen the shade cast by the fritted roof. Also, the glazed end of the central gallery projects forward from those of the galleries to either side, so people passing the pond on the entrance path can see into it as well as the gallery closest to them, thus extending this central gallery to accommodate an exceptionally long painting, one of Monet's Water Lilies series. Although this device somewhat emphasizes the

museum's central axis and the symmetry of this porch end, Piano welcomes such functional reasons to disrupt an overly classical or definite termination to a building, so tempering an abstract system with the 'indeterminacy' of the contingent.

The placing of the entrance lobby, and the cross axis implied by the gallery space and bookshop it expands into, might similarly offset expectations of classical symmetry; but though the resultant asymmetry is clear in plan, it does not register on the visitor. However, this asymmetry does lessen the length of blank wall visitors must walk past before reaching the entrance doors. Despite the longitudinal thrust of the lobby, lit only at its two ends, it comes to a serene stasis where it swells on one side into the bookshop and, on the other, into the more brightly-lit gallery space which basks in the sumptuous top light that pervades all the galleries.

This first gallery space, with its comfortable settees and the adjacent bookshop, forms a calm hub where visitors can browse and wait for each other before or after viewing the rest of the museum. From here the route turns back on itself to proceed

69

Beyeler Foundation Museum

5 The roof structure is secured to the heads of the external columns by the same cast-steel elements that perform a similar function along the heads of the walls.
6 Night view shows how surface of pond is at same level as gallery floor, accentuating interlocking of inside and out and the serene atmosphere.
7 Oversailing eaves shelter approach path to museum.

Overleaf

South porch at dusk. Not only the interior and exterior, but the essential organisation of the building in concept and construction is revealed in a single x-ray view.

6

7

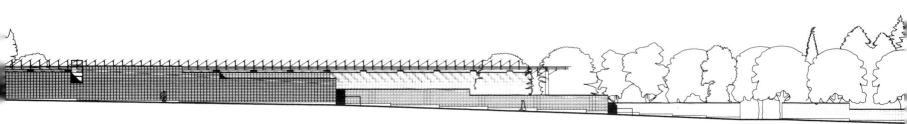

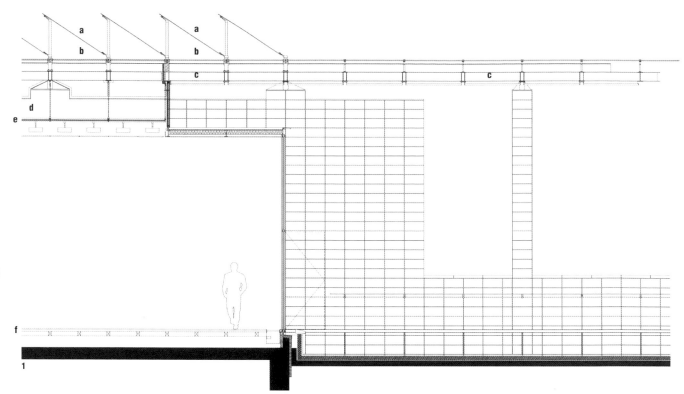

1

Beyeler Foundation Museum

South porch.

1 Detail section through end of loft, gallery and pond: **a** glass sunshades; **b** double glazed roof; **c** primary roof structure; **d** glass ceiling closing loft; **e** perforated steel ceiling; **f** raised floor with air-inlet ducts.

2 Temple-like aspect and interpenetration with pond suggest that the museum is a semi-sacred and contemplative sanctuary for art.

3 The sides and bottom of the window frames are concealed so that the floor and walls extend smoothly to pond and stone-faced walls outside, indivisibly interlocking interior and exterior, architecture and nature.

72

2

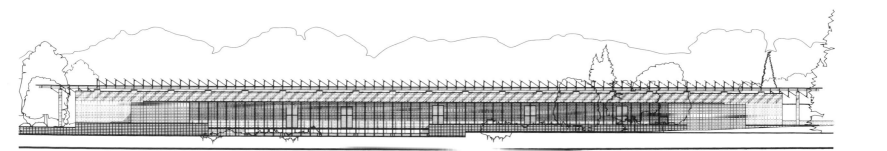

2

Beyeler Foundation Museum

Winter garden.

1 Detail of west elevation where winter garden steps down to basement. Concrete walls are simply faced in stone while elements of roof and glazing are expressed independently. Strip window separates roof from head of wall, while glazing mullions below are welded from three steel strips, the central one of which is recessed to give a sense of crispness and lightness.

2 West elevation. The inverted glass sunshades are not in the final building.

3, **4** Night views.

5 Detail cross-section through roof: **a** bottom of posts supporting sunshades; **b** double-glazed roof; **c** insulated gutter; **d** primary steel structural grid; **e** cast-steel junction element; **f** steel box beam over opening in main wall; **g** motorized aluminium louvres; **h** strip window; **k** suspension tie; **m** glass ceiling; **n** perforated steel ceiling; **p** artificial lighting units; **q** air extract; **r** concrete external wall; **s** stone cladding.

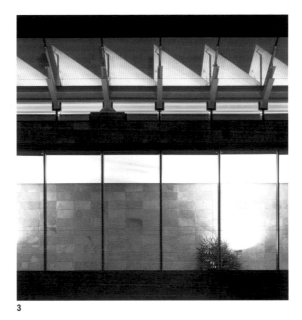

3

4

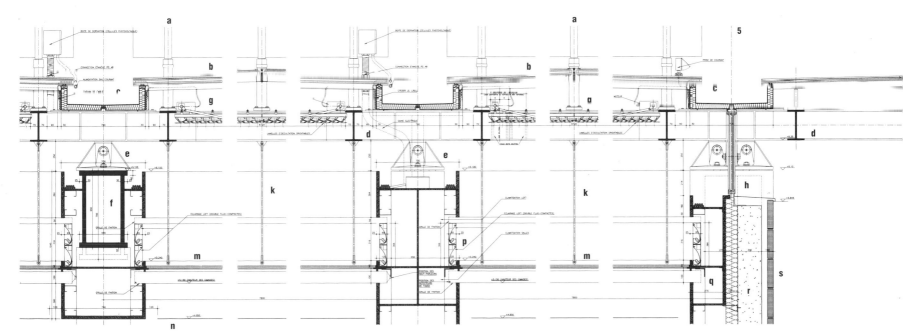

5

1

Beyeler Foundation Museum

1 Looking west in small double-width gallery, with views through openings across upper part of double-height portion of winter garden.

2 Cross section: **a** road to Germany; **b** elongated entrance lobby; **c** permanent collection gallery; **d** loft; **e** temporary exhibition gallery; **f** sunken portion of winter garden; **g** public footpath.

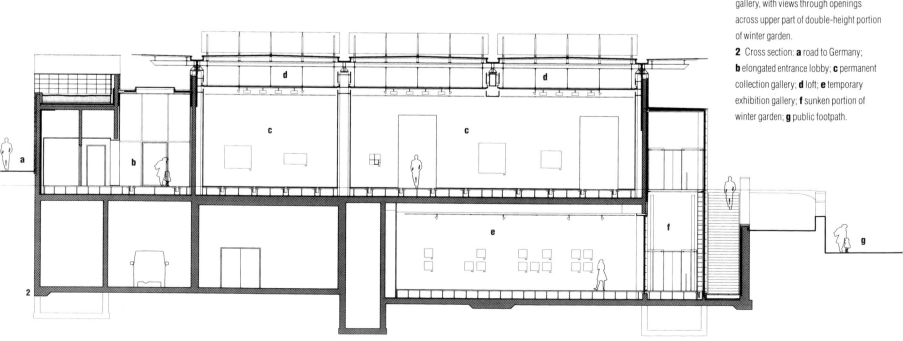

a   b   d   c   d

c   e   f   g

2

3

Beyeler Foundation Museum

Gallery interiors.

3 Enfilade view linking central aisle of galleries.

4 Same gallery as **1** on facing page viewed in opposite direction.

5 Sectional detail of glazed screen in double-height portion of winter garden. Horizontal strut between transom and stone-clad wall was eventually eliminated.

Overleaf

View of double-width gallery shows how the walls are kept devoid of incident and detail, with no skirtings or covings. Light switches and other distractions are restricted to the sides of openings between galleries.

4

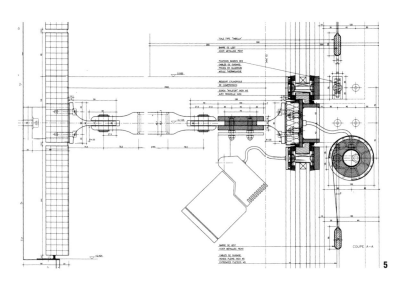

5

southwards to re-establish a connection with the pond and the garden beyond. This is a simple, obvious, but nevertheless masterly touch, as is the use of, and balance between, enfilade views and open and closed vistas. The enfilade views each extend through three rooms, linking them into coherent groupings and leading visitors through them. In the central row of rooms, the enfilades align with their and the building's central axis, and in the outer rows of rooms they are usually aligned close to the rooms' outer edges, thus subtly helping to orient visitors. The openings between the rooms – both those that frame these enfilades and others – define a meandering route gently leading visitors through the museum while also offering choices and short cuts. Also masterly is the way the enfilades restate the theme of linear aisles, a theme that has been compromised by the subdivision of the museum into rooms; and the balance achieved so that each room is both part of a larger aisle and fluid route, and yet self-contained enough to allow intimate and undistracted contemplation of the works it contains.

To reach the southernmost rooms, visitors first pass through a pair of the smallest rooms, each a single bay wide (7.10 metres) and shorter (at 12 metres) than some others of this width. (The Water Lilies room is 15 metres long and the Picasso room 18 metres.) So that nothing distracts from the artworks, the rooms are visually as clean and simple as possible, with no covings or skirtings to the plain white walls and all signage, as well as hatches and vents for technical equipment, such as temperature and humidity monitors, are restricted to the sides of the openings between rooms. The generous and handsome proportions add to the sense of luminous, contemplative calm. The only hint of colour, other than the art, is the floor of bleached French oak in which the continuous grilles of the air inlets are detailed with utmost simplicity.

Piano had originally considered stretched cotton ceilings like those in the Cy Twombly Gallery and the Atelier Brancusi. Beyeler vetoed these: to him they seemed cheap and makeshift, detracting from the timeless permanence that he sought. Instead the white perforated steel panels were designed. These appear mechanically brittle and distracting in some photographs, but are beautiful in reality. This is due to Piano's characteristic precision with proportions (including the relationships between the shape and spacing of the slots, the width of the unperforated edge of the panel around the slots and the spacings between panels) and to such small but telling subtleties as the barely-noticeable outer frame that surrounds all of the panels and is set close to them but further from the head of the walls. The ceiling eventually adopted brings another visual advantage: it is more distinctly different from the plain white walls than seamless stretched cotton would have been, and so distinguishes major elements in the rooms to give a definite character very different from the blandly disorienting all-white galleries of high Modernism. Concealed in the loft above this ceiling is the source of general artificial illumination (triphosphour

77

1

2

3

linear fluorescent fittings), and here and there slender stems drop through the gaps between the ceiling panels to support single low-voltage spotlights for focusing on individual artworks – particularly sculpture which needs directional lighting to bring out its forms.

The artworks in the southern-most rooms are chosen to relate to, or be able to stand up to, the natural backdrop visible through the wall-to-wall and floor-to-ceiling end glazing, and include several sculptures which benefit from the strong side light. Here it becomes apparent how the complex interpenetrations and overlappings of this porch end, already noted outside, pay immense visual dividends internally also. The outlook on the garden is not as if through a conventional window. Instead views are framed by the stone-faced walls and columns as well as the projecting roof, all of which are visible as they continue outside to interlock building and nature and draw the pool in as a smooth continuation of the gallery floor. The continuities between inside and outside are again aided by burying the outer window frame in walls, ceiling and floor. Yet again, transparency involves more than seeing through a glass screen: more important is revealing of the design's concepts and intentions – intellectual transparency, not just physical.

Like the loft above it, the perforated steel ceiling stops short of the glazed end wall and a plain plaster ceiling under the low roof ends the gallery. Without this, the ceiling and window frame would have come too close for visual comfort: the room might then have seemed rather cage-like; and though both ceiling and window are subdivided in four, only the central of these subdivisions would align. To avoid similar problems of slight misalignment, the lines of air-inlet grilles in the floor line up with the middle of the window panes. This brings another satisfying visual effect into play, as pairs of such rows of grilles, though briefly interrupted at the thresholds between rooms, can be seen converging in perspective, reinforcing each enfilade view as they align with the edges of the openings that frame them.

From these southern rooms, the route continues northwards along the westernmost wall. Every alternate (double width) room has a pair of openings through the wall into the winter garden. But Beyeler, quite rightly it seems, has chosen to close all, except those in the room on axis with the entrance lobby. Hence, on the route through the museum, the winter garden is discovered later than it might have been, when it offers more of a contrast to, and relief from, the enclosed galleries. It is a pleasant place to simply sit and perhaps consult a catalogue or gaze across the fields to the nearby hills and enjoy a respite from the intense experience of viewing such a fine collection. The winter garden's closed southern end is used for viewing videos.

At the winter garden's midpoint is the all-glass lift which descends into the sunken northern half of the winter garden. The double-volume height of this is also enclosed along its western edge by a glass wall, separating it, at this point, from a trench into which steps descend at either end. This arrangement not only brings

4

Beyeler Foundation Museum

1 The openings between the rooms define a meandering route leading visitors through the museum.

2 View from corner of one of the western-most galleries. On the right is the currently sealed opening to the winter garden. To the left is one of the independent structures within which graphic works are exhibited at low light levels.

3 The central of the southern-most galleries is longer than to those to either side so as to accommodate Monet's Water Lilies without end of painting coming too close to the real lilies in the pond outside.

4 The western of the southern-most galleries, showing how the views through the porch outside interlock architecture and nature.

5 Plan detail of glazing of end galleries. Note how mullion is made of three strips of steel, with the end of the central one recessed to increase the sense of crispness and lightness.

some side light into the basement temporary exhibition gallery, but the external stairs also provide independent access to this gallery when used for lectures and other events outside normal museum hours. A stair in the northern end of the winter garden also links the basement gallery with the temporary exhibition galleries on the main floor.

Comment has been made that access to the basement gallery is rather remote from the entrance and difficult to find. This is true, especially of the after-hours external route; yet when circulating through the museum the sunken part of the winter garden is discovered quite inevitably on the route through the museum, and both internal modes of access are at appropriate enough points on that route. In addition, some criticize the juxtaposition of the Water Lilies with the pond outside, deeming it too literal and distracting – even that the painting cannot hold its own against live nature. Some claim that the high and wide rooms are unsuited to smaller paintings, like those by Klee, which would be better in more intimate settings – though those can, in fact, be provided by inserting the independent structures used to display light-vulnerable works.

These seem reasonable, intellectually justified criticisms. Whether or not the juxtaposition of pond and painting is too literal and corny is a matter of opinion (and there are critics who strongly praise it, arguing that the external landscape is thus revealed to be as artificial as the painting, and that the great length of Monet's canvas was meant to suggest such continuities beyond its edges). But the other criticisms are not borne out by actual experience of the building and of the artworks in context. The quality of natural light on the Monet and the stretch of blank wall between it and pond allow attention to be focused solely on the painting, even when the low morning sun casts diverting reflections from the pond onto the intermediate wall. And the contemplative calm of the closed rooms is perfect for engaging with Klee's paintings.

Following comments by Piano himself, some critics have characterized the building as agricultural, its parallel walls recalling terracing and its glass roof reminiscent of greenhouses. Such characteristics certainly apply to Piano's own Laboratory-workshop at Punta Nave, Vesima (Volume two pp76–91), and were indeed generative concepts here; but it is difficult to fit such a description to even the distant view from the west, the only remotely viable candidate for such a reading. The building is too much a sumptuous sanctuary dedicated to art to be agricultural.

The museum's main problem is that, like the Pompidou, it is much more popular than anticipated and cloakroom space has proved to be inadequate. To enlarge this, the ticket office has been moved out of the strip between the entrance lobby and street wall and an independent kiosk built outside the museum's front door.

The museum's rapturous reception has caused Beyeler to consider extending the building northwards, expanding the ground-floor gallery space for temporary exhibitions so that these need not be split between the two levels. This is a good

81

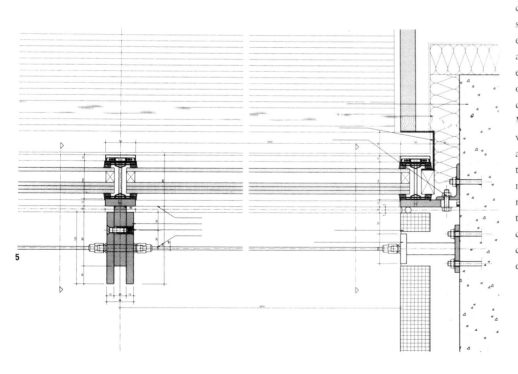

5

enough reason, but it threatens to spoil the design's beautifully poised balances: the asymmetry about the entrance might become too lopsided; the galleries opening on to nature might become too few in relation to closed ones and too remote from the centre of the building; the meandering route with its balance between choice and inevitability might become too extended for coherence; and the system of three gallery enfilades that hold the composition together would break down.

Ultimately the Beyeler Museum is one of the Building Workshop's most accomplished works. Seemingly straight-forward, it is much more than that thanks to the subtlety and surety of judgement of large and small design decisions, that has often entailed eliminating the inessential and refining to the simplest, most understated of solutions. What started as an austerely rigorous and abstract design concept has become richly nuanced to experience. To a large degree this is achieved by the way in which the design plays out a series of dialectical oppositions: archaic, earthbound walls, versus floating, mechanical yet ethereal, roof (or mass and materiality versus light and lightness); thick, hollow walls, versus hidden, load-bearing columns; the linear directionality of long parallel walls and enfilade views, versus serenely static rooms and a meandering route; the fluid continuities of the meandering route, versus the intimate stillness of the individual rooms; the abstraction of rooms enclosed in weightless white walls, versus an engagement with the earthy particulars of the locale; rooms opening extrovertly to nature (while their space remains serenely

static rather than rushing outwards), versus windowless and introverted rooms; intimate engagement with nature achieved by interlocking building and garden, versus the more disengaged enjoyment of the winter garden panorama; building as an adjustable mechanism, versus being a timeless sanctuary for the contemplation of art.

Untouched by fashion and the fad for ego-expression that have afflicted most recent museum design, the Beyeler Foundation Museum is both timeless yet very much of its time and place. Here architecture and technology are at the service of the contemplation of art as enhanced by natural light and nature and the constant subtle changes to which both are subject. Moreover the building exactly exemplifies the motto Matisse borrowed from Baudelaire and with which Beyeler briefed Piano: 'Luxe, calme et volupté'.

82 **Beyeler Foundation Museum**
The winter garden.
1 Detail section of glass-sided elevator.
2 Longitudinal section. Glazed screen in basement elevation encloses temporary exhibition gallery.
3 View down stairs from north into sunken portion of wintergarden with exhibits from a show on the architecture of the Building Workshop spilling into it from the temporary exhibition gallery.

Overleaf
Dusk emphasizes the essentials of the design: its sectional organization; the interweaving of inside and out; and its contemplative serenity as a sanctuary for art.

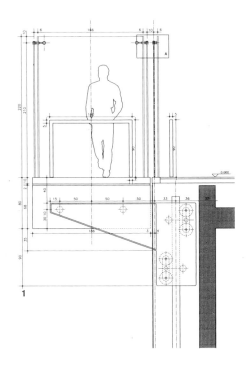

1

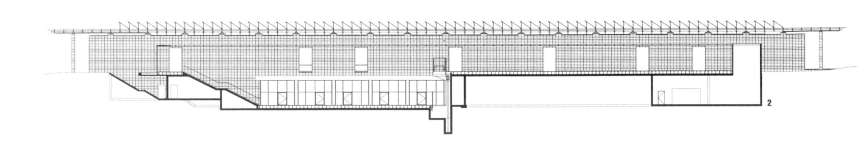

2

84   **Beyeler Foundation Museum**
Client Beyeler Foundation
Architect Renzo Piano Building
Workshop with J Burckhardt & Partner AG,
Basle (collaborating local architect)

Preliminary Phase, 1992
Design team R Piano, B Plattner (senior
partner in charge), L Couton (architect in
charge)
Assisted by J Berger, E Belik, W Vassal
Modelmakers A Schultz, P Darmer
Structural and service engineers
Ove Arup & Partners

**Design Development and
Construction, 1993–7**
Design team R Piano, B Plattner (senior
partner in charge), L Couton (architect in
charge)
Assisted by P Hendier, W Matthews,
R Self, L Epprecht
Modelmaker JP Allain
Structural and service engineers
Ove Arup & Partners, C Burger & Partner,
Bogenschütz AG, J Forrer AG (HVAC),
Elektrizitäts AG, Basel
Landscape architects J Wiede,
Schönholzer + Stauffer

Tjibaou Cultural Centre Nouméa, New Caledonia 1991–8

Stretched along the top of a promontory between the Bay of Magenta and a mangrove-edged lagoon on the South Pacific island of New Caledonia is a row of excitingly exotic structures, intermittently-spaced among the trees they emerge from and exhibit such affinity with, which are as enigmatic as they are evocative. They seem both archaic and futuristic, looking rather as if made of basketwork, yet are far too vast, and somewhat resembling radio telescopes, and yet they are made of wood. Such visual similes point backwards and forwards in time. They evoke simultaneously the indigenous Kanak culture whose artefacts, including huts ('cases', in French), are mostly made and woven from vegetal matter, and aspects of contemporary civilization which still signify a sense of cosmic awe. Symbolically, such associations are resonantly apt: these structures, also dubbed cases, are the most conspicuous parts of the Tjibaou Cultural Centre which has been built to conserve Kanak culture and help it evolve to face our times with replenished roots.

The tall backs of the cases crest a steep slope up from the sea. They enclose the centre's major spaces as man-made vegetal husks which, like the huts and artefacts of the Kanaks, establish an intimate visual connection with the surrounding vegetation, particularly the tall Norfolk Island pines. The cases engage in other ways with the nature the Kanaks worship. The tops of their tall vertical ribs comb the Alize, the predominant trade wind on which the Kanaks sail their outriggers, and which sighs as it blows through the slatted cladding to ventilate the building.

The rest of the centre is more low-key and nestles below a flat roof into the gentle slopes dropping to the lagoon. Here, rather than emulate the tall palms and pines, as do the cases, the building opens up to more obviously landscaped and cultivated vegetation. Indeed, a prime characteristic of much of the building (though not the cases) is how open it is, how blurred and minimal the sense of enclosure as the breezes pass through the centre which merges into the vegetation that is as intrinsic to the project as the architecture. Again, this is inspired by precedent, for the Kanaks live in the verdant tropical outdoors, and mostly only retreat into their huts at night and in inclement weather.

Although built by a western colonial government and

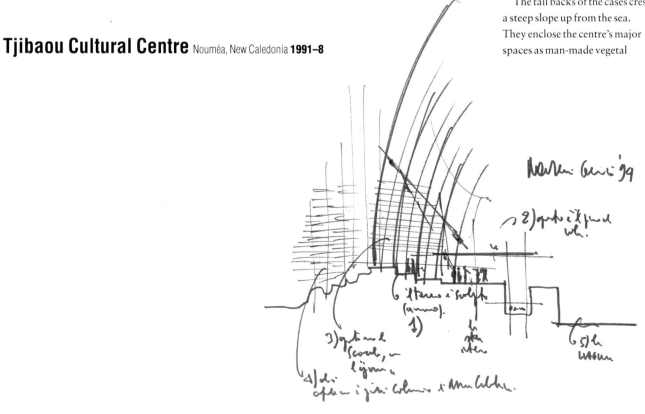

1

88   **Tjibaou Cultural Centre**

Previous pages The cases rise from the top of a steepish slope up from the sea to comb the trade winds that blow off it and establish a harmony with the surrounding vegetation, particularly the tall Norfolk Island pines.

Some key personalities:
1 Renzo Piano and Paul Vincent, the partner in charge, on site. **2** Renzo Piano with Alban Bensa. **3** Opening day: Renzo Piano with two Kanak women. **4** Jean-Marie Tjibaou and his wife, Marie-Claude. **5** Meeting of design team, consultants and clients at Piano's laboratory-workshop at Punta Nave, Vesima.

3

designed by a European architect who has evoked the forms of the local tradition, there is nothing patronizing, kitsch or fake about this building. Instead it is the product of a deep and extended dialogue as Piano and his team of colleagues and consultants studied local traditions and listened to, engaged with and even entered the mind-set of the Kanak clients. So there is no sense of the centre being only an imposed or beneficent 'gift' from a colonial power, a work of conventional contemporary

2

architecture handed down to, as much as over to, the Kanaks. Nor is it a modern building decked out with a few Kanak motifs and materials, what Piano has called 'a tank camouflaged with palm fronds'. Instead the design and its programme evolved organically from all aspects of the situation, including site and climate, the Kanaks' traditional culture and their aspirations for the future, and the design skills and technological expertise brought by the Building Workshop.

To modernist western eyes the resulting scheme might seem more romantic than rational. Of all Piano's many buildings, this might be the one where he dared most in following his design process of participative engagement into territory that is not only uncharted but threatens to transgress conventional critical criteria. Despite considerable trepidation, he has even flirted with the folkloric, evoking, if not imitating, the forms of traditional huts. But he has avoided the pitfalls of kitsch because every aspect of the building is true to itself and obeys its own very contemporary logic of construction and form. The resulting scheme appeals to something very deep inside of us. Not only does the building establish an intimate relationship with all aspects of its natural setting, but it evokes a dream of living in harmony with a paradisiacal nature as if part of, or in easy accord with, a culture that has always enjoyed that harmony. This is a seminal building: as we leave the industrial modern age we realize we must learn to live in

harmony with not just the earth and its ecosystems, but also with all its many cultures who are asking for recognition after having been subsumed into larger nation states or suppressed by colonial powers for so long.

New Caledonia has been an overseas territory of France since the mid-nineteenth century. The French have held onto it because its main island is the world's third largest supplier of nickel, extracted by opencast mining which brutalizes the mountainous landscape so revered by the local Melanesian people. Colonization has also stunted the traditional culture and population growth of the Kanaks so that they now constitute only 45 per cent of a population of 200,000. Europeans, mostly French, though a minority at 35 per cent of the population (the rest are of Asian extraction, or from elsewhere in the Pacific) have opposed independence from France to which the island is strategically so important.

The Kanak struggle for independence between 1984 and 1988 resulted in the Matignon Accords, negotiated by the Kanak leader Jean-Marie Tjibaou. These granted greater recognition to Kanak culture, but no independence as yet.

4

6

7

10

Because of this, Tjibaou and some of his followers were assassinated by Kanak extremists in 1989. This shamed the French government into building the cultural centre which now takes Tjibaou's name as the last of President Mitterrand's 'grands projets' – the only one to be built outside of Paris. Hence the big-budget, beautifully crafted and technologically sophisticated monument to a culture which had no lasting architecture or monuments as we know them. The Kanaks had only had huts, which were allowed to collapse and rot back into nature when their owners died.

The chosen site was the Tina Peninsula, just east of Nouméa, New Caledonia's capital. The location accords with Tjibaou's only recorded wish for any such centre that it should be near Nouméa, so that urban Kanaks might rediscover their roots, and non-Kanaks might discover what is universal in Kanak culture. The spectacular site, between sea and sheltered lagoon, has a dramatic backdrop of mountains and further headlands jutting into the Bay of Magenta.

8

9

Once selected for the international competition to choose the architect, Piano visited the site in early 1992. He was struck by the beauty and topography of the island, by its vegetation and the extent to which the Kanak huts and other artefacts looked at home amongst the plants they are woven from. He noted a path, curving along the promontory's ridge, whose alignment became that of the circulation spine of his scheme, and also three bare patches extending down the gentle slope to the lagoon. He resolved to restrict construction to these areas, leaving untouched the vegetation which was to be utterly integral to the design. He also noted the strength of the persistent trade winds and of the sun, and decided to work with, rather than resist them. Then, on returning to Paris, Piano sought out Alban Bensa, an ethnologist who had lived among and is an authority on the Kanaks.

Bensa became a consultant on the design and described the layout of a typical Kanak village to Piano and the rest of the team led by Paul Vincent (the Partner in charge of the project, who would work with Dominique Rat and William Vassal). The dominant element is an elongated communal open space, terminated at one end by the chief's hut. All other huts are set back from this space and largely hidden in the vegetation, some of which has been specially planted with species that convey messages such as marking the bounds of personal space or welcoming visitors. Such symbolism explained Bensa was important – as a pre-literate culture, the Kanaks invest their memories in things rather than writing. Memories and stories are thus projected into both natural and man-made objects, and to best convey a narrative the latter are made so that their parts are related in a clearly legible and easily understood manner. Thus a hut's central post is the 'big chief' who is protected by the 'lesser chiefs', of the wall posts which surround it, and the coconut-fibre cords which tie the latter together are the women whose function is to hold the tribe together.

The Building Workshop's competition entry (see Volume two pp190–209) was organized around a 230-metre-long covered

89

1

Tjibaou Cultural Centre

1 The backs of the ten cases, clustered to create three 'villages', seen from the sea.

2 North-west elevation towards lagoon.

3 South-east elevation towards sea.

4 Plan of upper level: **A** village 1; **B** village 2; **C** village 3; **a** approach path; **b** reception; **c** gallery; **d** upper volume of gallery; **e** exhibit of Kanak sculptures; **f** sculptures from Pacific region; **g** audio-visual; **h** cafeteria; **k** terrace; **m** multi-media library; **n** lecture theatre; **p** class room; **q** administration; **r** patio; **s** curators offices; **t** auditorium; **u** craft shop.

2

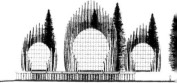

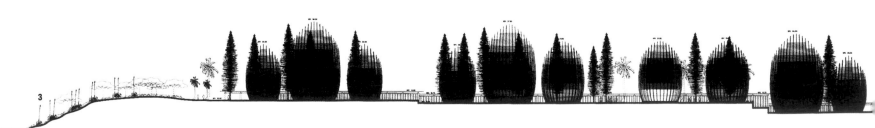

3

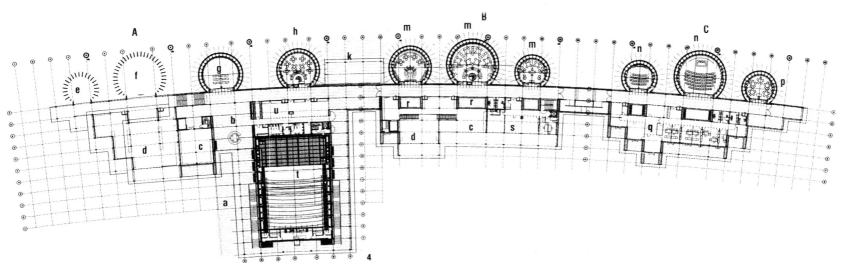

1

2

3

Tjibaou Cultural Centre

Site and context.

1 Aerial view during construction shows contrast between cases cresting rise from sea in foreground and flat-roofed parts on gentle slope to lagoon.

2 Besides vegetation and sea, the natural context includes a backdrop of mountains.

3 Initial view from car parking, with the flat-roofed parts forming a stable datum below the cases' upward thrusting ribs.

4 Aerial view of site at time of competition showing the bare patches where building was sited.

5 Site plan: **a** lagoon; **b** sea; **c** parking; **d** entrance gate; **e** view point; **f** entrance path; **g** Kanak path; **h** outdoor auditorium; **j** area for traditional ceremonies; **k** restaurant; **m** lodgings; **n** studios.

4

way that curved gently with the crest of the peninsula. To either side, the cases containing the centre's main spaces were clustered into three sub-villages exactly as dictated by the pattern of bare patches in the enclosing vegetation. At this stage the cases resembled the Kanak huts, with the vertical ribs of each case coming together in a common apex. The open portions of the cases also faced both into and away from the trade winds to function as wind scoops as well as convection chimneys (aided by the Venturi effect) to naturally ventilate the centre.

Despite reservations some jurors felt about excessive technical sophistication and constructional complexity, the Building Workshop scheme was the unanimous winner of the competition, not least because it was the only entry with which the Kanak jurors felt they could strongly identify. Yet Piano was uneasy that the cases were still too close in form to the Kanak huts and unsure that the passive systems of ventilation would work. But the Kanaks, represented by Octave Togna and Marie-Claude Tjibaou (a colleague of Tjibaou who was to become director of the cultural centre and Tjibaou's widow, respectively), were adamant that the cases had to remain and were reluctant to see them diminish in number, conspicuousness or evocativeness of form.

However, wind tunnel tests proved that the cases would not function as wind scoops. But eventually a version was devised with an inner, as well as outer, ring of vertical ribs, none of which met at their tops. The space between these rings of ribs now proved to work as a convection chimney as part of a larger strategy for natural ventilation. This meant that the cases would look less like Kanak huts, and should all be on the same side of the promenade with their backs to the trade winds. Significantly, this also meant the scheme once again closely resembled Piano's very first sketched response to the site. This reflected the site's sectional asymmetry: tall curved strokes resembling the ribs of the final cases, rose above the steep slope from the sea on what Piano called the 'hard' side of the site; and horizontal strokes, the flat roofs, descended over the less steep slope to the lagoon on the 'soft' side of the peninsula. Besides returning to this original generative impulse, the final scheme seems more rigorous than the competition design, which by comparison resembles a holiday village.

The evolution of the scheme from competition to final design, and its interim stages, is charted in detail in Volume two and is not repeated here. All that should be added is to emphasize the close involvement of the Kanak clients. They pointed out, for instance, that the approach path from the car park could not come directly to the end of the promenade. In their culture, only the chief was permitted such a direct approach – others arrive in a more round about, deferential fashion, as in the built scheme.

Later, in a big meeting in Paris between architects, clients, contractors and the engineers (from Ove Arup & Partners, GEC Ingénierie, Agibat MTI and CSTB Nantes), as well as consultants such as Bensa, Togna objected that although the design of the case seemed very clever, he could not identify with it and see himself in its forms. Bensa repeated to all assembled the story of the big and little chiefs and the role of the coconut fibre cord that represented the women. A few days later Piano presented sketches in which the previous structure was visually simplified to clarify the parts and their

93

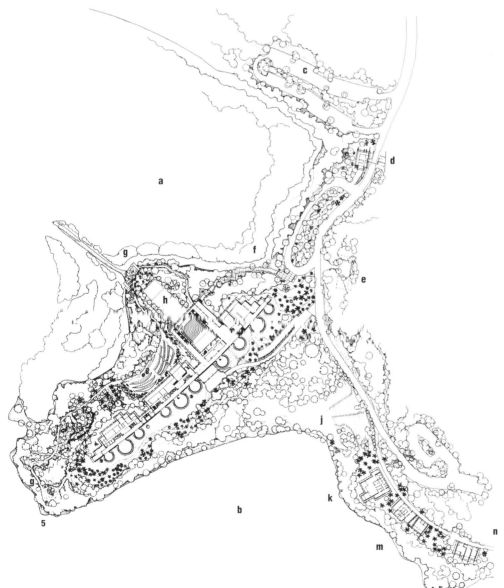

5

1

94 **Tjibaou Cultural Centre**

General views of the cases:

1 Sunset view from in front of village 3.

2 Cases of village 1 seen from lagoon.

3 View from slope above centre showing it with Nouméa, on the far side of hidden lagoons, in the background.

4 Backs of cases from the sea.

5 Fronts of cases from lagoon.

2

3

4

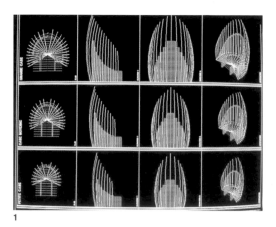

1

Tjibaou Cultural Centre

Structure and ventilation of the cases.

1 Comparison of the three sizes of case. Because the spacing of the structural ribs is constant, the larger cases have more ribs than the smaller ones.

2 Wind tunnel testing with smoke.

3 Diagram showing how ventilation is adjusted in response to different wind speeds and direction by opening and closing the louvres at the head, base and entrance to a case.

structural roles. Togna immediately accepted this and everybody reworked their designs. Thus were tradition and contemporary technology married in a novel hybrid devoid of pastiche.

In the final, built scheme there are ten cases in all, of three different sizes. The four smallest are 9 metres in diameter and 18 metres tall. The three medium-sized cases are 11 metres in diameter and 22 metres tall. And the three large cases are 13.5 metres in diameter and 28 metres tall. Around each of

these, forming three quarters of the circumference of a circle, are the two rows of vertical ribs made of laminated wood. Those in the inner row rise straight up, without curving, and support the roof, though they also extend up beyond it. These inner ribs also support the elements that fill the gaps between them to enclose the various rooms. The outer ribs curve more steeply at the bottom than at the top. These support only the screens of wooden slats which were preassembled into panels before being fixed into place.

The wood chosen for the ribs and slats, and indeed used throughout the building, is iroko. It is stable, termite-resistant and can be used laminated as well as unlaminated; it needs no finishes, and so is maintenance-free, and weathers to a silver grey, similar to the galvanized steel with which it used here. The tops of the ribs are splay cut and capped by stainless-steel plates to stop water penetration. At their bottoms the ribs are spliced to cast-steel elements pinjointed to cast-steel shoes bolted to the concrete foundations.

The laminated wood ribs are stabilized and braced by steel elements. Connecting each row of ribs are horizontal steel tubes, together forming an arc at regular vertical intervals. At every third arc there are also tubes between the inner and outer ribs and cross bracings, which all meet on cast-steel elements that reach around the sides of the ribs. Thus the various steel elements at each of these intermittent levels together form a curving horizontal truss. Such reinforcement is necessary

because during cyclones the cases are subject to enormous forces. From the inner ribs is suspended a tubular steel elliptical ring beam from which span the sloping steel I-beams of the roof. These support corrugated steel decking on which is insulation and a waterproof membrane, the whole being shaded by an outer layer of aluminium panels. Below the main beams is a flat plasterboard ceiling.

The number of vertical ribs varies with the diameter of the case so that the spacing of the inner ribs is the same for all sizes of case, allowing identical infill elements to be used throughout. These infill elements include fixed and louvred windows, opaque louvres of enamelled glass, wood panels slotted for acoustic absorbency, shallow niches and cupboards, and deeper cupboards. By varying the disposition of these, each case is tailored to its function and varies in its transparency to view and incoming light, a cafeteria being the most transparent and an audio-visual room the least. But no matter how transparent the case, the disposition of ventilating elements, whether clear or opaque, is the same. This is because this arrangement is crucial to the way in which the cases are ventilated in different wind conditions.

Computer simulation (by CSTB – the Centre Scientifique et Technique du Bâtiment – in

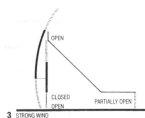

2

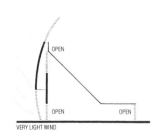

OPEN

OPEN | OPEN

VERY LIGHT WIND

OPEN

OPEN
CLOSED
OPEN | OPEN

LIGHT WIND

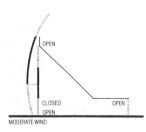

OPEN

CLOSED
OPEN | OPEN

MODERATE WIND

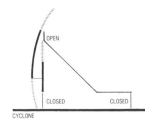

OPEN

CLOSED
OPEN | PARTIALLY OPEN

3 STRONG WIND

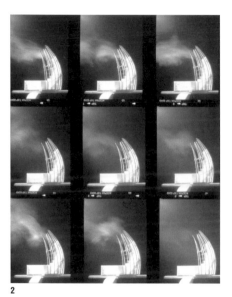

OPEN

CLOSED | CLOSED

CYCLONE

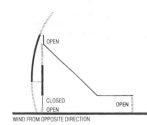

OPEN

CLOSED | OPEN

WIND FROM OPPOSITE DIRECTION

4

5

97

Tjibaou Cultural Centre

Ventilation of cases.

4 The cafeteria with its banks of glass louvres.
It is the case that admits most light and air.

5 Louvres facing onto a patio that admit
breezes into flat-roofed part of centre.

6 Spacing of outer layer of slats varies to
control flow of air horizontally through them,
or upwards behind them.

7, **8** Flattened-out internal elevations of two
medium-sized cases: **7** cafeteria;

8 lecture theatre.

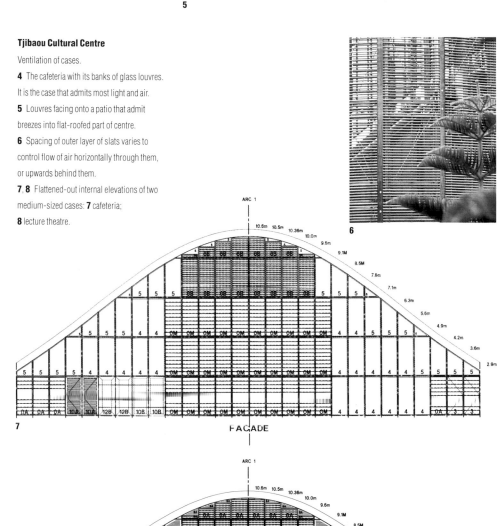

6

7

FACADE

8

FACADE

Paris following early advice from Ove Arup & Partners, GEC Ingénierie and Agibat MTI) and wind tunnel testing were used to refine the design of the natural ventilation system in which several elements act in unison. The cases, with their sloping ceilings and inner and outer enclosures, together with patios across the promenade all work as part of a single system that is adjusted to cope with different wind conditions. The slats on the outside of the cases are not merely for decorative effect: where spaced with relatively wide gaps towards the bottom, they allow the wind to pass through horizontally; where closely spaced midway up, they trap air to form a chimney in which the air must rise between the two layers of ribs; and where widely spaced at the top, they aid the Venturi effect which helps suck the air upwards. The inner walls of the cases have fixed louvres below the highest part of the ceilings, and a larger area of adjustable louvres below these. There are further adjustable louvres between the case and the promenade. All of these adjustable louvres rise from the floor to the 2.31 metre height of the promenade ceiling.

In normal conditions, with the prevailing trade wind blowing (some 90 per cent of the time), the adjustable louvres are left open (though adjusted to control the amount of ventilation with varying wind speeds). The breeze then passes through the outer slats and louvres, through the case and across the promenade to exhaust through the perforated roof of the patio. This prevailing breeze can also ventilate the offices and exhibition spaces under the flat roof, if the louvres between these and the patio and those opposite overlooking the lagoon are left open. However this natural ventilation is often insufficient, so these areas also have full air-conditioning.

When the wind is very light, the natural ventilation depends on convection. Warm air in the case rises under its sloping ceiling to exhaust through the louvres at the top of the wall. Another current of warm air rising between the inner and outer layers of the case helps this process by sucking the air

upwards through the louvres and out of the case. These upper louvres remain permanently open because they play a crucial role in equalizing internal and external air pressures during cyclones. As the wind picks up, sensors below the case's ceiling automatically close all the lower louvres to stop the wind howling through the building. Then if the cyclone blows from the sea to create a low pressure above the roof, air is immediately sucked out through the upper louvres. If the direction of the cyclone is reversed, putting pressure on the sloping roof, then wind is also forced down between the two layers of the case and in through the upper louvres.

The design of the cases was tested and further refined through erecting two full-size prototypes; both constituted slices consisting of three sets of structural members (outer and inner laminated wood vertical ribs, and steel roof trusses), the steel bracings between these and the glass and wood claddings they support. The first of these was erected in Angoulême near the south of France in July 1993 (Volume two pp205–09), the second was erected in Muttersholtz in northeast France in March 1996. Piano consequently adjusted the spacing and shape of the wooden slats to achieve precisely the visual vivacity and affinity with the surrounding vegetation that he sought. Thus

1

2

3

98 **Tjibaou Cultural Centre**

Constructing the cases.

1 Handling a panel of slats that will clad a case.

2, **3** Lifting a steel roof structure into position against the ribs of one half of the case. The rest of the ribs will be erected once the roof structure is in place.

4 Roof structure being fixed into position.

5 Attaching the cables prior to lifting the roof structure.

6 Workmen wait to fix the roof structure into position.

7 Erecting the inner row of ribs.

8 The structure is complete and the internal cladding in place. Only the outer layer of wooden slats is missing.

9 Positioning the cast-steel ends of the ribs prior to finally pinning them.

10 Hoisting the ribs into place.

4

5

6

7

8

9

10

1

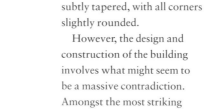

Tjibaou Cultural Centre

1 The second full-size mock-up in Muttersholtz, France, in March 1996.

Integration of architecture and nature.

2, 3 Cases emerging from and merging with vegetation.

4 Corner of the flat-roofed galleries of village 1.

5 Rock that marks the beginning of the narrative part of the Kanak Path.

6 Corner of administrative offices of village 3.

7 View from planted patio through flat-roofed part of centre.

2

3

4

5

6

7

the slat is no longer square in section, but is six sided and subtly tapered, with all corners slightly rounded.

However, the design and construction of the building involves what might seem to be a massive contradiction. Amongst the most striking aspects of the building is the openness of the main floor and how interwoven it is with the vegetation which, on all sides, comes right up to and even into it without the normal distancing intervention of roads or pavings for emergency vehicles. But this was only possible because rooms requiring solid enclosure are below ground where there is also a service road extending under the promenade. So beneath the light and airy building is a deep and heavy concrete substructure. (Between the theatre auditorium and the cafeteria case, the basement extends down through three levels, in part so that lorries might ramp down to the same level as the stage. And each case sits on a heavy circular concrete raft – 1.5 metres deep for the larger cases, 1 metre deep for the smallest – so as to resist buffeting in cyclones.) Thus construction involved carving into and carrying away much of the top of the promontory in what looked at times almost as brutal an intervention as the nickel mines. Yet, and these are the really critical issues, no plants of any size were dislodged, nor was any undegraded topsoil (that precious but vulnerable interface between earth and air).

As well as the Tina Peninsula, the eight-hectare site includes arms of land that extend northwards along the lagoon and southeastwards along the sea. Entrance to the site is from the north, with car parking between this and a gatehouse that controls vehicular access to the rest of the site. Beyond here, the road passes a vehicular drop off, which loops off the road between the gatehouse and the path leading to the cultural centre. The road then extends past a short road leading to the service tunnel beneath the cultural centre (from which an offshoot can take emergency vehicles to a terrace beside the cafeteria) to reach a group of flat-roofed buildings in the southerly arm overlooking the sea. These are a restaurant, accommodation for visiting school children and artists, and studios for the latter. In the bend between this southern arm and the peninsula is a clearing whose curving, sloping sides form a natural amphitheatre for 2,000 people to watch traditional ceremonies. Three traditional Kanak huts have also been built on these slopes.

Approaching the centre from a distance brings tantalizingly evocative views of the cases reaching from the tropical vegetation against the backdrop of sky or mountains. The sight really does evoke some new vision of what architecture might be: a flowering forth from the local natural forms and forces, with deep roots in tribal tradition and opening up optimistically to the future. From the gatehouse there is a spectacular view of the cases, with their vertical ribs combing the sky, seemingly bowed by the

8

prevailing winds. The variously spaced slats between the ribs create an effect of extraordinary visual vivacity, a shimmering optical flicker as when leaves rustle in the wind. Sloping up into the embrace of these wooden casings are the grey aluminium roofs of the rooms within each one; and providing a delicate but stabilizing visual datum are the flat roofs, the rafter ends forming dotted highlights against the shade below.

At the end of the looping drop-off visitors are greeted

by signboards. From here the paved access path descends to, and edges, the lagoon, before climbing through dense vegetation to meet the corner of the flat roof which projects forward furthest towards the lagoon. Here visitors are greeted by broad eaves projecting beyond a colonnade and offered a choice of routes. Plunging down into the vegetation is another path that leads to a key element of the whole scheme, the Kanak Path. In the opposite direction, a broad straight path, one side of which is sheltered by the colonnade, leads up to the main entrance of the centre.

Behind the colonnade a long straight flight of stairs drops into the ground, providing access to a 400-seat theatre, the centre's largest space, which is under the projecting flat roof. The stair (and a second stair symmetrically placed on the opposite side of the auditorium) descend from the head of a rectangular lawn sloping down to the lagoon. This outdoor auditorium, on the same axis as the theatre, can seat 800 people, its stage defined by a light framework of lattice beams supporting lighting, and whatever else a performance or other event may require. The internal auditorium is a straightforward rectangular space with a single bank of seating. The walls are of layered construction for acoustic isolation: a pair of concrete walls with a 40 millimetre cavity between them; external cladding

of iroko slats; a space inside for air-conditioning ducts, then acoustic insulation and a cladding of tatajouba wood panels, slatted like the iroko on the cases for acoustic absorbency.

As everywhere else in the building, the colonnade is of composite construction, combining wood and metal. The columns are flitched, with balks of laminated iroko bolted to either side of a steel core – a strengthening device needed to resist cyclones. Steel footings protect the bottom of the iroko from water penetration and steel capitals, linked by tubular bracing, support a spacing element on which sits an I-section steel beam. This supports I-sectioned steel rafters over which span aluminium panels that shade the inner weather-excluding roof as the outer part of yet another example of the double-roof construction used so often by the Building Workshop.

In the heat of New Caledonia the double roof brings immense benefits: temperatures above the outer roof have been measured at more than 50 degrees Centigrade while temperatures above the inner roof were only approximately 30 degrees Centigrade. The aluminium

Tjibaou Cultural Centre

8 Looking towards village 2 from the lawn in front of the end of auditorium.

9 Theatre as seen from its stage.

10 Section: **a** cafeteria; **b** promenade; **c** craft shop; **d** wcs; **e** service tunnel; **f** plant and store rooms; **g** theatre; **h** grid for scenery.

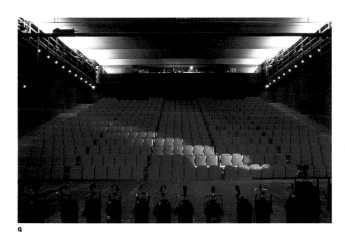

9

10

panels do not meet or overlap, as can be seen at the various eaves conditions around the building. Instead, they are spaced to leave a gap for air movement and to cast enlivening slivers of sunlight over the facades and columns below. These shafts, like the dappled effects of sunlight through leaves, do much to enliven the building.

The broad straight path leads to a circular reception desk immediately inside the entrance, beyond which is the promenade which forms the circulation spine for the whole scheme. Here visitors arrive at the first of the three 'villages' into which the cultural centre is subdivided, and which, besides the theatre, mainly consists of exhibition spaces. Directly across the promenade, a medium-sized case houses an audio-visual presentation introducing visitors to the Kanak culture and the physical setting which helped inspire it. To the left of this, the promenade descends a level with the slope of the land. Down here, are the first two of the row of cases, one small and one large, which house permanent exhibitions of Kanak sculpture and sculptures from this Pacific region. Under the flat roof are high-ceilinged galleries (up to 6 metres tall) for temporary exhibitions. These look down to the lagoon through floor-to-ceiling banks of glass louvres. Returning to the main level, and proceeding along the promenade past the audio-visual case, the next case houses the cafeteria, beyond which is its paved and partially covered terrace. Across the promenade from the cafeteria are shops for Kanak crafts, souvenirs, books and postcards. Like the other villages, the promenade is glazed in with large top-hung horizontal louvres, but these are set in sliding doors so that it can be entirely opened up.

The second village has three cases, one of each size, which together house a multimedia library where visitors can use books and computers to study the cultures of this Pacific region. Here the design's generating concept can be seen in its purest form. Across the promenade from each case are the planted patios, roofed with perforated aluminium panels – an essential part of the natural ventilation system. The floor under the flat-roofed area follows the lie of the land so that at one point it drops to form a double-height space. This is part of further gallery space that, together with offices for curators, fills this flat-roofed portion which overlooks terraces cultivated in the traditional manner as an adjunct of the Kanak Path.

The third village, set a few steps higher, has one large and two small cases – the first two serve as lecture rooms and the last one as a children's classroom. The flat-roofed portion houses the administration offices. A path connects this end of the promenade to the end of the Kanak Path.

The Kanak Path originated from Alban Bensa's idea of landscaping the grounds with traditional plants used for their symbolic associations. Devised in its final form by Emmanuel Kasarherou, cultural director of the new centre, and Bealo Wedoye, a local chief working for the New Caledonia Museum (both Kanak) and two French ethnologists (Roger Boulay of the National Museum of African and Oceanic Arts in France and Bensa) the Path recapitulates the major myths that underpin Kanak culture. Although there are now discreet boards of text explaining the

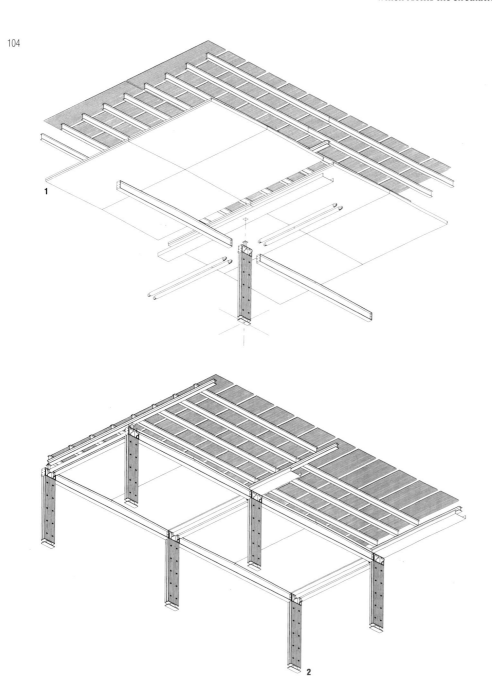

1

2

3

Tjibaou Cultural Centre

Previous page Backs of the cases seen above ramped road entrance to service tunnel.

1 Exploded worms-eye isometric projection of components of structure and roof of flat-roofed parts of centre.
2 Worms-eye isometric projection of oversailing roof of colonnade in front of lower-level galleries in the flat-roofed part of village 1.
3 Approach path along colonnaded side of sunken theatre.
4 The first case with exhibition of Kanak sculpture.
5 Medium-sized case holding part of the multimedia library.
6 Double-height gallery on lower level of flat-roofed part of village 1.

4

5

6

symbolism, it is a narrative told through plants and their symbolic associations, and two rocks with distinct forms. The rocks are at the beginning and end, like a prologue and epilogue of the narrative which passes through five chapters or thematic landscapes: creation, agriculture, habitat, death and rebirth.

From the outside corner of the theatre the one-kilometre route drops down to a water garden at the edge of the lagoon. Here the first rock rises from a pond of water lilies to represent the moon's tooth that fell to earth, leading to the creation of the Kanak people. The second theme tells of the cultivation of plants and centres on irrigated terraces where yams and taro are grown in the traditional manner. Around these are planted sugar cane and bananas. The third zone evokes the ancestral habitat of the Kanaks. A gravel clearing between coconut palms leads to rings of stones, both the first stage in building a hut and all that remains after it has been abandoned and left to decay. The fourth zone is a sacred grove of the spirits and death. It is entered through a gate marked by a kaori tree and a Norfolk Island pine which signify that it is a taboo space; and it centres on the spreading shade of a Banyan tree which (because its self-propagating roots ensure that it will never die) symbolizes rebirth and regeneration. The last zone, 'rebirth', culminates in a rock with a hole in it. Through this visitors can look down to the sea and imagine that after death the soul will follow their gaze as it passes through the hole to return to the sea from whence it came and to which it will return again.

Together building and landscaping evoke timeless essentials about the culture of this part of the Pacific, enticing visitors into a better appreciation of that culture. Crucially, that culture is not commemorated as something dead or historical but as still vital and evolving. The Tjibaou Cultural Centre should help the Kanaks face the future on their terms, keeping alive, rather than forsaking their roots, their culture both influencing and taking its place in the global mosaic of the new millennium. The public no doubt will be entranced by the building, grounds, exhibits and other activities. But for some architects and critics the response to the building might be more ambivalent. While not immune to the scheme's enchantments, and also admiring Piano's courage in straying so far into such fraught territories as symbolism and the vernacular, they may also find aspects of the building, particularly the cases, to be too extreme. They are intensely, poetically evocative – but also so huge, especially in relation to the relatively modest spaces they enfold that they affront fundamental credos of functionalist and utilitarian modernism. But any truly creative work must expand, or step outside of, the conventions of its time. Like other works by the Building Workshop, the Tjibaou Cultural Centre transcends, rather than forsakes, mere functionalism to herald a new age that must, if it is to survive, forge a new compact with nature and whose global electronically-enmeshed culture will, in contrast with the monolithic modernism of the industrial and colonial era, be an ecology of many local, even traditional, cultures. The functions of the cases transcend those of shelter and climate control to serve and express the spirit in all of us that wishes to merge into nature, tune into the cosmos and engage harmoniously with deeply-rooted local cultures.

105

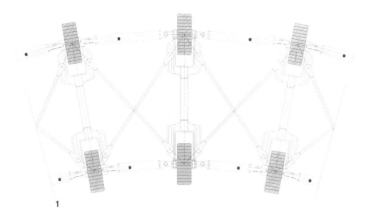

1

2

Tjibaou Cultural Centre

Structural details of cases.

1 Plan detail of the system of steel struts and ties that brace the ribs and form curving horizontal trusses.

2 Looking down onto system of bracings seen in **1**.

3 Plan of structure of medium-sized case.

4 View up between the inner and outer structural ribs.

5 Exploded isometric projection of the elements that come together at the foot of each pair of ribs.

6 Tightening the pin that secures the cast-steel tip of the inner rib to cast-steel shoe.

7 The elements securing the bottom of the ribs fully assembled.

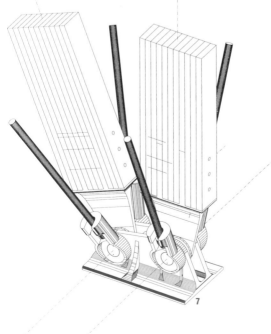

4

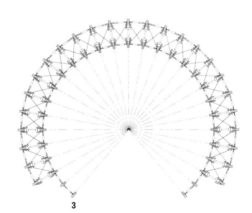

3

5

6

7

8

9

Tjibaou Cultural Centre

Structural details of cases.

8 Exploded isometric projection of all the elements that connect at a single junction of the bracings that stiffen the ribs.

9 The bracing elements coming together behind an outer ribs without the slat cladding.

10 Isometric projection of junction without vertical bracings.

11, 12 Views of junction of bracings shown in **8**, as well as in **1** and **2** on opposite page.

13 Junction shown in **10**.

14 Detail showing how panels of slats are held slightly away from the structural ribs.

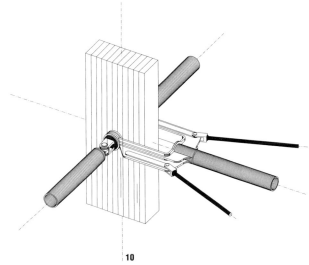

10

12

11

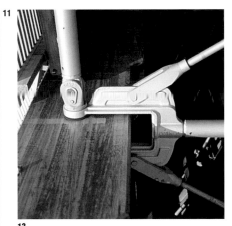

13

14

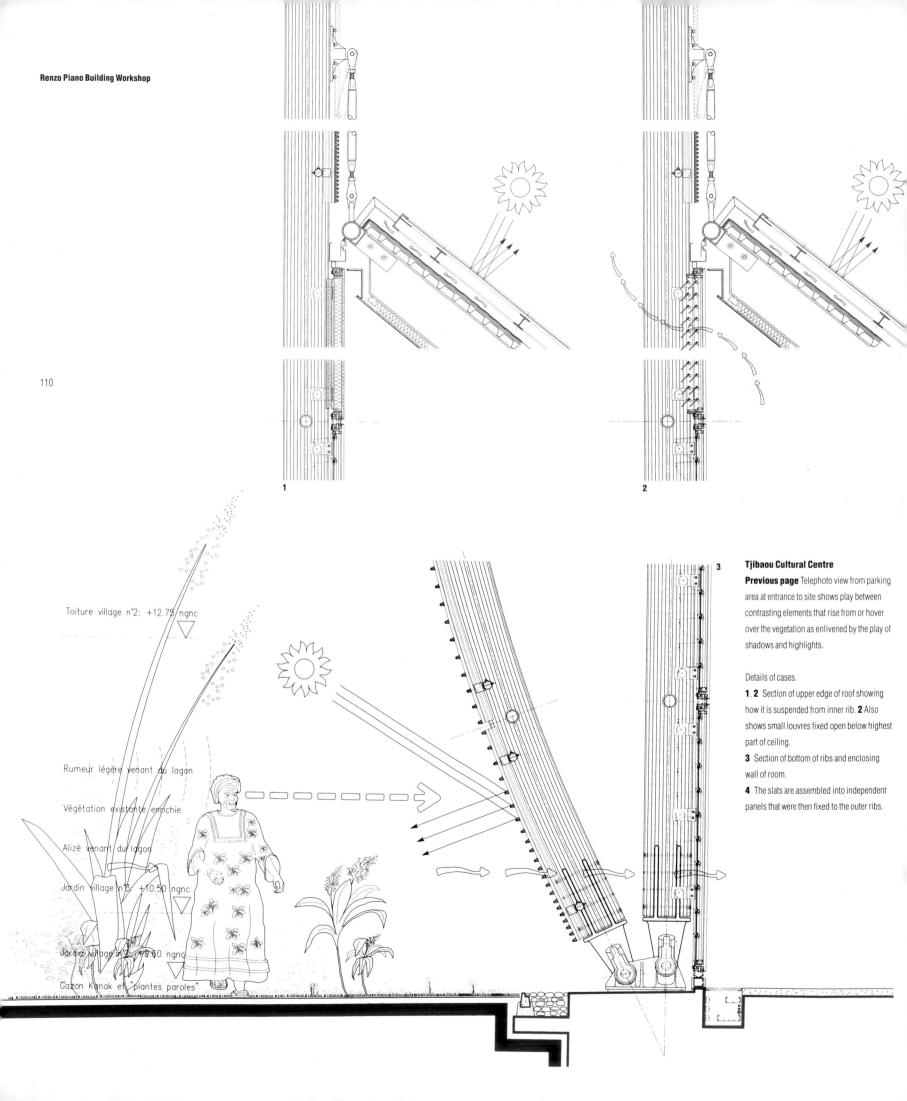

110

1

2

3

Tjibaou Cultural Centre
Previous page Telephoto view from parking area at entrance to site shows play between contrasting elements that rise from or hover over the vegetation as enlivened by the play of shadows and highlights.

Details of cases.
1, **2** Section of upper edge of roof showing how it is suspended from inner rib. **2** Also shows small louvres fixed open below highest part of ceiling.
3 Section of bottom of ribs and enclosing wall of room.
4 The slats are assembled into independent panels that were then fixed to the outer ribs.

Toiture village n°2: +12.75 /ngnc

Rumeur légère venant du lagon

Végétation existante enrichie

Alizè venant du lagon

Jardin village n°3: +10.50 ngnc

Jardin village n° +9.60 ngnc

Gazon Kanak et "plantes paroles"

1

2

Tjibaou Cultural Centre

1 Approach path with reception straight ahead, sunken theatre behind colonnade to right and temporary exhibition galleries of village 1 behind colonnade to left.

2 Paved and shaded patio off promenade on lower level of village 1. Behind the glass louvres is the temporary exhibition gallery.

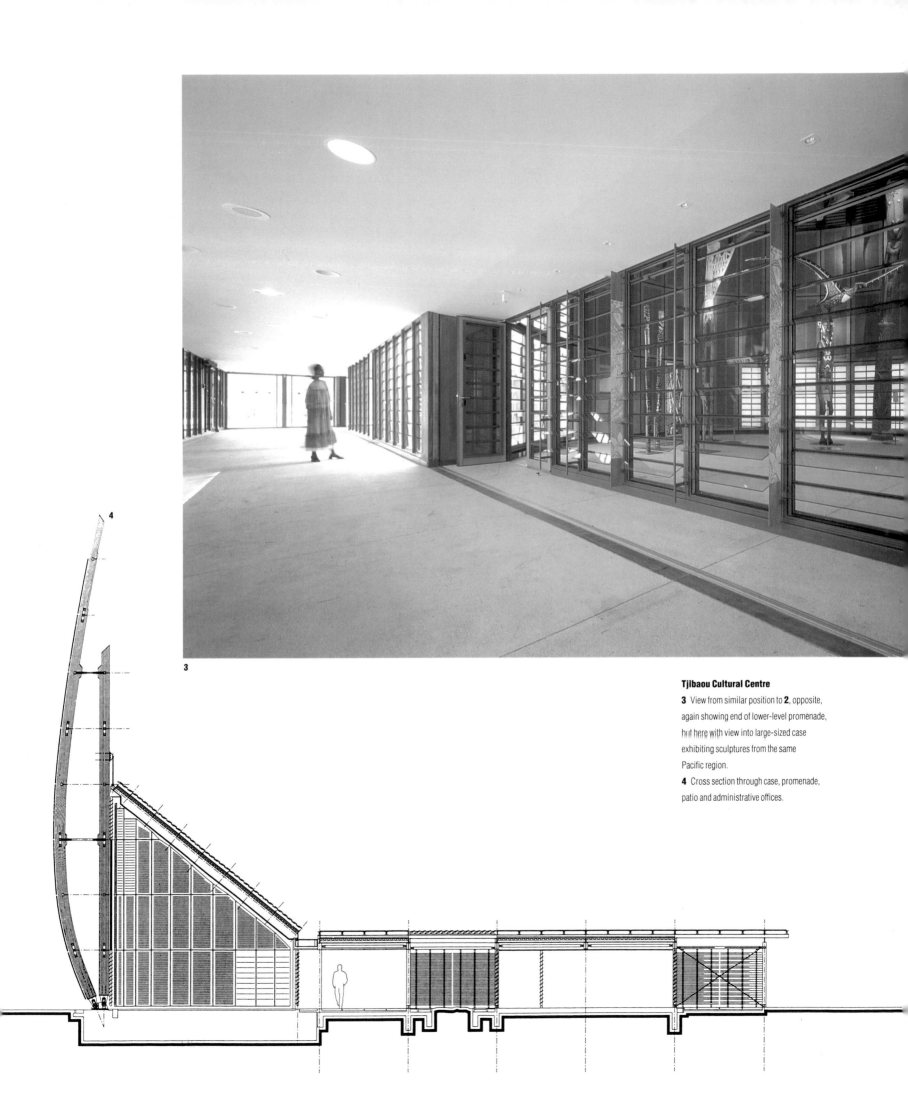

Tjibaou Cultural Centre

3 View from similar position to **2**, opposite, again showing end of lower-level promenade, but here with view into large-sized case exhibiting sculptures from the same Pacific region.

4 Cross section through case, promenade, patio and administrative offices.

1

Tjibaou Cultural Centre

Interiors.

1 Lower-level gallery in flat-roofed part of village 2.

2 Plan of cafeteria.

3 Large-sized case on lower level exhibiting sculptures from the same Pacific region.

4 Large-sized case with multi-media library.

5 Medium-sized case, with more light and ventilation than others, housing cafeteria.

Overleaf View at dusk past back of cases and over the sea to Nouméa.

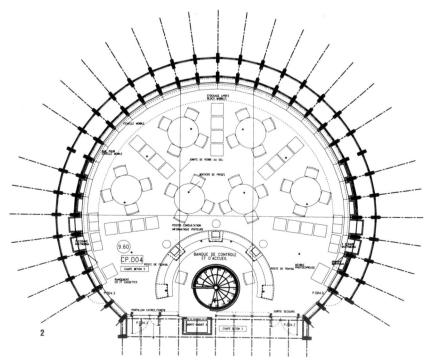

2

3

4

5

Tjibaou Cultural Centre
Client Agence pour le Développement de la Culture Kanak

Preliminary Design, 1992
Design team R Piano, P Vincent (senior partner in charge), A Chaaya, D Rat (architects in charge)
Assisted by JB Mothes, AH Téménidès, R Phelan, C Catino, A Gallissian, R Baumgarten
Modelmaker P Darmer
Ethnologist A Bensa
Cost control GEC Ingénierie
Structural and MEP engineering concept Ove Arup & Partners
Environmental studies CSTB
Structural engineers Agibat MTI
Stage equipment Scène
Acoustics Peutz & Associés
Security Qualiconsult
Planting Végétude

Design development and construction phase, 1993–8
Design team R Piano, P Vincent (senior partner in charge), D Rat, W Vassal (architects in charge)
Assisted by A El Jerari, A Gallissian, M Henry, C Jackman, P Keyser, D Mirallie, G Modolo, JB Mothes, F Pagliani, M Pimmel, S Purnama, AH Téménidès
Modelmaker JP Allain
Ethnologist A Bensa
Cost control GEC Ingénierie
Structural and MEP engineering concept Ove Arup & Partners
Environmental studies CSTB
Structural engineers Agibat MTI
Stage equipment Scène
Acoustics Peutz & Associés
Security Qualiconsult
Planting Végétude
Signage Intégral (R Baur)

118

Ferrari Wind Tunnel Maranello, Modena, Italy 1996–8

The Building Workshop's clients include mass production motor giants Fiat (VSS Experimental Car, Volume one p64, Lingotto Factory Rehabilitation, Volume two pp150–167 and Volume three pp40–53 and various exhibitions), Renault (L'Île Seguin, Volume three pp98–101), Daimler Benz (Mercedes-Benz Design Centre, p124–35, and Potsdamer Platz, p156–213). So maybe it is inevitable and particularly apt that another client is now the much smaller and more specialized Ferrari – that Italian epitome of a thrilling fusion of leading-edge technology with immaculate craft and elegance. The first of an intended series of buildings is now complete and operating more or less continuously at the Ferrari plant in Maranello. It is a wind tunnel for the testing and development of Formula One racing cars – again an apt subject for an architect who tests many of his prototypes in wind tunnels.

A wind tunnel facility is largely made up of machines, monitoring equipment and other elements that are designed by independent experts and which each come with stringent functional requirements that must be met. Hence, for instance, the various parts of the Ferrari wind tunnel required three independent sets of foundations so that vibration in one part should not be transferred to, and interfere with, delicate electronic equipment in another. Minimizing the time taken to service the various machines, to change and adjust parts, exerts further crucial design constraints. Yet, despite all this, the architect still has some options as to how to house all this equipment, as well as the people working with it or making test models and components in the workshops.

One logical solution would be to mount the various elements on separate foundations and cover the whole with a simple shed, highly insulated acoustically and thermally. This would dampen noise transmission from the wind tunnel itself and also prevent temperature fluctuations that cause structural movement and changes in size from upsetting delicate measurements. But the Building Workshop opted for a solution that is almost the antithesis of this approach. This is because, although the wind tunnel is at present tucked away deep into the Ferrari lot behind all the other buildings, it will flank the planned new main entrance to the Ferrari works. So a more eye-catching solution

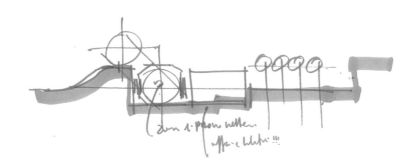

1

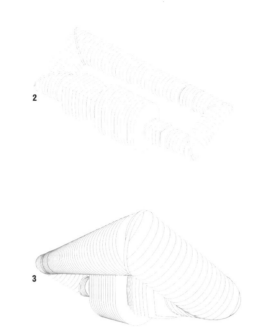

2

3

4

120   **Ferrari Wind Tunnel**

Previous page   Night view of wind
tunnel with test chamber to left and fan in
enlarged portion at top of slope.

1   Renzo Piano studying model
of building.
2–4   Computer perspectives of wind
tunnel element. (Built design differs from
that shown in **1–5** in that fan is in arm
opposite test chamber rather than
beside it.)
5   Site plan.

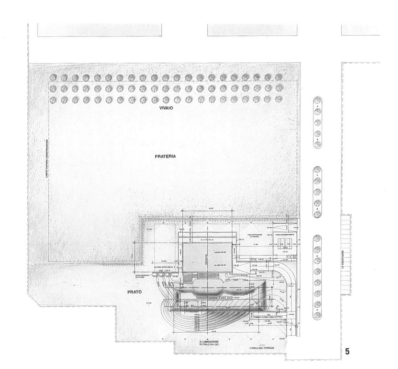

5

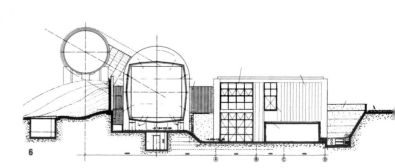

6

has been devised, precariously
perching the major mechanical
elements above mounded
landscaping.

The rectangular ring of the
wind tunnel has been exposed to
view and clad in its own close-
fitting insulating jacket. But,
more than that, it is raised off
the ground and tilted up so that
the fan sits conspicuously high
on a planted hillock – which
hides the top of its 200-tonne
foundation that, together with
the springs and shock absorbers
between fan and foundation,
stabilizes the fan's vibrations.
Consistent with a trend in
Piano's designs, this solution
was adopted purely as an
expressive gesture to context,
despite the complications of
cladding the tunnel and fan
independently, and of gaining
access to them for servicing.
And, as is so often the case, the
solution often results in
architecture and landscaping
being inextricably interlocked.

To emphasize their
mechanical nature, tunnel and
fan are clad in Alucobond (an
aluminium-finished sandwich
panel), as is the vaulted test
chamber. In the test chamber,
cars (usually half-size models)
and components are studied at
differing wind speeds and, if
required, at different alignments
with the wind. To test a car,

conditions must simulate reality
as closely as possible, and so the
tires must turn and bounce on a
road surface. This, as well as
ensuring that the wind at floor
level is not reduced by friction,
is achieved by placing the car or
model on a rubber belt that
moves at speeds equal to the
wind. Just as the model can be
turned, pitched and yawed by
mechanisms controlled by the
observing engineers, so the road
belt can be manipulated to
simulate banking and other such
conditions. The belt must move
at speeds up to 250 kilometres
per hour, and also resist the
strong upward suction due to
lowered pressures that racing
cars are designed to create
below them. So the belt endures
considerable wear and must be
replaced every fifty hours of
running time. Yet it can be
replaced in only twenty minutes
by lowering the whole belt
mechanism into a basement

8

Ferrari Wind Tunnel

6 Section through wind tunnel with building in elevation.

7 Engineers in control room monitoring a test.

8 Engineers setting up a car prior to testing.

9 Car in test chamber awaiting testing.

10 Testing aerodynamic flow with a smoke stream.

11 Section through office, laboratory and workshop block with wind tunnel in elevation behind.

12 Section through wind tunnel with building in elevation.

9

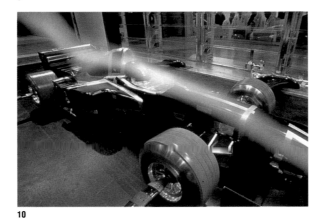

10

room below the test chamber where there is ample space to work.

Abutting the test chamber is a conventionally rectilinear, flat-roofed block with a ground floor and basement. On the upper level, adjacent to and overlooking the test chamber, is the control room. Like the rest of this level, and the observation room on the other side of the test chamber, this is set a few steps below the floor of the test chamber. Hence seated engineers are precisely level with the test car with its flying cotton tabs revealing the exact direction of air flow. The remainder of the upper floor houses office and laboratory space for engineers. On the floor below are the workshops for making models and mocking up components.

A large goods lift raises models and components, and even complete racing cars, from the basement to the test chamber. The racing cars are brought down to the workshop by a service road that descends between the wind tunnel to the rectilinear block, thus further dramatizing the raised and tilted tunnel and the mound it hovers above. A trench descends from this service road into the mound to give access to the electricity sub-station concealed below it. This delivers the 15,000 volts necessary to run the 2.2 kilowatt output fan which from start brings the winds up to stable speeds within only fifty seconds – another crucial factor in minimizing turn around times in a facility that is in almost constant use.

121

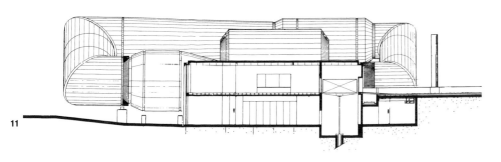

11

12

1

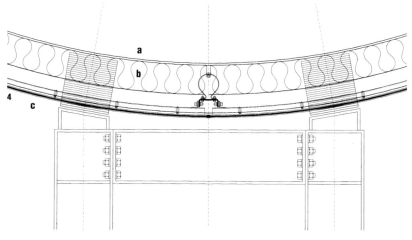

2

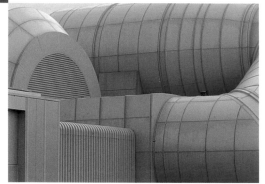

3

122 **Ferrari Wind Tunnel**

1 View from proposed new entrance to Ferrari works.

2, 3 Close-up views of cladding of wind tunnel.

4 Section detail through bottom of wind tunnel: **a** steel lining of wind tunnel; **b** insulation; **c** curved sandwich panel cladding.

5 Close-up view of outer corner of wind tunnel.

6 Large-scale plan detail of junction between cladding panels.

7 Main entrance to testing facility is over bridge, seen here with wind tunnel behind.

8 End-on view of wind tunnel and test chamber.

9 Part elevation of wind tunnel.

10 Section through wind tunnel.

5

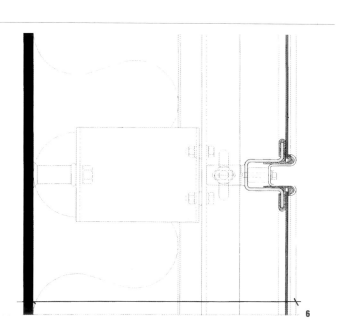

4

6

7

8

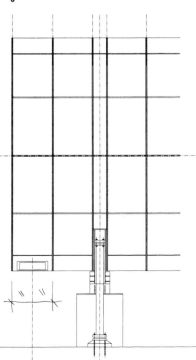

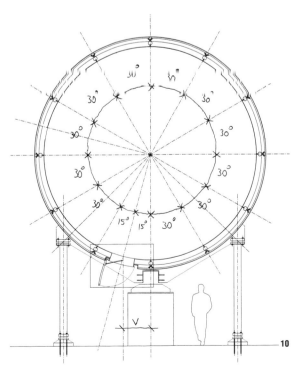

9

10

Ferrari Wind Tunnel

Client Ferrari SpA

Design team R Piano, P Vincent (senior partner in charge), M Salerno (architect in charge)

Assisted by JB Mothes, N Pacini, M Pimmel, D Rat, E Rossato Piano, S Lee, G Modolo and S Abbado, T Damisch and JC M'Fouara

Modelmaker JP Allain

Wind tunnel consultant CSTB

Structural engineers Agibat, MTI

Planting Végétude

Cost control Austin Italia

Acoustics Peutz & Associés

Interiors F Santolini

General contractor F lli Dioguardi SpA

124

Mercedes-Benz Design Centre Sindelfingen, Germany **1993–8**

In many ways, the Mercedes-Benz Design Centre is a particularly apt commission for Renzo Piano. The immediate client is a fellow Italian designer of international repute, Bruno Sacco, Chief Designer for Mercedes-Benz. He and the teams who work under him in this building are world leaders in designing products that fuse leading-edge engineering with elegant styling. Even more aptly, the brief was to provide the ideal environment to facilitate a collaborative creative process, that of designing the various ranges of Mercedes-Benz vehicles. This process extends from initial conception, through all stages of design and technical development (including building models and full-size mock-ups), to presenting and photographing the final product.

To stimulate this creative process, designers working on sketchpads and computers have to be constantly in touch with each other and with the craftsmen making models and full-size prototypes. Hence visibility, transparency, ease of communication – qualities dear to Piano – are all crucial to generating the sense of participation in a common undertaking which requires constant interaction. Sacco

recognized these qualities as abundant in Piano's own workshop-studio at Punta Nave (or Vesima as it was known in the earlier volumes). Sacco wanted the same atmosphere, but in a much larger building, in a very different context. But he was also keen that the design department should not appear spoilt and elitist, and so the budget was kept modest.

To compete today, vehicle manufacturers must develop new models faster, and to higher standards, than ever before. To ensure that it can do this, Daimler-Benz is building the vast new Development and Preparation Centre at Sindelfingen outside Stuttgart. Here 7,500 designers and engineers will work together developing new models in close collaboration with another 3,000 engineers – who develop the engines and powertrains at another plant at Untertürkheim – thus bringing together, on just these two sites, staff who had been spread between eighteen locations. The overall masterplan of the Sindelfingen site, and all other new buildings on it, have been designed by Christoph Kohlbecker (Mercedes-Benz's regular architect and the collaborating architect on the Design Centre) to encourage the

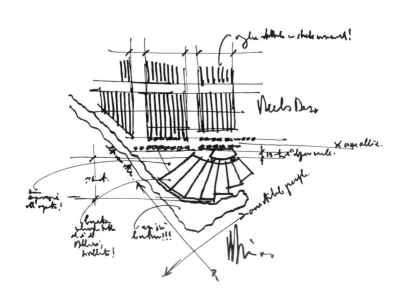

1

126   **Mercedes-Benz Design Centre**
Previous page Fanning roofs, which
taper to a crisp channel fascia, oversail
clerestoreys and glazed west walls of
studio bays.

1 Aerial view from west shows how
fanning forms of Design Centre, set in a
corner of the new Sindelfingen plant,
contrast with the orthogonality of the other
new buildings.
2 Computer diagram showing how one of
the fanning roofs is excerpted from the
surface of a toroid.
3 Computer diagram of structural system
supporting fanning roofs.
4 Face presented to the rest of plant to the
east. To the right is the entrance forecourt
and to the left are the administrative offices.

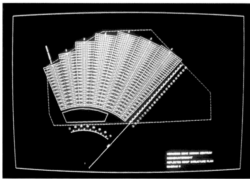

2

3

4

creative interaction necessary for rapid and effective product development. This is achieved by adopting an orthogonal grid that interweaves, around shared courtyards, a warp of engineers' offices with a weft of workshops. Opportunities for interaction are provided wherever these intersect, and engineers must now pass through the workshops and so receive instant feedback from developments there. But though such openness is encouraged within its boundaries, the Sindelfingen works are, of commercial necessity, closely guarded against any form of industrial espionage.

This paradoxical tension between openness and defensiveness is most extreme in the Design Centre, where 300 members of staff now work. Here the designers are working from the earliest conceptual stages, and are furthest into the future in terms of how far ahead they are of when their creative efforts will finally manifest in the market place. So the Design Centre, the first building completed at Sindelfingen, is in the projecting southwest corner of the site where it is isolated and most easily guarded from being overseen. It was this corner location, as well as the shape of the site allocated to him, that led Piano to the fan-like configuration so that the building contrasts with, and forms, a terminating flourish to the orthogonal grid of the other new buildings.

The first sketch proposals, however, were of an orthogonally organized building. This deferred both contextually to the other buildings on the site, and to the rectilinearity of major elements in the interior: the gantries and parallel strips of lighting under which the full-size mock-ups are sculpted. But Sacco protested that the prestigious design department deserved a building that was less conventional, more free in form and feeling, and more appropriately expressive of its purpose. Hence Emanuela Baglietto (who speaks German well and was architect-in-charge throughout the project) and Shunji Ishida worked with Piano to devise the radial layout, while the geometry of the roofs was developed by Geoff Cohen working at this early stage with structural engineers from Ove Arup &

Partners. (Johannes Florim later represented the Building Workshop on the construction site.) The radial plan and the disciplined curves of the roof, which are simultaneously sensual and sober, are equally apt but more celebratory responses to context than the original proposal. Moreover, the hand-like configuration fits the internal functions like a glove.

Analogous in form and location to the heel of the hand, and detached slightly from the rest of the Design Centre, is a four-storey block housing the administrative offices, with an entrance and reception lobby on its ground floor. This block, which is as far as those not working in the Design Centre may penetrate (except when invited into the presentation hall), presents a relatively mundane face to the rest of the works. It thus suggests a connection to the larger body of buildings to the east, while also screening the fanning fingers behind it. Across a small courtyard from this block are the seven fingers of studios. Each finger, or bay, is progressively longer than the one to its south. The two northern-most of these bays extend beyond the administration block to define a triangular forecourt from which the building is entered. The presentation hall extends across the court-side ends of three of the shorter bays (thus forming the palm of the hand). Within the space left in the fingers, the departments responsible for designing each kind of vehicle are allocated the number and the length of studio bays they require. Beyond the ends of the

5

fingers, and providing outlook for the studios, is a landscaped area. And around this is a dense hedge between a pair of fences – a loose-fitting mitt that excludes prying eyes.

This basic plan has been elaborated in its three-dimensional form, section and cladding to be even more appropriately tailored to function. The roofs over the studio bays are curved in both directions and resemble the blades of a fragment of a gigantic turbine. In cross section the roofs curve down from

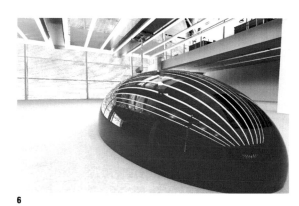

Mercedes-Benz Design Centre
5 View from across road on west.
6 One of a series of computer simulations made by Arups to ensure that the reflections of the rows of strip lights above the mock-ups will be undisturbed despite changing natural and artificial lighting conditions through the day.
7 Site and roof plan

6

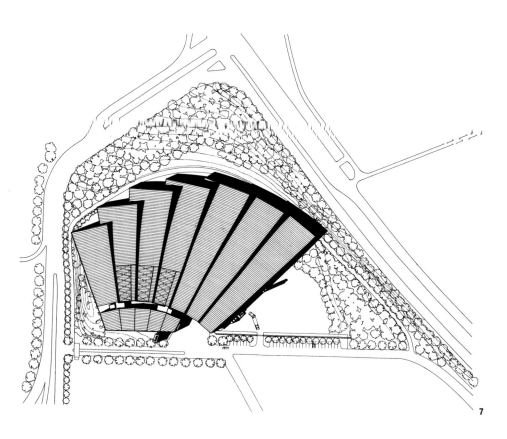

7

leaning north-light clerestoreys. In the longitudinal direction, they curve down much more gradually from a three-storied zone on the east, towards the office block, to a single-storied but double-height portion on the west, at the end of each studio bay. In concept, though the reality is inevitably more complex (not least because of the constant interaction and feedback this layout deliberately encourages), design proceeds from the top-floor design studio down to the ground-level workshop floor where the full-size mock-ups are made. The design process thus follows the flow of space downwards and outwards under the twisting roof – which together with the lean of the glazed end wall adds a further centrifugal impetus to this spatial flow – towards the garden which everybody overlooks and into which the full-size mock-ups are sometimes wheeled for critical contemplation.

As usual with the Building Workshop, the character of the building does not come only from the shape and generous scale of its spaces, and how these flow into each other; just as important is the expressive role of the elegantly refined and internally exposed constructional elements, the 'pieces'. Here, the 'pieces' particular to this building alone are to be found principally in the structure of the studio roofs (which was developed with Arups, though later modified by the contractor). The roofs are held aloft by the thick, 675mm, in situ concrete walls that radiate at a constant nine degrees to each other from a common centre to define the studio bays. The internal faces of these walls are simply plastered and painted white and externally they are faced with

tall, narrow panels of Alucobond, a composite sheeting whose aluminium face is held rigidly smooth by a polyethylene backing. The curving roofs span clear between the heads of these walls, which at lower levels also support the edges of the concrete floors that are supported elsewhere by intermediary concrete columns.

Running along the gently curving heads of the walls are channels folded from 10mm steel and welded together in short lengths to take up the curvature. Inside these channels is 100mm of insulation and a waterproof lining that forms gutters into which drain the southern edges of the roofs and the sloping clerestoreys of the adjacent roof. Welded to both outer sides of the steel channel are double brackets. These support the roof structure consisting of tubular struts, tension rods and cast junction elements, all of steel.

Because the span, and so the weight, of the roofs increase towards the west these brackets are spaced progressively 100mm closer together. Hence the eastern-most brackets are 5.1 metres apart, the next are 5 metres apart and so on until the western-most brackets of the northern-most roof are only 2.3 metres apart. Pairs of 194mm-diameter tubular struts are pinned to each of the brackets on the northern sides of each wall (via junction elements that are in turn pinned to the brackets). Together all these struts form a structural web that leans in from the head of the wall to support a chord of tubular elements set in from the

127

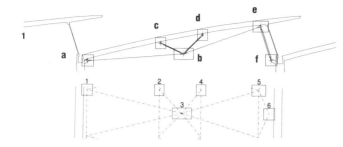

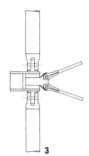

Mercedes-Benz Design Centre

Details of roof structure.

1 Key section and plan.

2 Sectional elevation and **3** plan, and **4** full-size mock up of junction **a** at head of wall.

5 Full-size mock up, **6** sectional elevation and **7** plan of junction **b**.

8 Sectional elevation, and **9** inverted plan of junction **d**.

10 Sectional elevation, and **11** inverted plan of junction **d**.

12 Sectional elevation, and **13** plan of junction **e** at head **d** clerestory.

14 Sectional elevation, and **15** full-size mock up and **16** plan of junction **f** at head of wall.

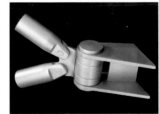

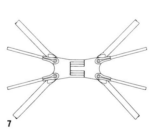

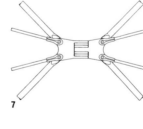

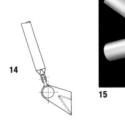

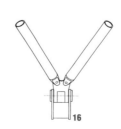

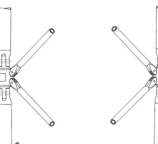

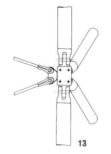

northern edge of the roof. The struts, and the clerestorey glazing set just outside of them, become progressively taller towards the west because the head of the wall curves down less gently than the roof above. Thus the clerestoreys, placed high up, to preserve secrecy, not only follow the downward-stepping work levels inside, but admit more light as the studio bays widen.

The precise geometry of the studio roofs is toroidal, like that of the boarding wing of the Kansai International Airport passenger terminal (Volume three pp128–229). But here each roof represents only a very tiny portion of the toroidal ring of which it is part, and the cross section of the ring is circular. Because of the toroidal geometry, the curves in both directions remain constant so that, though the spans vary, the radiusing of the ribbed steel sheeting that forms the roof itself is also constant throughout. The toroidal form also accounts for the differences in the curves of the upper and lower edges of the roofs: the latter is further from the equatorial circumference of the toroid and cuts across its surface at an angle that increases its curvature, while the angle of the former diminishes its curvature.

Despite spanning up to 30 metres at the ends of the longest bays, the roof structure is pared to an elegant minimum. (It could be seen, and indeed started design, as a further-evolved relative of the roof of the Thomson Optronics Factory, Volume two pp34–45.) The two layers of curved steel sheeting (used as a sandwich of two layers separated by 180mm of insulation) form the main compressive element that works together with a web of ties and struts below it as a three-dimensional structure. The chord of tubular members propped from the head of each wall by the web of struts, and the tubular members between the brackets on the wall-top channel opposite, support the long edges of each roof. (The inner of the two ribbed sheets of the roof deck is bolted to a steel bar welded with intermediary spacers to the tubular members of the curving chords.) The junction elements to which the tubular members are pinned also provide anchorage for the tie rods that crisscross diagonally beneath the roof to support at their midpoint more tubular struts. These in turn splay out to support another pair of tubular chords that prop the middle of each curving roof. As always with the Building Workshop, the detailing of the joints between these brackets, tubular members and ties is unfussily understated yet extremely elegant. Because of the differing spans, the junction elements (which were cast in Spain) are hinged so that the same elements can accommodate the different angles of the ties.

Outside, Alucobond sheets are fixed with coverstrips to the upper layer of sheeting to provide a smooth, silvery but matt finish to match the external walls. Along their northern edges, and supported by concealed tapering rafters, the roofs extend by up to six metres beyond the clerestoreys to shade them. These projections taper to the east in proportion to the diminishing height and inward lean of the clerestoreys below. This, and the upward slope of the inner sheet, as it follows the concealed tapering rafters that support this cantilever, add

17

further formal nuances to the exterior.

At the western ends of the studios, the roof structure extends out by a full structural bay beyond the glazed end wall, so revealing the structure externally as well as internally. The roof cantilevers by a similar distance again, tapering in section to terminate in a small channel fascia that has become a favourite Piano motif. All this, together with the outward lean of the glazed end wall which is set at 90 degrees to the roof to align with the radius of the toroid (like the structural ribs of Kansai's boarding wing) enhances the dynamic impression of the huge, light and tensely-curved roofs twisting and floating free of the walls. The shade this porch provides for the west-facing glass is supplemented, when required, by motorized external fabric blinds. A typical Building Workshop detail, these are identical to those shading the east facade of the administrative block. Inside the glazing are mesh blinds. These allow views out but block views in, as well as protecting against glare.

Inside and under the embrace of these roofs, the layout of each of the studio bays is somewhat different, not least because of their varying length. Yet they follow a similar pattern. The main designers' studio, with its computers and drawing boards, is in the eastern end of each bay and on the top, second floor where flooded with northlight from the clerestorey. Directly below this on the first floor are storerooms for clay and other model-making materials. Also on this level are galleries around three sides of a well, which extends in from the western end of the studio bay where space rises unobstructed from ground level to roof. On these galleries, which again are brightly lit from the clerestorey, are more designers.

The ground floor is the workshop. Under the galleries, small-scale models and full-size components are made. In those parts of the workshop that open up through the full height of the building, and which constitute more than half the area of most studio bays, designs are mocked-up at full-size and then steadily refined by sculpting their thick outer layers of wet clay. Here this painstakingly slow process of refinement, which is at the heart of the whole design method (which like that of the Building Workshop is a collaborative process drawing on the interactions of various professional skills as well as of brain, hand and eye), can be watched and commented on by everybody, whether elsewhere in the workshop, in the galleries overlooking the well or in the second-floor studio.

The full-size mock-ups are sculpted below special gantries, the tops of which rise through the well to above first-floor level. Under these gantries hang long, straight and parallel strips of fluorescent tubular lighting. The reflections of these bright lines on the wet clay clearly reveal any flaws in the modelling, such as curves that are not smoothly fluent, or asymmetries between the two halves of the vehicle. Once the provisional or final form of the design has been agreed upon, the clay can be left to dry and then its contours charted by electronic pantagraphs suspended from tracks that span between the gantries. These measurements are fed directly into the designers' computers to

129

Mercedes-Benz Design Centre
Erection of roof.

17 Laying the upper of the two sheets of ribbed decking over the insulation that separates the sheets.

18 Fixing structural frame for glazing at end of studio bay.

19 Roof structure over the exhibition hall with trusses spanning across it and curving ribs to support the sun-excluding roof glazing.

20, 21 Fixing propped purlin to underside of ribbed sheeting. Temporary props from floor support suspended hinged junction during construction.

18

19

20

21

2

3

1

4

5

130 **Mercedes-Benz Design Centre**

1 Night view into studio bay through western glazed wall.

2 Hinged junction supporting props which is suspended at mid span of roof.
3 Part plan of structural system.
4 Last bay of structure over porch outside end wall of studio bay.
5 Sun-excluding glazing of roof over exhibition hall.
6 Peeled-away axonometric view of roof structure, decking and finish.
7 Detail of bottom edge of roof over western end of studio bay.

6

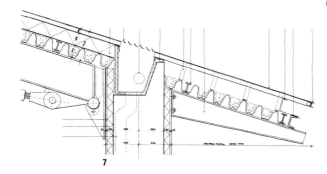

7

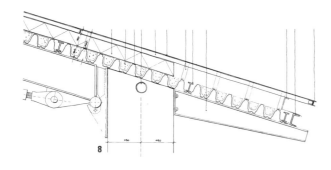

8

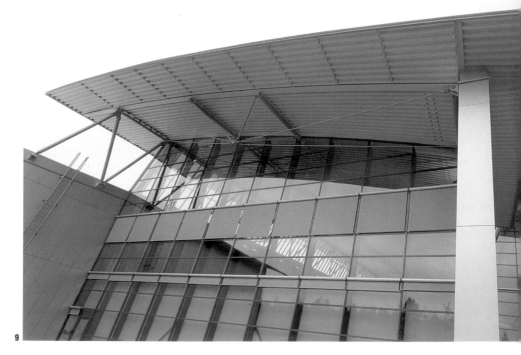

9

10

Mercedes-Benz Design Centre

8 Detail of bottom edge of roof over porch outside western end of studio bay.

9 One bay of roof structure extends outside the glazed west wall, and beyond that the roof cantilevers yet further.

10 Each of the fanning studio bays extends further westwards than that to its south.

11 West elevation showing glazed ends of fanning studio bays

12 North elevation showing how clerestory increases in height with increasing width of studio bay.

11

12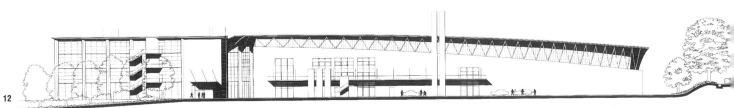

1

2

132 **Mercedes-Benz Design Centre**

1 Upward view of typical clerestory.

2 Ceiling of exhibition hall: huge louvres with spindly aluminium structures and sheathed in white and clear polythene sheet pivot to adjust light levels.

3 North–south section through studio bays.

4 West–east section through studio bay and administration block.

5 Sun-excluding glass roof and clerestory over exhibition hall.

3

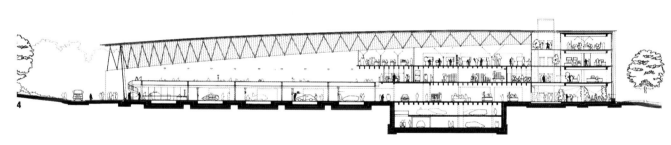

4

6

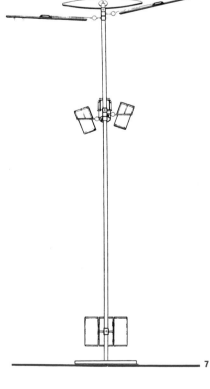

7

5

Mercedes-Benz Design Centre

6 Gallery at first floor level in typical studio bay is abundantly lit from clerestory and has views out through glazed west wall and down to full-size mock ups made under gantry projecting up through well.

7 Elevation of standing light fitting seen in **6** and designed by the Piano Design Workshop.

8

Mercedes-Benz Design Centre

8 First-floor gallery in studio bay looking towards second floor studio in narrow eastern end of bay.

9 Section detail of gutter at head of radial wall: **a** Alucobond sheathing; **b** outer layer of ribbed steel decking; **c** insulation; **d** inner layer of ribbed steel decking; **e** steel bracket supporting tubular purlin; **f** grille; **g** double-glazing of clerestory; **h** tubular strut to purlin at head of clerestory.

10, **11**, **12** Louvres in exhibition hall pivoted at different angles to vary the light.

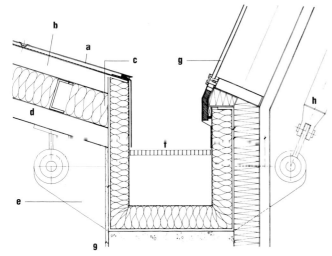

9

update their drawings as part of the constant process of feedback and refinement.

During design of the building, Arups (who were also responsible for the services engineering) made computer simulations of the lighting under various conditions in both studios and workshops. This was partly to ensure that neither natural nor artificial light would interfere with the crucial reflections from the strip lights. The artificial lighting solution is to use background lighting reflected off the curved ceilings from uplighters – the same units that the Building Workshop originally designed for the Lingotto Factory Renovation (Volume two pp150–67) and now have used in numerous Piano projects. This is supplemented by local task lighting from standard lights designed for this project by Piano and his product designer son, Matteo, who now constitute the Piano Design Workshop. (These lights are now on general sale.) Each light fitting consists of a central post rising from a circular base to support three circular reflectors lit by cylindrical lamps secured lower down on the post. The building is air-conditioned with incoming air in the studio bays admitted from a horizontal cylindrical duct attached to the radial walls above each work level. The main plant room is in the northern-most studio bay, outside of which stand a pair of tall cylindrical chimneys and a pair of shorter air intakes.

When ready, new models – whether as mock-ups or fully engineered prototypes – are exhibited and photographed in the presentation hall. This huge space was a fairly late addition to the programme. It was accommodated by eliminating the eastern end of two of the radial walls and spanning triangular-sectioned trusses of tubular steel across the resultant openings to support the roofs, clerestoreys and gutters. To show the vehicles to best effect requires variable conditions of both natural and artificial light, allowing a range from soft diffusion to very bright. The clerestoreys alone could not provide the desired light levels, so the hall is roofed with a recently developed translucent sheet. This follows the same form as the steel sheeting; but because the new material cannot function structurally like steel, it is made up in framed panels supported by curved steel rafters.

The translucent sheet was especially developed for the roof of an exhibition hall by architect Thomas Herzog with Christian Bartenbach, in collaboration with Siemens who now manufacture it. Basically, the sheet consists of a plastic grid set between two panes of heat-absorbing glass. The grid, which is only 16mm deep and has a very thin coat of pure aluminium to achieve a 90 per cent reflection value, is made up of parallel inclined blades with parabolic shaped surfaces that are stabilized by lateral counter

strips. The result is a grid of miniature 'northlights' that admit light directly only from that direction and intercept and diffuse all direct sunlight. Light in spaces below it can be a third as bright as outdoors, which is remarkable considering all direct sun is excluded.

Underneath the roof and its supporting structure, and forming a ceiling to the hall, are large aerofoil-shaped louvres that each span the full width of a structural bay. These motorized louvres are used to modulate the incoming natural light, as well as that from luminaires set directly below the roof. To keep weight down, each louvre is formed of a spindly aluminium frame that is enclosed in a sleeve with an upper surface of transparent polythene sheeting and a lower surface of a white polythene sheeting. These sheathings are impermeable to air, and the smooth aerofoil shape of the sleeves is maintained by keeping the air inside pressurized. This is done by pumping air through clear plastic piping into each sleeve. By adjusting these louvres, the perfect light conditions can be created to highlight the sleek form of any vehicle. So that the silhouettes of viewers, photographers and their equipment are not reflected distractingly in the vehicle's high gloss paintwork, the floor is dark grey carpet and the bottom 2.5 metres of the white walls are masked with charcoal-coloured panels. These are set forward of the wall to conceal

133

10

11

12

1

134

Mercedes-Benz Design Centre
1 Interior of administration with fully-glazed partitions.
2 Exploded isometric of glazing frame, structural stiffening and blinds.
3 Workshop at bottom of well where full-size mock ups are made under the lines of strip lights.

4 Section through early version of end glazing of studio bay which leans so as to be at right angles to the roof.
5 End of a studio bay.
6 View from helical stair in **5** with the end of the gantry over the mock up area seen between the galleries for designers.

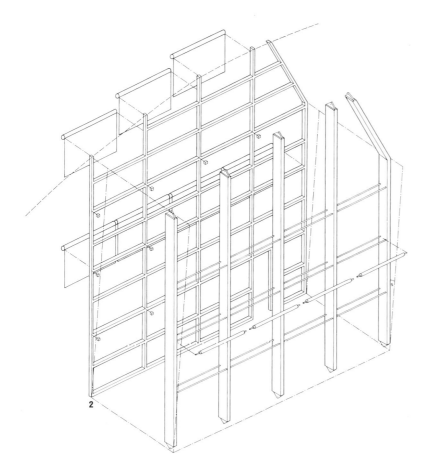

2

air-conditioning ducts and inlets, as well as strip lights that light the white walls above.

The Design Centre is a big building whose activities are shrouded in secrecy. Indeed the client will not even allow plans and the internal layout to be published. Few members of the public will ever see it, and even fewer of the Building Workshop's fans will have a chance to visit. This is a pity because it is a building whose generosity of scale, space and spirit needs to be experienced to be fully appreciated. Then too it can be seen that the hand-like configuration, with its fanning fingers, and the double-curved toroidal roofs are no mere formalist conceits. Besides the achievements of functional fit and spatial flow, and despite the thick concrete walls, the result exemplifies Piano's ideal of lightness, both in the sense of being flooded with light and seeming weightless.

Outside, the building is monochromatic in shades of silver and grey. Piano has said that he wanted it to seem as though a single casting of aluminium. Yet there is no sense of mass, only surfaces, and these seem wafer thin. The tall narrow sheets of Alucobond are absolutely flat, and where these end in the long curves at the heads of walls the aluminium angle flashing that caps them is so small as to be invisible from below. (Particularly fine is the north elevation, where crisply detailed stainless-steel chimneys and air intakes stand forward to

form vertical counterpoints to the slow downward-sweeping curves behind.) Above the clerestoreys and beyond the porches, the roofs fly free and taper to the sharp shadowed line of the channel fascia. The combination of thinness, tense double curves and tapering overhangs seems to set the outsides of the studio bays in a slight spinning motion led by the twisting motion of the fanning roofs that seem caught in some fragile equilibrium between resting serenely in place and straining to lift off.

Yet what really matters is the interior and the working of, and atmosphere in, the studio bays. Here, designers and craftsmen allocated to various tasks can be deployed to enjoy ideal relationships to the light, flow of work and each other. They are all brought together, overlooking and immediately in touch with each other, on their different levels around the central well. At the bottom of this well, all design effort finds final form under the constant scrutiny of all involved – as is the garden, and so the presence of nature, outside. In these big, generous-feeling spaces in which space expands and unfolds lengthways and downwards below the soaring curves of the roofs, which also reflect down the abundant light entering from the tall clerestoreys, the imagination is set free and people feel themselves as part of a single collaborative enterprise that thrives on interaction and participation.

3

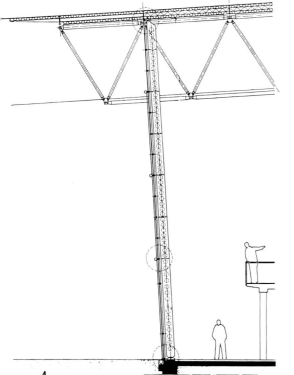

4

5

6

Mercedes-Benz Design Centre

Client Mercedes-Benz AG

Architects Renzo Piano Building Workshop in association with C Kohlbecker (Gaggenau)

Design team R Piano, E Baglietto (partner in charge), S Ishida (senior partner), G Cohen, J Florin, A Hahne

Assisted by C Leoncini, S Nobis, C Sapper, L Viti

CAD operators D Guerrisi, M Ottonello

Structural and services engineering consultants Ove Arup & Partners

Structural engineers IFB Dr Braschel & Partner GmbH

Mechanical engineers FWT Project und Bauleitung Mercedes-Benz AG

Acoustics Müller BBM

Interiors F Santolini

Although on a much smaller scale, the new Banca Popolare di Lodi headquarters shares several key features with the Potsdamer Platz scheme (p156). Both designs are about 'building a piece of the city' – creating an urban precinct of mixed uses around an outdoor public realm. In doing this, both schemes also connect dislocated parts of their surroundings, by direct physical means and by establishing visual links with nearby buildings. In Berlin, the music theatre and casino building formally resembles the adjacent National Library and so associates itself with it. In Lodi, cylindrical towers echo both that of a nearby medieval castle and the silos of farmsteads in the surrounding countryside. Moreover, as in Berlin, as well as with other recent Building Workshop schemes, a sense of urbanity is conveyed not just by the forms of buildings and urban spaces but also by enriching the facades with terracotta cladding.

Lodi is a small town 30 kilometres southeast of Milan, to which many of its residents commute daily. Yet it is ancient too, having started as a Roman castrum, the typical grid of which is still detectable in the street layout. In medieval times it was a walled city that rivalled

Milan in importance. The new headquarters of the flourishing Banca Popolare di Lodi lies a little outside the old city wall, between the town's medieval castle and the railway station used by many commuters. Here, on a site that previously had been occupied by a dairy products factory, the bank has consolidated its various departments that had been spread around the town. Piano (aided by Building Workshop architects Giorgio Grandi and Vittorio di Turi) has exploited this location to design a complex that also helps to consolidate the town's fabric, giving it a new civic completeness and dignity while enhancing the bank's image as agent and exemplar of this new civitas.

The new buildings and urban spaces are thus designed so that their forms and materials signal for the bank an appropriate image of status and security, as well as belonging to the town and its region. The scheme enhances and reintegrates the town formally and functionally, not least in forming a new gateway to it. Indeed, it links the station near its southeast corner with the old town core to the north with two new routes of distinct but contrasting urban character. One is a rather formal vehicular and pedestrian street

Banca Popolare di Lodi Lodi, Italy **1991–8**

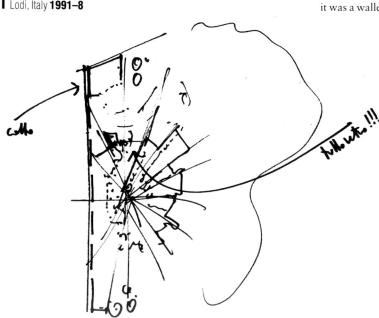

138 **Banca Popolare di Lodi**
Previous page Central precinct sheltered by glass canopy.

Context.
1 Typical farm and silos in surrounding countryside.
2 Looking past one of the new towers, with its glass cornice, to the castle.
3 Site and location plan: **a** station; **b** new street; **c** precinct; **d** garden.

along an edge of the site, the other a more intricately intimate pedestrian precinct that forms the core of the complex. Together these lend an intensified sense of urbanity to the town. The scheme also includes a hall for meetings and concerts, a civic amenity to be used by the town's people as well as the bank. (A precedent in Piano's work for a bank headquarters contributing very similar resources to a town is the Credito Industriale Sardo scheme in Cagliari, Sardinia, in Volume two pp140–9.)

In lieu of half of the urban development tax it would have had to pay, the bank ceded a strip along the western edge of the site and built there the broad street with tree-shaded pavements and, below it, two levels of underground parking to be used by commuters. (The new complex has a separate underground parking garage reached by ramps in the northeast and southeast corners of the site.) This side of the site is edged by a five-storey block, scaled to the width of the street. Its 250-metre length is broken down to read as a row of smaller blocks, each of similar size but with variations in their fenestration. The terracotta cladding continues past these windows as grilles that screen them against the fierce westerly sun, giving the facade a defensive demeanour suggesting the security that banks prefer to project. Yet the articulation of the blocks, fenestration and terracotta which lend the facade its urbaneness also ensure that it is not too unfriendly to the passer-by. And below the bastion-like wall of the upper storeys, there are several openings on the ground floor which allow pedestrians and views through to the central pedestrian precinct that extends behind the long block.

This precinct connects to the streets to the north and south through narrow gaps, between the long block along the street and lower blocks on the precinct's opposite (eastern) side. From these entrances, the lower blocks step back in plan and down in height as the precinct widens in its central portion into an elongated piazza. Here it is edged to the east by low walls, beyond which is a raised garden, lushly planted on the roofs over the parking basement, and some ancillary ground floor accommodation. This garden serves as a buffer between the new development and its neighbours, as well as an attractive outlook for both. It also hints at the presence of, and so implies, some connection with the public park a short distance to the northeast.

Placed rather randomly in the piazza are three freestanding cylindrical towers, two with

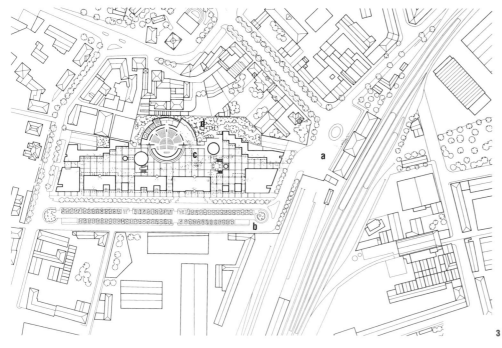

4

adjacent more slender towers housing helical stairs. There is also a less tall circular building of greater girth, half of which bulges into the piazza's edge, and half of which rises from the garden. The form, scale and positioning of the towers is reminiscent of the baptisteries and campanile in some medieval Italian piazzas – with the projecting semi-circle of the widest building perhaps recalling a church apse. This rather medieval precedent contrasts with what might be seen as the more classical

Banca Popolare di Lodi
4 Free-standing circular towers in the central precinct.
5, **6** Sketch sections through central precinct.
7 Raised garden, and beyond it the precinct, canopy and long block on western edge of site.

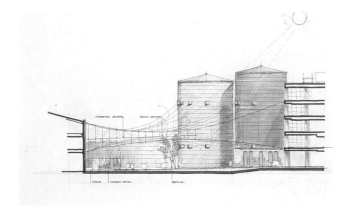

5

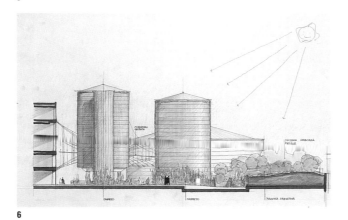

6

character of the broad street, thus accentuating the differences between the two new routes linking station and old town.

The contrast between the rectilinearity of the buildings edging the piazza with the roundness of those rising from within it reflects their very different functions: the former contain conventional subdividable space for offices and shops, while the round buildings accommodate specialized functions – as does the round helipad, the edges of which project visibly from the southern end of the long tall block. The banking hall is on the ground floor of the rectilinear buildings, but occupies only the northwest corner leaving the rest for a variety of functions that enliven the complex. Besides shops, there is an exhibition gallery just south of the banking hall and the local produce exchange, an important institution in market towns like Lodi. On the upper floors, the bank's administrative offices fill the top (fourth) floor of the long west block and all but a quarter of the other floors which is let to other tenants.

The two silo-like towers do not store grain, but are part of the bank and show off the storage of the town's riches. The precedent or 'memory' evoked is

again medieval or even earlier and further afield, of ancient treasuries and defensive round towers, such as those of the Irish. One tower houses safety deposit boxes retrieved by a computer-controlled belt system. A somewhat fatter tower contains private vaults for the storage of larger items, including fur coats. The third tower is raised on round columns and partly shelters an entrance to the underground parking. It houses mechanical plant, including the back-up generators essential to the bank's security and computer systems. The lowest and broadest of the circular buildings is the 850-seat meeting/concert hall, the interior of which has yet to be fitted out.

The bank needs a hall for occasional uses such as shareholders' meetings, and, as a civic gesture, it will also offer for it to be put to more frequent and various uses by the town

139

7

and its citizens. Besides echoing the towers, the circular embrace of the cylindrical form will give the hall a feeling of intimacy. The inherent acoustic problem of the central focus will be resolved easily by lining the inside of the drum with convex wooden panels that will scatter the sound. (Some of these will also be slotted to absorb certain frequencies.) However the main acoustic reflectors will be partially hidden from sight above a honeycomb steel mesh ceiling that will be about 50 per cent permeable to sound. The

reflectors are to be inverted domes of various sizes, laminated from wood so as to be absolutely rigid, arranged around a central rooflight that crowns the flattish conical roof to admit some natural light into the hall. This solution was tested on a 1:10 wooden model by the acousticians, Müller Bbm, and proven to perform well.

Only the upper volume of the hall is cylindrical, though smaller in diameter than it is perceived externally because it is ringed by rooms for changing, plant and storage – apart from around the lower part of its northeastern half. Here tiered seats will surround those on the flat central portion of the floor and extend back under the upper ring. An entrance lobby, opening off the piazza and lined with information and cloaks counters, and then a corridor will together curve around the back of these seats to provide access to the hall. Across the corridor will be meeting rooms of various sizes and lavatories, and at its opposite end to the lobby will be a bar that also opens off the piazza. All of these spaces around the lower part of the auditorium are already mounded over with earth and planting as part of the landscaping that edges this side of the site.

From the outside of the half of the drum that bulges into the piazza, suspension ties – forming both downward- and upward-curving catenaries – radiate out to the towers and the long rectilinear block. These

support the glass sheets of a large canopy which shelters much of the mid-portion of the piazza for such uses as an outdoor market or extension to the hall foyer. As with a number of other elements designed by the Building Workshop (such as the mast-stiffened glazed screen on the sides of the central terminal block of the Kansai International Airport, Volume three pp128–229), this suspension system was developed with, and made by, the French engineering subcontractors, Eiffel. It includes elegant cast elements, of the sort expected from Piano, which join the cables and tie-bars to each other and support the gently sloping, frameless glass sheets.

In contrast to the pared-down, and understatedly elegant, minimalism of material and detail of this system, the anchorings where the cables are secured to chunky blocks projecting through the terracotta cladding are quite crude. Yet this only reveals, and is consistent with, the very pragmatic strategy central to the whole design. This entails elevating relatively crude, conventional construction (of in situ concrete structural frame, square-gridded standard windows and so on) into something refined and urbane

140 **Banca Popolare di Lodi**

1, 2 Canopy under construction.

3 Elevation and section of front portion of a terracotta-clad bay of the west facade of long block.

4 Terracotta cladding is omitted to expose the anchorages of the canopy cables.

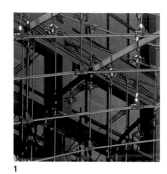

1 2

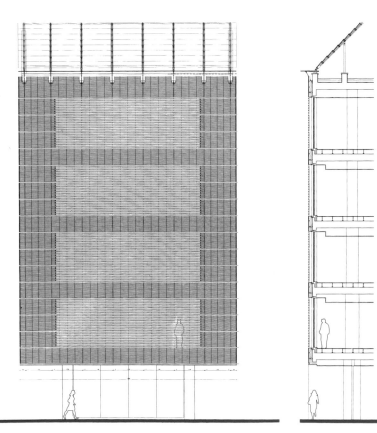

3 4

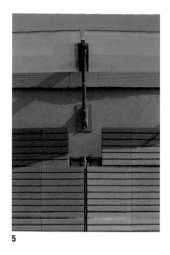

5

by dressing it in an impeccably tailored coat of terracotta, accessorized with such details as frosted glass cornices. This strategy is more explicitly revealed here than in other terracotta-faced schemes by the Building Workshop, both by exposing the underlying building at the cable anchorages and, in particular, by leaving unclad the whole mid-portion of that facade of the long rectangular block which faces the central piazza. Here the undressed building can be seen in its inelegant, raw banality.

Banca Popolare di Lodi

5 Close-up view of canopy, supporting bracket and terracotta cladding on top of auditorium drum.

6, 7 Assembling terracotta units that will form the corners of windows and grilles across them, as seen in **8** and **11**.

8 Worms eye isometric projection

9, 10 Construction views with the elements that terminate the terracotta cladding under the oversailing first floor being set in place in **10**.

11 Close up view of corner of window shielded by terracotta grille.

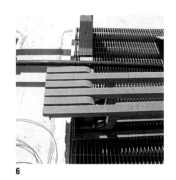

6

7

The terracotta is, as is also clearly revealed, not an integral part of the building's structural and weather-excluding fabric, but only a protective and decorative rain screen projecting 200mm from the building behind.

Although the Lodi scheme is one of a series by the Building Workshop which are clad in terracotta, there are always differences in the way this cladding is handled, as well as in the colour of the terracotta (which darkens and intensifies in hue with longer firing). Besides revealing the Building Workshop's urge to always explore and experiment further with a material, these differences reflect those of the buildings themselves, such as scale, proportions, function and context. Here the terracotta is a mellow, orangy-pink. And the basic cladding unit is not made up of small brick-sized elements assembled into larger metal framed panels as at the IRCAM extension (Volume one pp202–13) or Genoa docks (Volume two p122). Nor is it a large unit spanning self-supported between vertical rails as at the Lyon Cité Internationale (Volume three pp74–97) or Potsdamer Platz (p156) – although a square-sectioned unit, similar to those

used for grilles in those two projects, serves the same purpose here. Instead, it is a large unit, with regularly spaced horizontal grooves giving it a more delicate scale, as if it were several smaller units. And each of these is supported by being bolted to a pair of hollow steel rails. These are attached to brackets that clip onto pegs on the sides of the stainless-steel vertical supports set at 1.1 metre spacings.

Besides this basic unit, there are others for dealing with specific conditions, such as the square-sectioned grille unit. There are two sorts of L-shaped units. One is used to turn external corners, and a smaller version of this turns in to form the external reveals of windows. The other special unit terminates the bottom of the cladding just below the projecting first floor of the largest block and aligns with the soffit of the external ceiling. It is at this point, a little above eye level, that any imprecisions of alignment are readily evident.

Other than at this visually vulnerable spot, the cladding is yet another considerable success. Once again this is achieved largely through the precision of proportions and spacings and the hierarchy of scale that is given to the building. Here the fine-scale horizontal emphasis of the grooves is counterpointed by the vertical gaps in which the stainless-steel supporting rails are visible. The long west facing block is given a hierarchy of

141

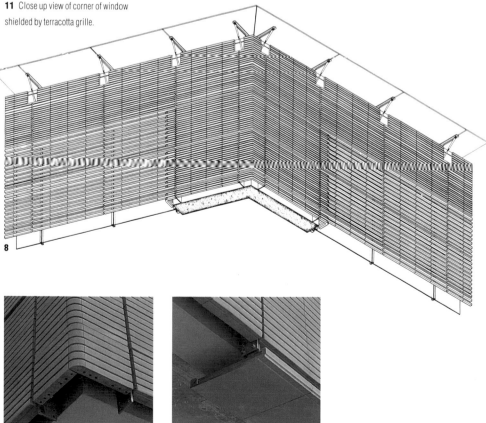

8

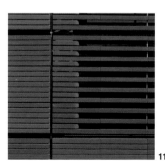

9

10

11

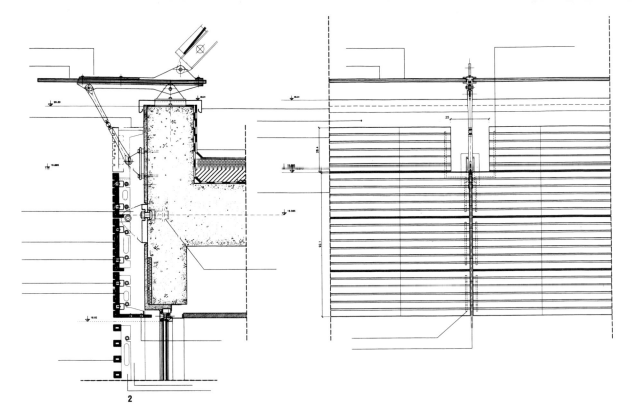

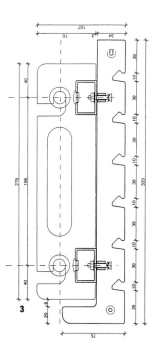

3

2

Banca Popolare di Lodi

Terracotta cladding.

1 Portion of long west facade showing three different types of cladding units: large grooved units facing solid parts; square-sectioned units creating grilles in front of windows; and units that fold in towards the window frames.

2 Section and elevation details at head of external wall showing fixings of claddings and glass cornice.

3 Section through large grooved terracotta unit and aluminium support rails, with bracket by which units are clipped onto pegs projecting from vertical support rails shown in elevation.

4 Staircase behind grille on western facade.

5 Plans, elevations and sections of the various terracotta units and their fixings.

4

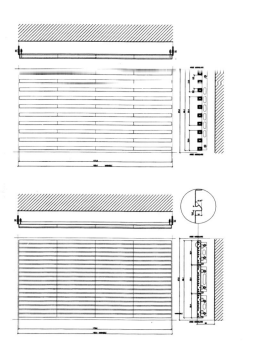

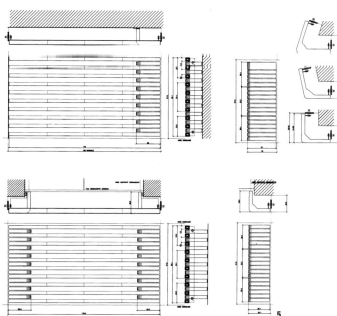

5

1

144 **Banca Popolare di Lodi**

1 Mobile water sculpture by Shingu stands in a pool below the canopy.

2, 3 Elevation and section of frosted glass louvres that conceal plant on roof of long western block.

4 Section of glass cornice and louvres on roof of circular towers.

5 Looking along cornice of western block.

6 Looking down on cornices of tower and auditorium.

7 Looking past drum of auditorium, to right, and across raised garden over its ancillary accommodation to canopy and towers in southern part of precinct.

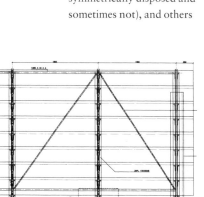

3

4

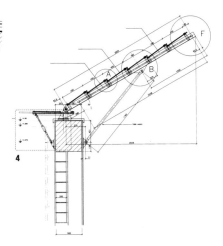

intermediary scales between that of its large bulk and the delicacy of the cladding: it is broken down into the smaller blocks, and these are articulated further by sharing and repeating between them a few patterns of fenestration in which all windows are screened by the grilles of horizontal units that continue in the same planes as the rest of the terracotta cladding. Some blocks have individual windows expressed on each floor (sometimes symmetrically disposed and sometimes not), and others feature a single four-storey glazed panel.

One element is totally new for Piano: the cornice that caps the cladding (such as one misses on the street facade of the Rue de Meaux Housing in Paris, Volume one pp214–27). This cornice is of glass panes fritted with white dots and held in propped steel brackets. The delicate, yet emphatic, termination against the sky is visually very successful on the lower blocks, but is perhaps a touch too small for the high long block. Large fixed louvres of similarly fritted glass step back behind the parapets of several roofs to conceal air-conditioning and other plant.

The paving of the precinct and the sidewalks of the broad street add another urbane texture to the scheme, and complements that of the terracotta facades. They are cobbled with grey porphyry stone set within a larger and more warm-toned grid of pietro dorata that continues the column grid. Here and there within this are beds of floral shrubs; and against the curving auditorium wall is a pond in which stands a specially-commissioned, mobile water sculpture 'fiore d'acqua' (water flower) by Shingu, a sculptor who often collaborates with Piano. Extending below this precinct and the buildings that frame it are the two levels of the basement parking garage. The upper level, with its pedestrian entrance below the tower raised on columns, serves the public; the lower level is for bank employees and security vans.

Tucked away in a sleepy little Italian town, the Banca Popolare di Lodi scheme provides lessons for cities everywhere. Following the fragmentation of urban fabric wrought by so much of modern architecture, the task now is to reintegrate our towns and cities and reinvest them with a sense of urbanity. This scheme achieves this, not just through its forms and mix of functions which tie together and bring life to the town, but also with the rich warmth and fine-scale articulation of its terracotta cladding and its partially-roofed public precinct.

5

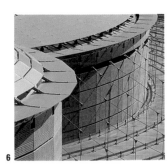

6

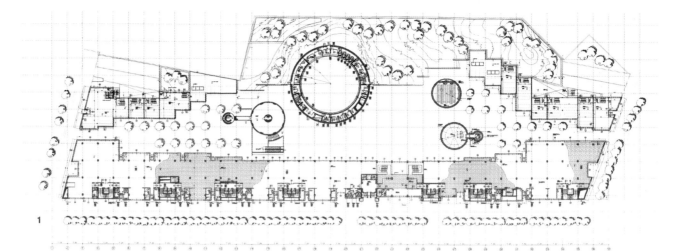

1

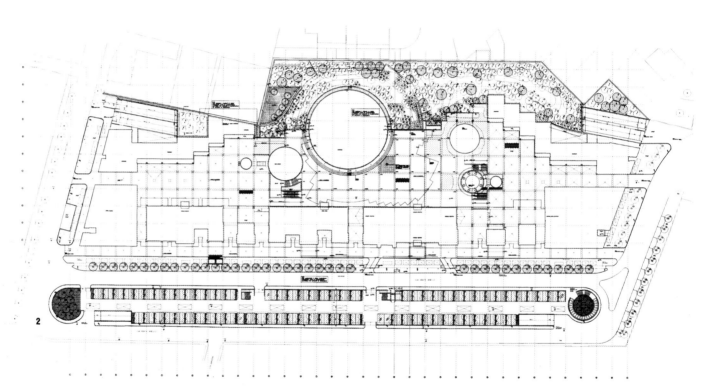

2

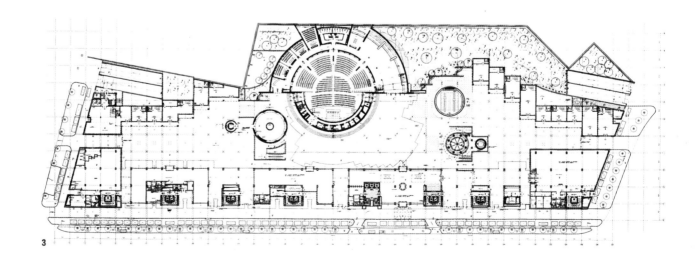

3

4

Banca Popolare di Lodi

1 First floor plan.

2 Ground floor plan showing treatment of broad street to west as well as of hard and soft landscaping.

3 Ground floor plan.

4 Facade of long west-facing block is articulated into smaller bays with differing fenestration, all of which is screened by terracotta grilles. Capping the facade is the frosted glass cornice, above which banks of frosted glass louvres slope back to conceal roof-top plant.

5 West elevation.

1

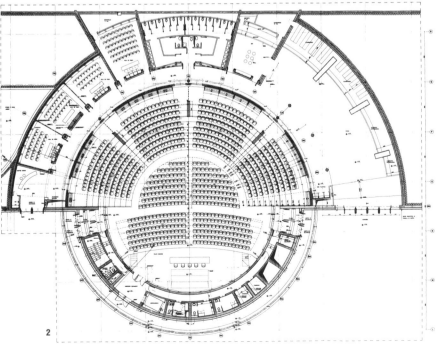

2

Banca Popolare di Lodi
Previous pages Portion of the west
elevation showing the sense of crisp
lightness achieved by use of terracotta and
frosted glass.

1 Central precinct viewed from north. Central
portion of facade of long block on west (to
right) is left without terracotta cladding.
2 Ground floor plan of auditorium.

Banca Popolare di Lodi

3 Central portion of precinct looking north. One reason middle portion of long block on left is left without terracotta cladding is because so many of the canopy cables are anchored to it. Ahead are escalators and stairs down to the parking garage, and on the precinct floor are cobbles set in a grid of grey stone.

4 Cross section looking north through long western block, precinct, auditorium and raised garden.

3

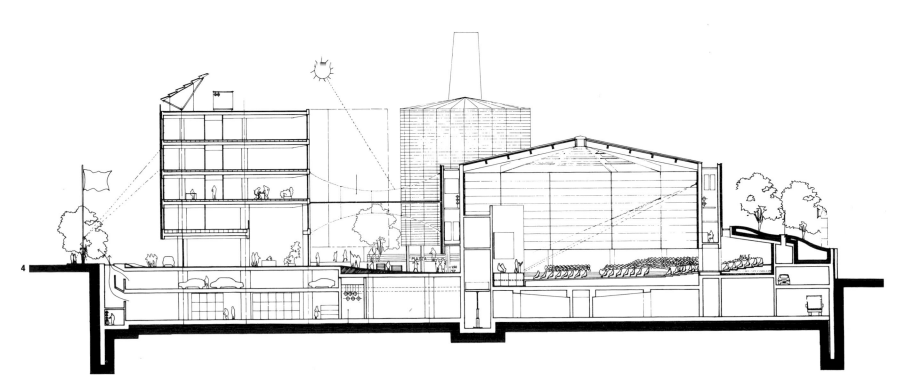

4

Banca Popolare di Lodi

Canopy details.

1 Close-up view of junction between connecting tie shown in **2** and lower arched cable.

2 Details of the ties that connect the upper and lower cables, with their turnbuckles that adjust length and tension and the quatrefoil elements that hold the glass.

152

3 Close-up view of the circumferential bars that help stabilize the structural system and support the the edges of the glass planes that do not lie under the radial cables.

4 Details of the cast-steel quatrefoil elements that secure the glass panes.

5 Glass cornices, screening louvres and canopy seen from above.

6 Plan showing radial cables, anchorages and different sizes and shapes of glass.

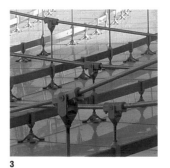

1

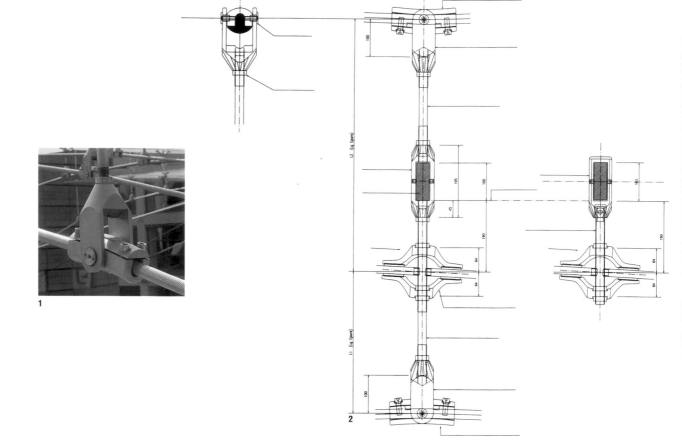

2

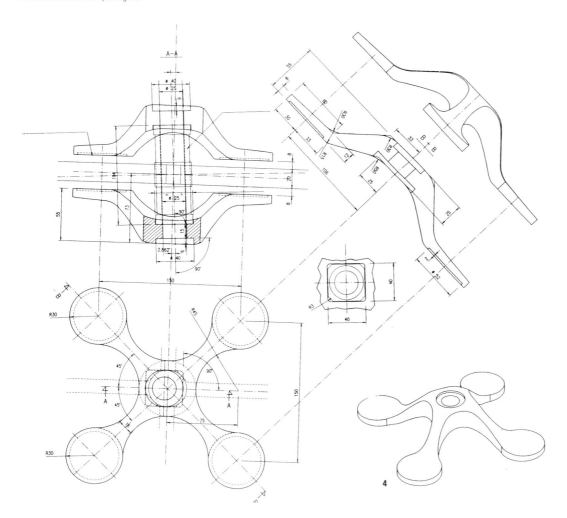

3

4

5

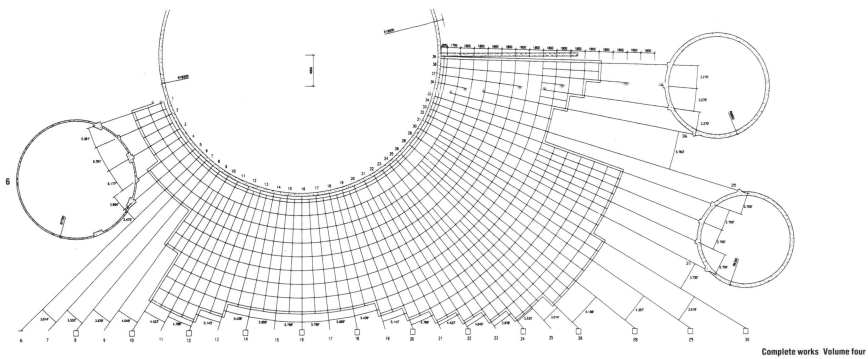

6

Banca Popolare di Lodi

Rooflight at top of tower.

1 Upward view of rooflight with glass roof
and a flat glass ceiling supported by structure
of suspension ties and struts.

2 Hall ringed by fat columns and capped
by rooflight.

3 Section: **a** glass roof; **b** flat glass ceiling;
c structure of suspension ties and
compression struts.

4 Typical interior in bank's administrative
offices as fitted out by the Building Workshop.

5 Plan of rooflight.

1

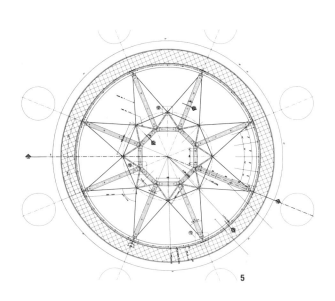

2

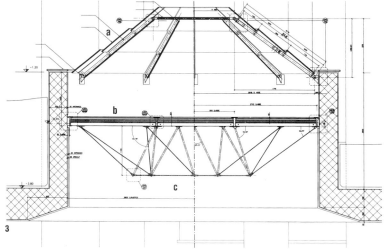

3

4

5

Banca Popolare di Lodi

Entrance lobby to bank's offices.

6 Detail of stair seen in **8** and **9**: cast-steel bracket supports nose of tread above and back of tread below.

7 Suspended stair in lobby with glass balustrades and treads.

8 Lobby with circular reception desk.

9 View through suspended stair.

7

8

9

Banca Popolare di Lodi
Client Banca Popolare di Lodi

Preliminary Design, 1991–2
Design team R Piano, G Grandi (senior partner in charge), A Alborghetti, V Di Turi, G Fascioli, E Fitzgerald, C Hayes, P Maggiora, C Manfreddo, V Tolu, A Sacchi, S Schäfer
Cad Operators S D'Atri, G Langasco

Design Development and Construction Phase, 1992–8
Design team R Piano, G Grandi (senior partner in charge), V Di Turi
Assisted by A Alborghetti, A Belvedere, C Brizzolara, S Giorgio Marrano, D Hart (partner), M Howard, H Peñaranda
Cad Operators S D'Atri, G Langasco
Structure and services engineers
MSC, Manens Intertecnica
Acoustics Müller Bbm
Lighting P Castiglioni
Graphic design P Cerri
Interiors F Santolini

156

Potsdamer Platz Berlin, Germany **1992–9**

The huge Potsdamer Platz project faced Piano with daunting challenges and conundrums. The prime challenge was to reweave together not just the rent fabric of a city, but what had been East and West Berlin as then separated by a broad swathe of dereliction populated only by memories and the terrible ghosts of history. The major conundrums were: whether it is possible (despite the ample positive evidence of historic examples in cities like London and Paris) to instantly create a vibrant, organic piece of the city at such a large scale; and to what extent is it possible, or appropriate, to resurrect the character of urban fabric and city life in an area that lives on vividly in memory, art and legend? This latter conundrum is compounded if, as here, that character is intrinsically of a bygone age and is associated with some of the sleazier aspects of urban life as well as the more glamorous.

Potsdamer Platz, and the area around it, had been the liveliest hub of Berlin. But for 45 years it was reduced to a bleak wasteland traversed by the infamous Wall. Now vast reconstruction projects are underway or recently completed. Of these, one stands out as a new urban quarter with the vivacity of mixed functions and architectural articulation usually associated only with old urban areas. The masterplan and about half the buildings occupying this huge tract – which extends from Potsdamer Platz in what became East Berlin to the Kulturforum in what was West Berlin – were designed and executed by the Building Workshop, who won the invited urban design competition in 1992. That scheme and its evolution towards the final masterplan, as well as early versions of the buildings, are shown and discussed in Volume two (pp210–19).

The scheme is not of the sort guaranteed to grab immediate international attention. It lacks the fashionable prestige of, say, a high-profile, big-budget museum; although energy-efficient, its offices and housing break no new ground in their internal arrangements, and there are no spectacular visible feats of engineering. Instead the scheme achieves something much more important, and which modern architects have so often failed at. It has recreated a simultaneously varied, yet integrated, chunk of urban fabric and city life, of what Renzo Piano would call 'normality', which for him is the highest of all goals to strive for today.

For Piano normality is not the merely mundane, though it is that too, but daily life as it should be – in this case in a mixed-use quarter of the city that is vibrantly alive day and night. Yet the scheme realizes this in an area that has been subjected to the most abnormal of recent histories and has been designed under conflicting but almost equally strong urges to both forget and remember aspects of that history. Hence it not only lies between, but ties back together, what had been East and West Berlin, while resurrecting some of the spirit of the area when it had been the throbbing heart of prewar Berlin.

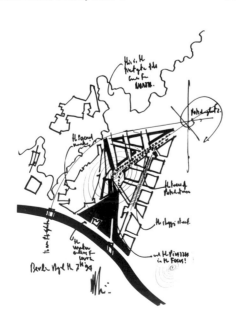

The scheme also continues Piano's explorations into terracotta cladding. Once again it has been used in a contemporary manner to achieve visual warmth, delicacy and a hierarchy of scales suitable to viewing from any distance. And refining the approach taken at the Lyon Cité Internationale (Volume three pp74–97), this cladding, supplemented in some places with a secondary skin of glass louvres, is part of a comprehensive energy-saving strategy.

Realized here is nothing less than an urban vision for the twenty-first century, one that marries the best of traditional urban forms and conviviality with contemporary functions and technology. A compact quarter in which to live, work, shop and be entertained, it is also a place in which it is a pleasure to just loiter, where differing sorts of public spaces, both internal and external, shelter a range of urban experiences. From the big and bustling – such as a broad tree-lined street, focal piazza or triple-level shopping arcade – these range to the quiet and intimate – such as narrow side streets and an elevated tree-shaded court. Design attention has obviously been as much on shaping the network of spaces between the buildings that form the public realm as on the buildings themselves.

Historical background

In these postmodern times, large-scale redevelopments such as the Potsdamer Platz project are shaped by more than the functional demands of present and future. As we seek to recreate a less alienated and alienating environment, they tend also to be conditioned by, or intentionally reflect aspects of, local history. Here, memories of Potsdamer Platz and the area around it, as well as generalized memories of Berlin's historic urban fabric, influenced design in direct and indirect ways. Although reduced to a wasteland, Potsdamer Platz retained its legendary status as the interwar epitome of metropolitan glamour and gaiety; and Berlin's reunification and impending reinstatement as the capital was provoking widespread debate about the city's identity and how this had been, and could be, encapsulated in built form.

Berlin's origins extend back 750 years, but only comparatively recently has it become a large city. It has also had a turbulent history, having had to rebuild itself each time after devastation in the Thirty Years War, the Napoleonic invasion and the Second World War. Now with the post-Cold War reunification, much of the city is once again a building site. However, besides being rebuilt after devastation, Berlin has also been refashioned with increasing frequency over the last 200 years or so in accord with contrasting architectural visions, including Neoclassicism, the pompous Wilhelmine style, Modernism and as Albert Speer's Germania, capital of the Third Reich.

Postwar partition then brought the pursuit of two very different urban visions: West Berlin retained the grain of the traditional city while East Berlin which pursued an

1

Potsdamer Platz

Previous Page The heart of the Potsdamer Platz scheme is the Marlene Dietrich Platz, seen here is shadow with the theatre edging it to the right and the Debis Headquarters beyond to the left.

1 Aerial view of Potsdamer Platz in the interwar period.
2 Potsdamer Platz in its interwar heyday and
3 the same view just after World War Two.
4 The Potsdamer Platz area after the destruction of the Wall. Alte Potsdamerstrasse lies roughly on a diagonal in the centre of the photograph. On the left is the Kulturforum with the National Library just beyond the end of the Alte Potsdamerstrasse.

2

3

erratically applied policy of architectural amnesia, razing vestiges of 'a decadent bourgeois lifestyle' along with Hitler's Reich Chancellery. These were replaced by gargantuan socialist realist blocks in a crudely neoclassical style; later came an equally gargantuan and crude modernism.

Berlin's reunification has provoked further forms of amnesia. Nothing is left of the Wall: only its route will be commemorated with discreet markers, and the pattern of historic streets and squares is being reinstated as seamlessly as possible.

Besides removal of traces of the recent past, Berlin's city architect, Hans Stimman, pursued a policy to reinstate an abstracted and generic Berlinische Architektur, maintaining the traditional street wall with masonry construction and a constant parapet line at 22, 28 or 35 metres, and adopting the courtyard layout of the nineteenth-century Mietskaserne built to house Berlin's then rapidly expanding population. (Once dank slums, these are now desirable urban housing, thanks to modern technology, such as central heating, and less dense occupancy.)

Some take the Berlinische Architektur theme further and advocate a 'new heaviness': stone-faced buildings in a starkly stripped classicism, reminiscent of buildings from the end of the Wilhelmine as well as the Nazi periods. This has provoked a reaction in those who advocate a similarly extreme form of contemporary architecture that exaggerates, rather than ameliorates, the fragmentation of

the modern city. Much of the debate about the future of Berlin has been a slanging match between these simplistic and overly polarized positions. Part of the significance of Piano's Potsdamer Platz scheme is that the latter camp might rightly recognize the architecture as contemporary (if too conventionally urban for its taste), while the former might also legitimately claim it as showing sympathy for their position (even if too lightweight for their tastes).

At the turn of the century, Potsdamer Platz station was much the busiest in the city, and the neighbourhood was Berlin's most popular district for drinking and dining as well as music, theatre and night life. By the 1920s, traffic was so congested that, in 1924, Europe's first traffic lights were installed on Potsdamer Platz. The square was then not only among the busiest in Europe but known throughout it for its bustling attractions. Later it was known for its sleaze of prostitutes and pimps as well as for its glamour.

Allied bombing in the Second World War left most of the buildings as torn and roofless shells. With the Allied Occupation, Potsdamer Platz became the point at which the American, British and Russian sectors converged. Later the Wall ran through it and the remnants of the buildings on either side were removed to accommodate the broad 'death strip' on the east and a planned motorway on the west. But though a desolate wasteland, what the area once was lived on in memory and legend, literature and art.

Even before the Wall came down, Daimler-Benz had decided to build the corporate headquarters of Daimler-Benz InterServices AG (Debis) in Berlin and had purchased land between the Wall and the Kulturforum. Following reunification, as other multinationals rushed to buy other sites nearby, this was consolidated into a 6.8-hectare holding stretching from the Potsdamer Platz in its northeast corner to the National Library in the west and extending down to the Landwehrkanal to the south. Crossing this site were two lines of trees that extended southwest from where Potsdamer Platz had been, to where the National Library resolutely turns its back on former East Berlin and the Wall. These trees had been preserved as a historic monument because they marked the route of the Alte Potsdamerstrasse, once lined by many of the area's famous establishments. Of these only the Winehaus Huth was still standing.

Competition and masterplan

Daimler-Benz held an invited international competition to develop a masterplan for the site. Competitors had to comply with an earlier competition-winning masterplan for the whole area around Potsdamer Platz and Leipziger Platz. Prepared by architects Heinz Hilmer and Christoph Sattler, this in turn conformed to city architect Hans Stimman's edicts on street and block pattern, and restricted building heights. But there is a crucial weakness to Hilmer & Sattler's plan,

4

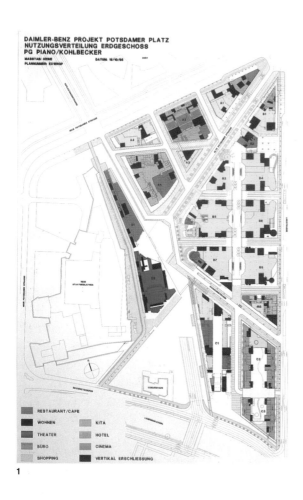

DAIMLER-BENZ PROJEKT POTSDAMER PLATZ
NUTZUNGSVERTEILUNG ERDGESCHOSS
PG PIANO/KOHLBECKER

RESTAURANT/CAFE
WOHNEN   KITA
THEATER   HOTEL
BÜRO   CINEMA
SHOPPING   VERTIKAL ERSCHLIESSUNG

1

Potsdamer Platz

1 – 3 Plans of the final scheme showing:
1 ground floor functions (yellow indicates
retail; red, vertical circulation); **2** overall
functions (olive green indicates offices; blue,
housing); **3** roof plan.
4 Plan from competition entry report showing
scheme in context of central Berlin. In the
centre is the large park of the Tiergarten.
South-east of this is the Kulturforum and
Potsdamer Platz site with the octagonal
Liepziger Platz to the east of these.

which affects the Daimler-Benz site in particular. This was planned as an island with no immediately adjacent urban tissue and activities to connect up with. To the west is the scarcely urban Kulturforum with its buildings floating dislocatedly in space, and to the east a new linear park, the Ostpromenade. To the north is a busy road with a broad central island, Neue Potsdamerstrasse, and to the south the Landwehrkanal. Even the Potsdamer Platz as reconfigured by Hilmer & Sattler offers no real chance of forging connections. Buildings terminate on it in sharp points, so it has none of the frontage necessary to both define it as a space and house the activities to enliven it as an urban node. (Fortunately the Daimler-Benz site enjoys very good subterranean connections to Potsdamer Platz station – serving German Railways, s-Bahn and u-bahn lines – which to a large extent mitigates this island condition.)

Other competitors accepted the site as an island and treated it accordingly. The Building Workshop scheme (submitted with Christoph Kohlbecker, with whom it was already collaborating on the Mercedes-Benz Design Centre p124–35) was quite different. Recognizing the relative isolation of the site and the dislocated layout of the Kulturforum, Renzo Piano and Bernard Plattner (the Associate in charge of the project) focused much of their design energy outside the competition site. Their scheme placed new and unasked-for cultural buildings abutting the inhospitable back of the National Library.

These were in a similar architectural language to the Library, so as to relate to it visually, and framed a new piazza (which like the cultural buildings was also outside both the brief and the competition site) that formed a climactic termination to Alte Potsdamerstrasse.

Besides being thereby the only entry to restore real significance to this historic street, these additions also cemented a firm connection between the Daimler-Benz site and the Kulturforum. The Building Workshop scheme made further off-site proposals to improve its integration into its larger setting. Extending northwards from the Landwehrkanal was to be a lake (into which dives the new Tiergarten road tunnel that passes under the site). This marked the competition site boundary and further clarified that the pivotal new cultural buildings were as much part of the Kulturforum as of the new urban quarter.

Despite flouting the competition conditions, these proposals were so inspiring and convincing that the Building Workshop scheme was voted winner by 20 of the 21 jurors. Daimler-Benz thus commissioned Piano and Kohlbecker to work up their scheme, designing and detailing the public realm of streets and squares, as well as about half the buildings. The rest of the buildings were assigned to some of the unsuccessful competitors.

As with any good urban design, as much attention has gone into shaping the spaces between the buildings, and the network these form together, as on determining the footprints and functions, height, bulk and finishes

DAIMLER-BENZ PROJEKT POTSDAMER PLATZ
NUTZUNGSVERTEILUNG NORMALGESCHOSS
PG PIANO/KOHLBECKER

2

3

of the various buildings. Here Piano and his team have created a carefully crafted network of public spaces of contrasting character. This not only forms a richly differentiated public realm but also articulates a range of locations well suited to different functions. These public spaces and their configuration as a network determines the character of the whole scheme as much as the architecture does.

The dominant spaces in this network are the broad tree-lined Alte Potsdamerstrasse and the piazza, now named the Marlene Dietrich Platz, that it leads to and which forms a focus for the whole scheme. (This piazza in turn focuses on a covered porch between the two buildings that mediate between this site and the Kulturforum.) A smaller street, Eichornstrasse, wraps around the edge of this and connects it to the major streets edging the north and east of the site: Neue Potsdamerstrasse and Linkstrasse respectively. The next most dominant element in the public realm network after the Alte Potsdamerstrasse and Marlene Dietrich Platz is the Arkade, a triple-level shopping arcade, of which the north end of the basement level connects with the Potsdamer Platz station. Another covered public space is an atrium in the Debis Headquarters in the south of the site.

Within the masterplan area, the architectural guidelines for central Berlin have been somewhat modified. Because Piano preferred to maintain the 2:1 ratio between building height and street width once common in the streets of this area, yet also to have some more intimately narrow streets than a 35-metre cornice line would allow, the parapet line was set at 28 metres. (Floors are set back above this to achieve the same built volume as the usual 35-metre height would have allowed.) And instead of being faced in stone or brick Piano preferred unglazed terracotta, a material now deemed acceptable elsewhere in Berlin. This reflects his continuing penchant for lightness, his successful experiences with the material and that it can be used as a flexible kit-of-parts in a language of clearly expressed 'pieces'. He also stipulated that each building have a colonnaded arcade set back in the base of each building, which, as much as possible, should contain such pavement-interactive uses as shops and restaurants.

At prominent locations on the site perimeter, the guidelines change. At the extremities, against Potsdamer Platz and the Landwehrkanal, where Debis built their own headquarters, office towers arise to address the open spaces before them, as well as Berlin beyond. The two towers built by the Building Workshop have a sheathing of glass outside the terracotta, not only for energy savings, but also to emphasize that this is no longer conventional 'street architecture'. The buildings between the rest of the Potsdamer Platz scheme and the National Library are clad with both terracotta and metal panels similar to, though much less vulgar than, those on the Library. These dual finishes recognize the mediatory role of these buildings.

On the site is now an extraordinary mix of functions bringing the round-the-clock life that Piano sought. On the 6.8-hectare site, only about 50 per cent of the 340,000 square metres of the gross floor area above ground (there is a further 210,000 square metres underground) is offices (which total 175,000 square meters). Another 20 per cent (70,000 square metres) is housing. The remaining 30 per cent is a mix of uses to which the public have ready access. There is a large 1,800-seat theatre for musicals, with a 700-seat theatre for dinner and cinema tucked below it, a casino with 8,000 square metres of high- and low-stakes gaming, a 350-room hotel with ballroom and conference facilities, a 440-seat IMAX cinema and a 19-screen multiplex cinema with 3,500 seats in total. There are 40,000 square metres of shopping and eating facilities that range from fast food outlets to high-class restaurants. Also, there is parking for 4,000 cars – 2,500 on site but underground, and 1,500 in a parking garage built south of the canal. Besides those who live on the Daimler-Benz site, some eight to ten thousand people work there and up to 100,000 people are expected to visit the commercial and entertainment attractions each day. From the year 2000, this will be the site of the Berlin Film Festival. This will take advantage of all these facilities and cinema screens (the music theatre also has a screen, and screens could also be erected in the Debis atrium and in the big porch off the Marlene Dietrich Platz).

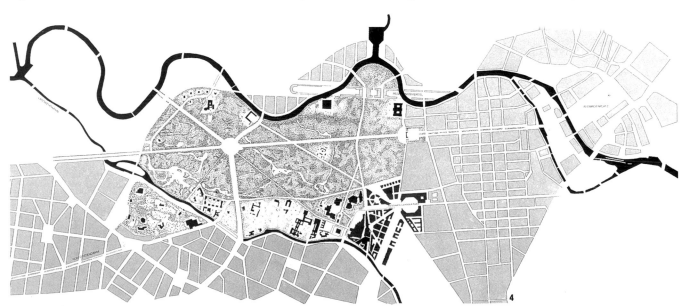

4

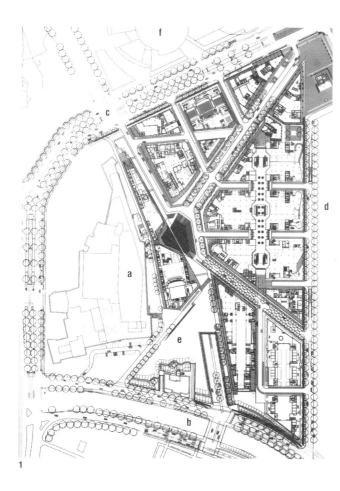

The allocation of buildings between the various architectural practices has been shrewdly handled. Those assigned to the Building Workshop have allowed Piano to create a considerable coherence within the whole scheme, despite the other architects being constrained only by the stipulation of function, parapet height, and preferred cladding material. The Building Workshop was responsible for a continuous string of buildings along the whole east side of Alte Potsdamerstrasse, including an office tower on Potsdamer Platz and the renovation of the Winehaus Huth as offices, which continues around the east side of Marlene Dietrich Platz as a pair of housing blocks and an IMAX cinema, to terminate in, and include, the Debis Headquarters. Also by the Building Workshop are the buildings between the Kulturforum and the rest of the Daimler-Benz site: stretching north from the covered porch is the casino and south of it is the large theatre for musicals. Lastly, the shopping arcade, which abuts the back of the housing blocks and the IMAX cinema, is also by the Building Workshop.

On the opposite, east side of the shopping arcade are a pair of office blocks and a housing block by Richard Rogers. South of these is a small housing block by Munich architects Lauber & Wöhr, and a large office complex by Arata Isozaki. On the northern corner of Marlene Dietrich Platz is a large hotel by Rafael Moneo, and between the hotel and the big road to the north is an office block, also

by Moneo. East of the offices is a multiplex cinema complex with housing above, and south of this another small housing block, both again by Lauber & Wöhr. East of these, and opposite Piano's tower on Potsdamer Platz, is another office tower by Hans Kollhoff.

Kollhoff's tower will look as if built with rough brick, though this is a cladding of terracotta tiles. But though the cladding of Moneo's hotel is easily mistaken for large terracotta tiles baked a dark brown, it is actually a German sandstone. The same architect's small office block is faced in what is unmistakably a yellow stone. Isozaki's office towers are faced in glazed ceramic tiles organized in alternatively dark and light brown panels. Lauber & Wöhr and Rogers have used terracotta, but more conventionally than Piano, as a simple tile facing.

Unlike the other architects, the Building Workshop developed a whole range of cladding units to be applied inside, as well as outside, to achieve various effects. This system is a further evolution of that used at the Banca Popolare di Lodi (p136–55) and the Lyon Cité Universale (Volume three pp74–97). As with the latter, the units are narrow and long, though without the rounded arris along top and bottom. There are three basic types of terracotta units that are similar to those used in both these previous schemes: flat units to face walls; square-sectioned units to form grilles in front of windows; and corner units. Here too these units

Potsdamer Platz

1 Plan of all open spaces and ground floors of buildings: **a** National Library; **b** Landwehrkanal; **c** Neue Potsdamerstrasse; **d** Oostpromenade; **e** new lake; **f** Sony site.
2 Elevation of the continuous string of buildings by the Building Workshop with, from the left, the office tower B1, the Winehaus Huth, the residential blocks B3 and B5, the IMAX cinema and the Debis headquarter. Behind the central buildings can be glimpsed the shopping arcade.

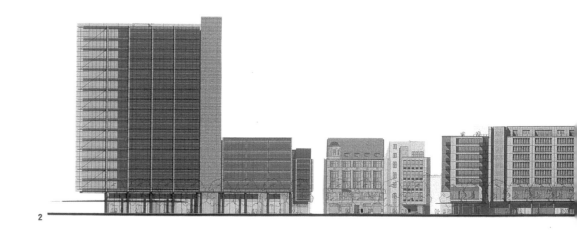

2

span between, and clip to, vertical aluminium rails that support them, although here the rails are usually hidden. (As a result, where the terracotta units face columns or stretches of blank wall they may be mistaken for tiles.) There is also a fourth, more complexly-shaped type of terracotta unit used to flank and conceal the vertical rails where they would otherwise be exposed in front of window frames. In such places it becomes clear that the cladding is set forward from the weather-excluding face of the building to form a continuous flat-fronted screen, which has solid areas as well as framing openings in front of windows that are in places unobstructed and elsewhere covered by grilles.

There are two basic cladding grids, 900mm (used only on the housing blocks) and 1350mm. The basic flat unit comes smooth faced or grooved to create a finer scale. The square-sectioned grille units are nick-named 'baguettes'. Outside office windows, these units span between the shapely vertical terracotta units concealing the aluminium rails. But where they pass in front of recessed balconies, their aluminium supports (which are pvf2 coated to match the colour of the terracotta) are clearly expressed. A refinement on earlier terracotta-clad schemes is that where the cladding ends at the parapet line or over the recessed arcades, this termination is clearly expressed. On the Debis building, this is achieved with large grc (glass reinforced cement) units coloured to match the terracotta. On the other buildings, grc is

used to create a slight cornice at the parapet, but above the arcades a small aluminium extrusion is used with a baked pvf2 coating also matching the terracotta. The walls above the arcades are supported on steel beams, whose projecting flanges create a neat channel fascia, which sits on concrete columns still clad in the cylindrical steel sleeves in which they were cast, and painted metallic grey like the beams.

The pavements within and outside these arcades have been handled with commensurate care, and follow the historic pattern for Berlin. Within the arcade, and forming a walkway in the broad pavement outside of it are smooth rectangular granite flagstones. Between these, and extending out to the kerb, are granite cobbles. Within this latter area are the trees lining the streets and benches.

Full appreciation of the success of the Potsdamer Platz scheme will require prolonged familiarity with all parts of it and its changing patterns of use and moods with time of day and the seasons. But much of what has been achieved visually by applying (even to a somewhat limited degree) the Building Workshop's design guidelines, as well as the way buildings were allocated between architects, can be well appraised by looking around from Marlene Dietrich Platz. From here everything by the Building Workshop can be seen; but the only building visible by another architect is Moneo's suitably urbane hotel. The continuous string of buildings by the Building Workshop, run-

ning down the east side of Alte Potsdamerstrasse, around Marlene Dietrich Platz and culminating in the Debis Headquarters, asserts a unifying order on the whole site. It screens the buildings by other architects behind them, which coincidentally include the architecturally and urbanistically least satisfactory, as well as creating a dialogue with the more plainly clad, less delicately animated buildings (by Moneo and Lauber & Wöhr) in front of them. Also, by forming 'book ends' marking the extremities of the site, the glassy towers at each end of this string help give a sense of the unity to the whole development.

The wall of buildings edging the eastern side of the Marlene Dietrich Platz are amongst the triumphs of the scheme. The cladding and window patterns are disciplined, yet animated (even more so when the yellow awning blinds are unfurled). Suavely urbane, the facades also have an earthy mellow warmth of colour and texture, as well as a shimmering vivacity and rich delicacy of detail. Some critics have complained that the architecture at Potsdamer Platz is too thin and lightweight, and verging on the scenographic. This is to utterly misunderstand Piano's intentions. These are not to impose upon urban life the dead hand of an inert and heavy architectural frame, but rather to provide an enlivening, almost pointillist backdrop. He is seeking not to recreate the historic city, but to find urban and architectural forms that draw on aspects of the past and

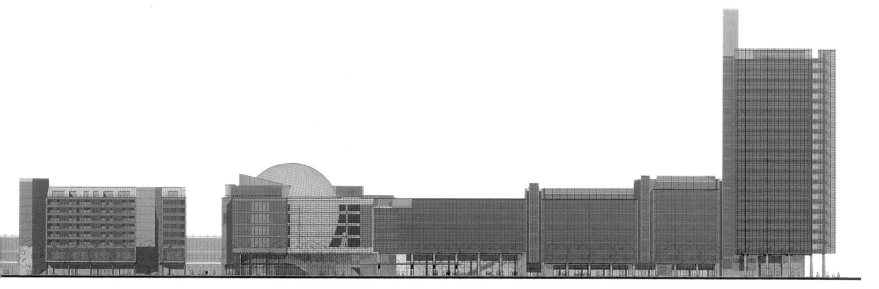

1

2

Potsdamer Platz
Construction.
1, 2 Divers at work tanking the basements,
2, even working under ice.
3 Aerial view of site during construction with
National Library in left foreground and the
site of the old Potsdamer Platz in the centre
of the photograph.

the potentials of the present to create a hybrid suited to contemporary conditions.

However, the success of these as urban buildings goes beyond the handling of the cladding. The ground floor uses – shops, fast food restaurants, entrance to the IMAX cinema – along with the bars and restaurant in the base of the hotel and various activities in the music theatre and casino, all help animate the square day and night. Piano has been unafraid of permitting the signage and advertising for these commercial uses to be on his buildings, so providing further visual animation. Up a small side street leading off the piazza can be glimpsed the shopping arcade that is even more conspicuous after dark. And above some stairs rising directly from the piazza edge can be seen the tree-shaded courtyard of a housing block whose facade gracefully curves away from the end of Alte Potsdamerstrasse.

To turn and look in the opposite direction is to be confronted by the music theatre and casino, and the huge porch between them, that mediate both formally and functionally between the rest of the site and the Kulturforum. This mediatory theme is confirmed by the cladding. The lower parts of the buildings and the back of the porch are clad in the same terracotta units as the rest of Piano's buildings. But the upper parts and ends of both buildings are sheathed in gold anodized aluminium panels that are a tasteful version of those on Scharoun's buildings: they have the same diamond motif pressed

into them but at a finer scale and are of a softer, cleaner, more silvery-gold colour than the brassy tone selected by Scharoun.

The bottom of this metallic sheathing angles upwards towards the porch, focusing attention onto it in much the same way as do old-fashioned theatrical curtains when pulled to the sides and upwards. This visual metaphor is most fitting, for the porch is the climax of the whole Potsdamer Platz scheme. It is an urban stage, on which the dishing of the piazza focusses further attention while also serving as an auditorium. Even when almost empty, this space is animated by the vistas and activity visible through the glass walls to either side. But it is so inviting that it is impossible to imagine it not being used more or less constantly for all sorts of performances. All in all, this is an apt resurrection and reinterpretation for our times of the legendary spirit of Potsdamer Platz.

Construction, logistics and ecology
Although the structure of the buildings is conventional enough above ground, the scale and complexity of the whole Daimler-Benz scheme posed problems to those constructing it, as did the ground water. The project involved the near simultaneous construction of eighteen buildings (including the renovation of the Winehaus Huth, and if counting the shopping arcade as a separate building and the music theatre and casino as two buildings) by seven architectural practices. At the same time, major road and rail tunnels

3

4

5

were built under the site and a new regional railway station under Potsdamer Platz. Also constructed were pedestrian tunnels to the stations, basements for service, storage and parking and all the ramps up and down to these from the streets on the site and the road tunnel beneath it. All this required the involvement of more than 100 contractors and sub-contractors with up to 4,000 construction workers.

Berlin was built on swampy land and environmentalists were worried that, at this scale, conventional construction involving pumping of excavations would disturb the water table in the surrounding area with all sorts of unpredictable and unwelcome consequences, such as drying out the trees in the Tiergarten park. To avoid such problems, all initial subterranean construction was undertaken by divers, up to 80 at a time, who even worked throughout winter in heated suits under the ice. Once the site had been cleared of fragments of bombs and other weaponry, as well as of the remnants of cellars and bunkers, a sequence of huge ponds were dug by floating dredgers. Around these were cast diaphragm walls 1.2 metres thick and 25 metres deep. Then the column footings and the lowest slabs were cast and anchored against uplift before the basements were pumped dry.

Daimler-Benz, like other German corporations and their government, is committed to ecological responsibility. So further measures were taken to protect the environment. Nonpolluting materials were used as a matter of policy, all rainwater is being reused and a range of energy-saving measures were mandatory. Hence rainwater is collected from the roofs of all the buildings and used for irrigating plants, topping up the lake and flushing lavatories. It is estimated this will save 20,000 cubic metres of purified tap water each year.

Energy is saved in a number of ways. Heat from a new power plant is to be used throughout the Daimler-Benz site (as well as others around Potsdamer Platz) for both heating buildings and providing the energy for refrigeration. On this site alone this will save emissions of 48,000 tons of carbon dioxide each year. All the buildings are highly insulated up to standards that are only recently required by law (so need not have been complied with), and use heat-insulating rather than double glazing. All rooms are naturally ventilated and only on exceptionally cold or hot days will require heating and mechanical ventilation. (There is no full airconditioning.) Where a lot of electronics will be installed, cooling is supplied by flushing cold water through ceiling panels. Together all these measures should reduce energy consumption to half that of buildings using yearround air-conditioning. The two Building Workshop office towers at the opposite extremities of the site apply further measures, in particular the secondary skin of glass louvres, so that air-conditioning is not required even in such tall buildings.

165

Potsdamer Platz

Construction.

4 Early phases of construction were done under water before, **5**, the basements were pumped dry.

6 The scheme in context when nearly complete, just beyond the Sony site left of centre.

Overleaf Potsdamer Platz scheme in context, with the Landwehrkanal in the foreground and Scharoun's National Library to the left.

6

2

Debis Headquarters

The first Building Workshop design to be completed was the 45,000 square metre headquarters for Debis, a subsidiary of Daimler-Benz whose property development division was the client for the whole Potsdamer Platz. The building was occupied and functioning while everywhere else was still a construction site. Its overall massing is largely a response to the shape of its lot and to its location. (There was hardly a context, in terms of existing neighbours, to respond to.) The lot and location no doubt suggested the tower rising 21 storeys from the narrow, southern end, above a larger, lower and broader portion where narrow arms of offices along a central corridor are wrapped around an atrium. Yet this same configuration is also consonant with the prime intention to exploit natural light and ventilation as much as possible.

The resultant, rather cumbersome massing has been crisply articulated and given vertical emphasis by expressing the vertical circulation elements of lifts and stair shafts. The way this is done, though necessitating rather more external wall, also brings natural light and views into the lift lobbies as well as a visual connection to the outside and city around. The tallest shaft, 106 metres high and capped by the green Debis logo, ventilates the Tiergarten tunnel, an entrance to which plunges into the lake against the building's west side. The southern elevation of the tower in particular, conspicuous above the Landwehrkanal, is given a thrusting vertical emphasis by being expressed as a cluster of shafts of differing height and flanked by projecting escape stairs. Adding visual drama to the opposite end of the building is the acute angle in which it terminates, as emphasized by the horizontal thrust of a sharp-pointed, cantilevered canopy.

Both a multi-purpose, semi-public facility and an energy-saving device, the atrium is the building's dominant space. Seven storeys high, 82 metres long and 14 metres wide, it has much the same dimensions as the nave of Notre Dame in Paris. As did the cathedral in medieval times, the atrium houses many functions. These include concerts and large meetings, as well as its day-to-day function as a place for casual meetings for the public and employees, perhaps before eating in the cafeteria or the staff canteen that open off the base of the atrium. Also opening off it, in the building's northern corner, is a Mercedes-Benz showroom with its own mezzanine in the northern corner, and some pockets of space along the atrium's eastern edge are used by a commercial gallery to display artworks.

At the atrium's southern end, the grey granite floor extends under the offices above to end in a pool that seems to extend inwards, through the base of a multi-storey shaft of glazing, from a large pond outside. Forward of this pool, but still under an overhanging boardroom that looks back down the length of the atrium (as well as between the walls on which moving shafts of sunlight are reflected), are the circular Debis reception desk and security turnstiles. Those entering here turn east to use the lifts whose shaft adjoins that ventilating the tunnel. At the northern end of the atrium and

169

Potsdamer Platz
Debis Headquarters

1 Portion of southern end of tower seen from the east. This shows the lively filigree and paradoxical sense of both lightness and depth achieved by the terracotta set forward of the windows and external aluminium Venetian blinds pvf2 coated to match the terracotta. Towards the end of the escape stair shaft the terracotta horizontals are progressively thinned out, like the threads towards the tassled end of a piece of cloth.

2 Looking across Marlene Dietrich Platz and past the end of the theatre to the Debis building.
3 Debis tower seen from west along Landwehrkanal.
4 Ground floor and context plan: **a** atrium; **b** reception; **c** car showroom; **d** lake; **e** entrance to road tunnel; **f** Eichornstrasse; **g** shopping arcade.

3

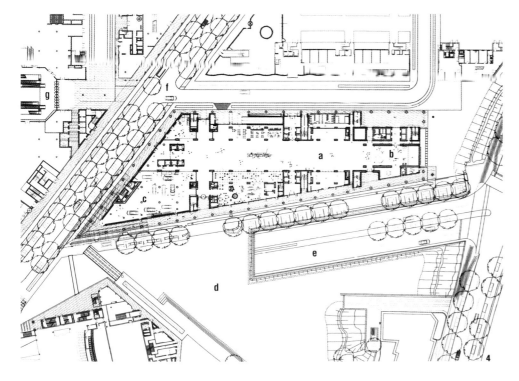

4

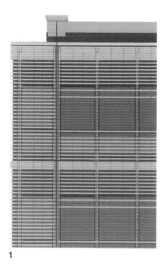

1

170   **Potsdamer Platz**

Debis Headquarters

Terracotta cladding: evolution from drawing to
prototype to final result.

1 Drawn study of portion of terracotta
clad elevation.

2 Full-size mock up of portion of facade
on site.

3 Built reality: a portion of a typical facade.
Note how the column grid is articulated at
every sixth window, further enriching the
articulations of the facade.

4 Portion of west facade of tower with outer
layer of glass louvres and escape stair to right.

5 Bottom corner of screen of glass louvres
showing how it is held away from the
terracotta facade.

2

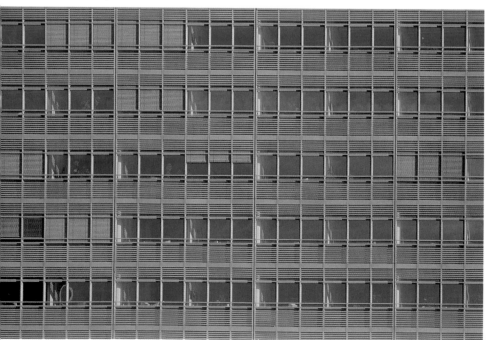

3

on both its long sides are
secondary entrances to the
offices, where security is
provided by swipe cards. The
lifts serving these secondary
entrances and against the atrium
are glazed, so they and their
occupants can be seen moving
behind grilles in the terracotta
cladding which extends in from
outside. Each lift landing is open
to the atrium so that people on
these further animate the tall
sides of this huge space.

Doing their bit to enliven the
space are two large artworks.
Set in the middle of the floor is a

Jean Tinguely sculpture that
judders to life briefly twice a
day. (These times are restricted
to prolong its life and because it
is noisy.) And arcing across the
atrium's sides and floor are the
blue neon tubes of a piece by
François Morellet. A video and
neon installation by Nam June
Paik animates the entrance foyer
between the atrium and
Eichornstrasse to the north.

The architectural treatment of
the atrium is as a semi-outdoor
space (hence the unpolished
granite floor and terracotta
cladding) assembled from parts
that are, to a greater or lesser
degree visually autonomous.
Defining the edges are terracotta-
clad piers that narrow at first-
floor level to carry steel channel
beams similar to those outside.
Above this, bands of windows
stretch between the piers. Across
the tops and bottom of these, as
well as across the intermediary
spandrel panels, are ranged rows
of white fritted glass shelves
tilted upwards. These serve
several functions. All of them
break up sound reflections and
diminish any acoustic echo, an
effect aided by the fact that the
metal spandrel panels behind the
tilted shelves are perforated and
front slabs of rockwool. The
shelves across the bottoms of the
windows also provide privacy,
while those across the heads of
the windows reflect the light
descending from the glass roof
above deep into the offices. This
device adds to the energy-saving
functions of the atrium, as a
space intermediate in
temperature between inside and
out from which offices can be
naturally lit and ventilated
through single glazed windows.
But, as much as anything, the
shelves are there for aesthetic

reasons, to soften these tall
internal facades and
paradoxically combine a
crystalline quality with a misty
indistinctness that together
create an affinity with the glazed
roof. From the tops of the piers,
slender tubular-steel posts rise to
support the grid of steel beams
that carry the roof glazing.
Suspended in rows at an angle
below this are panes of glass
fritted with a pattern of white
dashes. While allowing
northwards views of the sky,
these serve as solar sunshades –
and also as reflectors for
spotlights secured to each cast-
steel piece that supports the
bottom corners of two adjacent
panes. This roof, with its
supporting and lighting systems
(which can only be studied from
the top landings of the
circulation cores) is the most
refined part of the atrium. Its
equivalent is only found in the
handling of the various cladding
systems used outside.

As the first and biggest of
Piano's buildings in Berlin,
considerable effort was invested
in developing the Debis
building's terracotta cladding
system (which has been used on
all the other Building Workshop
designs), as well as in
researching an energy-saving
approach to the design of the
facades. The latter aspect was
funded by the European Union
as part of the Joule II research
programme administered by the
Directorate-General for Science,
Research and Development of
Non-nuclear Energy.

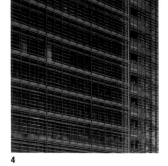

4

5

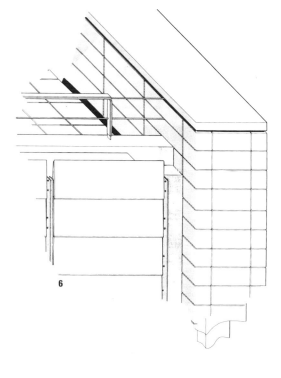

6

Potsdamer Platz
Debis Headquarters

6 Isometric study of top of southern facade of tower, where glass external louvres terminate in front of roof balustrade and terracotta cladding ends in coping of same material.

7, **8**, **9** Sections of alternative ways of handling external wall, terracotta cladding and outer layer of glass louvres, and relationship of these to channel beam that terminates facades of ground floor arcades. **9** is the solution adopted.

10 Close-up of part of the west facade where double height arcade on left ends beside bottom of stair shaft on right. Here a range of the terracotta units can be seen, from grilles of 'baguettes' to large flat units that are grooved on projecting elements and smooth on back wall of arcade. Note too how the bottom of the office facade ends on a terracotta coloured smallish channel while the stair ends on a larger channel in the same dark metallic grey as the big channel beam set back under the office facade.

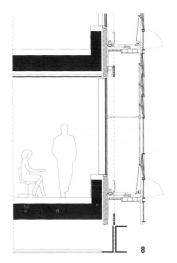

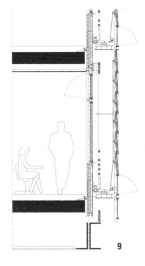

7   **8**   **9**   **10**

The cladding and energy-saving systems are the same as those first developed at the Lyon Cité Internationale, but applied in a more rigorously researched and comprehensive fashion. Two types of facades are used, depending on building height and orientation, which the architects call the 'opaque' and the 'transparent' (or 'ventilated') facades. The former is clad in a rain screen of terracotta units, behind which is the weather-excluding, highly-insulated wall and conventional openable windows, which are an economical off-peg product. These facades provide some of the modulation of solid and void, incidence of detail and mellowing with weather and age associated with traditional urban architecture.

The transparent facade is built and clad in much the same way, but projecting forward on a steel framework from this is another layer of adjustable glass louvres.

The transparent facade is applied to the west and south elevations of the tower at the building's southern end. These are the facades most exposed to wind, rain and traffic noise. The less-exposed east elevation of the tower is clad in the same opaque facade as the rest of the building. These two types of facades, along with the internal facade with the sloping light shelves around the atrium, are all part of a strategy to maximize the use of natural light and ventilation – although, just as artificial light is provided, so there is also a mechanical ventilation system to be used in extreme temperatures.

Research for developing these facades was conducted with the aid of two purpose-made items, the 'solar box' and 'climate box', as well as with full-size mock-ups, both in Vesima and on site. Various forms of computer simulation were also used by Ove Arup & Partners and Drees & Sommer, the two engineering consultants who collaborated with Roger Baumgarten of the Building Workshop on various aspects of this research. The solar box consisted of a 1:5 scale model of an office that could be tilted and turned in direct sunlight so as to match light conditions at various times of the day and year. With it, various facade devices for modulating light could be compared for their effect on conditions inside. The climate box was used to study more local conditions, immediately inside the facade, resulting from different facade treatments. It is not a device to be used for accurate predictions about exact performance, but is very useful for immediate feedback to confirm or contradict the designer's intuitions.

The opaque facades were designed to admit maximum light while also giving a sense of secure containment, as well as modulated degrees of glare not achieved by floor-to-ceiling glazing. Various sorts of lightshelves that would project light deep into the building, a solution common in the tall narrow streets of Genoa, Piano's home city (Volume one pp38–44), were investigated. Various of these systems worked by reflecting, refracting or diffusing the light, and each was of a different shape and surface treatment. These were all tested in different orientations and groupings, sometimes in conjunction with optimally-shaped ceilings that helped reflect the light deeply and evenly into the office. But although the research proved the lightshelves to be effective, they were used eventually only on the sides of the atrium and, for economic and aesthetic reasons, not on the outside. But, doubtless, all of this unapplied

171

1

Potsdamer Platz
Debis Headquarters

1 West elevation with lake in foreground and end of theatre on left.

2 Lower portion of west facade of tower whose screen of external glass louvres is constantly brought alive not just by louvres opening and closing but by the play of reflected sky and refracted sun light.

3 Looking west past bottom of southern end of tower.

2

3

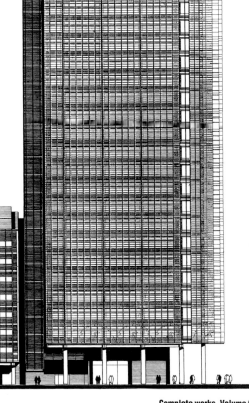

4

Potsdamer Platz

Debis Headquarters

4 Looking north towards centre of scheme
along west elevation.

5 West elevation.

5

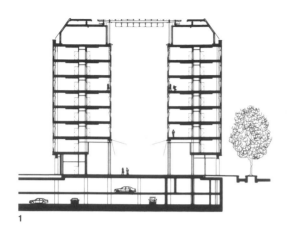

1

Potsdamer Platz
Debis Headquarters

1 Cross section through lower office block
and atrium.
2 First-floor board room overlooking atrium
from its southern end.
3 Longitudinal section through tower, atrium
and lower block.

research will bear fruit in future Building Workshop designs.

The transparent or ventilated facade is a refinement of that used at the Cité Internationale, which was devised to provide energy savings while also allowing people inside to have a sense of direct contact with the outside. The outer layer of glass louvres reduces wind pressure and intercepts rain so that the windows can be left open at all times and in all weathers, no matter how high up the building – thus naturally ventilating the offices when occupied, and cooling them at night when unoccupied. The louvres also attenuate the noise of the traffic entering and exiting the tunnel at the foot of the tower. In winter, the louvres can be closed to trap an insulating layer of warmed air

against the offices. In summer, the louvres can be opened in varying degrees while the gap between them and the windows serves as a thermal chimney convecting away warm air to escape from the top, while sucking in cool fresh air.

The research also contributed to the refinement of this system, testing various configurations of opening elements and their performance at various orientations at different times of the year, and in different wind conditions. This confirmed that the secondary glass skin considerably increases the period of the year during which the offices can be naturally ventilated. It was predicted that in summer, natural ventilation (extending into the night to purge heat from the building fabric) would produce better conditions than mechanical ventilation (with comfortable temperatures and more than three air changes an hour) when external air conditions are below 30 degrees Centigrade. Above that, mechanical ventilation and chilled ceilings (for which provision has been made for their installation wherever requested) are enough to keep temperatures down. Mechanical

ventilation and heating are also required when external winter temperatures drop below five degrees Centigrade. The research also predicted that the double, ventilated facade would allow offices at the top of the tower to be naturally ventilated for nearly 40 per cent of the year and those towards the bottom for 55 per cent of the year. If users fully exploit this capacity it would reduce the energy needed to heat and cool this part of the building by 40 per cent.

For all their simple repetitiveness, both kinds of facades are quite rich visually. The opaque facades soften the insistent rhythm of the verticals by interweaving them with the filigree of the grilles of baguettes across the top and bottom of each band of windows. Despite the large flat stretches that are obviously thin and relatively lightweight, the space between the terracotta and the windows is animated by external aluminium venetian blinds of the same biscuit colour as the terracotta, which emphasize the depth of the facades. Also satisfying are the contrasts between the various terracotta-faced parts: the office facades emphatically terminated top and bottom with the grc elements; the continuous grilles on the stair shafts terminated with grey aluminium channels; and the simple elements that face the insides of the arcades and the atrium. The stretches of external glass louvres are enriched by the play of light as they reflect a mosaic of the sky, and their bevelled edges refract rainbow glints.

2

3

Potsdamer Platz
Debis Headquarters

4 Northern end of atrium. Behind the terracotta grilles can be seen the movement of the glass-sided lifts, and below the balcony of the first floor lift lobby is the main entrance and way out to the shoping arcade. The corner to the left leads to a car showroom and on the extreme left is the entrance to a cafeteria. Note also that though the sky can be seen through the clear glass roof when looking north, the lift shafts and atrium are semi-shaded from southern sun by rows of fritted glass panes suspended at an angle below the roof.

4

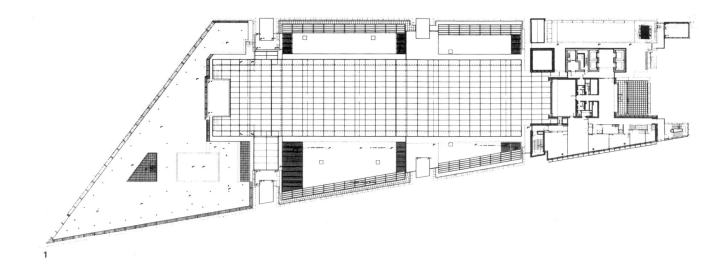

176   **Potsdamer Platz**

Debis Headquarters

1 Plan of top floor of tower and of roof of lower parts.

2 First floor plan: **a** atrium void; **b** cellular office; **c** board room; **d** ventilation shaft.

3 West-facing office in tower with screen of glass louvres outside.

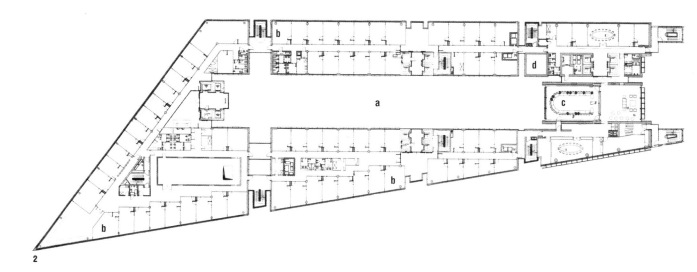

4

5

Potsdamer Platz
Debis Headquarters

4 Night view from Marlene Dietrich Platz.

5 Internal pool behind reception desk at southern end of atrium.

6 Section through car show room.

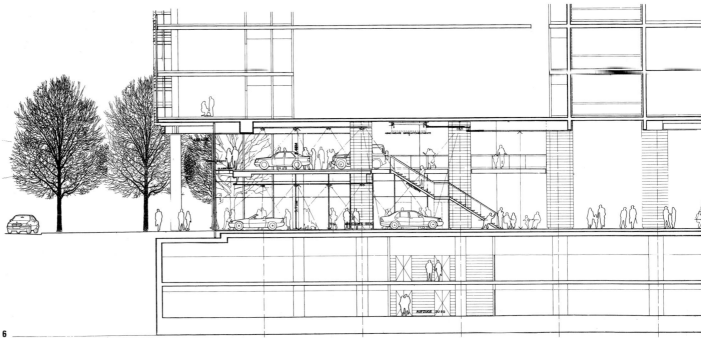

6

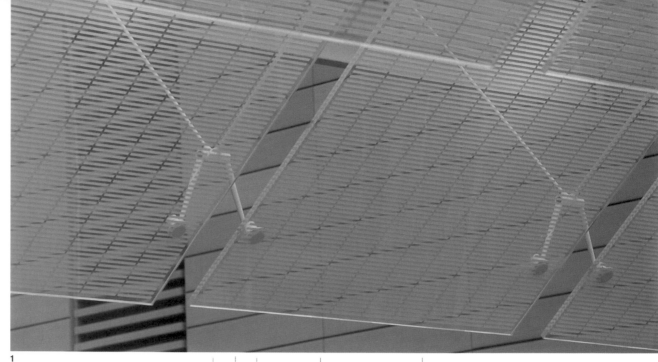

1

178 **Potsdamer Platz**
Debis Headquarters

Atrium roof.

1 Close-up view of the panes of fritted glass
that are suspended at an angle under the roof
to serve as sun shades and reflectors of
artificial light.

2 Detail elevation showing how tops of
reflector/sun shades are supported, as well as
the end of the arm supporting a spot light.

3 The rows of suspended fritted glass panes
and the spot lights they reflect diffusedly
downwards.

4 Looking straight up at part of the view at
dusk. Powerful downlighters along the edges
of the roof supplement the light relected down
from the spot lights by the rows of inclined
panes of fritted glass.

5 The atrium looking south, a view in which a
direct view of the sky is obscured by the rows
of sloping panes. Reflecting the spot lights
these create a glowing ceiling at night. The
space has roughly the same dimensions as the
nave of Notre Dame de Paris and is enlivened
by a Jean Tinguely sculpture set in the
middle of its floor and arcs of blue neon by
François Morellet.

2

3

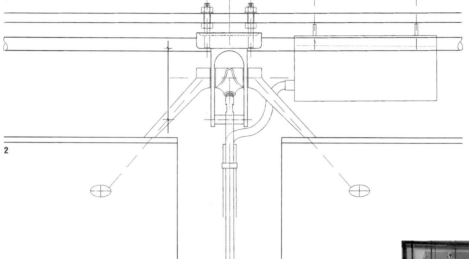

4

1

Potsdamer Platz

Previous pages The northern end of the west elevation of the Debis heaquarters with most of the Venetian blinds closed against the sun. On hot summer days such as this, children make good use of the lake.

Shopping arcade

1 Banquet held in the immense arcade to celebrate the opening of the Potsdamer platz scheme.

2 Looking down on the roof and entrance of the arcade from the Debis tower.

3 View from office tower by Hans Kollhoff, looking along the arcade roof to the Debis tower and along Alte Potsdamerstrasse to the theatre and the porch in front of it.

4 Secton of arcade from ground level upwards. In elevation behind it are, from the left, the IMAX theatre, the larger residential block B5 and the smaller residential block B3.

5 View through entrance of arcade showing bridges spanning across length of interior.

Shopping arcade and adjacent buildings

As a piece of exemplary, 'normal' (in Piano's terms) urban fabric, which could be repeated in other contexts, the most successful part of the Daimler-Benz development is probably the central portion of the long string of buildings by the Building Workshop and the shopping arcade that connects them along their backs. Besides the arcade, this group of buildings includes the renovated Winehaus Huth, two blocks of housing and the IMAX cinema.

2

3

These buildings are seamlessly integrated with each other and their newly built context. But they do not make explicitly gestural responses to their context, as does the tower and cantilevered canopy of the Debis headquarters or the faceted polygonal forms and metal sheathing of the music theatre and casino. Nor are their forms in any way 'styled' or unnecessarily distorted for formal purposes, as is the fragmentation into vertical shafts of the Debis tower, or the raked angles that terminate the metal sheathing on the theatre and casino. Moreover, in this chunk of formally-modest urban fabric there are semi-public spaces of very different character, as exemplified in the contrast between the bustling arcade and the quiet refuge of the housing courtyards.

There are further reasons to admire this cluster of buildings, not least the lively urban facades created by the terracotta cladding system and the elegance of the engineering elements that enclose and open up the arcade. Here the terracotta cladding system has produced its best urban facades to date. The colour is a mid-toned orangey-brown, and its treatment is far more varied than it is on the Debis Headquarters, but this

richness is achieved with uncompromised rigour.

Articulated into a coherent whole, that is lively rather than mechanical, the facades include balconies, and windows of various sizes for housing as well as, to a lesser extent, other uses. (The only place where the application of this system falters somewhat is on the smaller housing block where there are too many 900mm-wide windows in a row and the effect becomes a bit cage-like.) These facades are also satisfyingly terminated top and bottom, with a slight cornice at the top and a channel at the bottom. Both are of aluminium with a baked pvf2 coating to match the terracotta. A similar recessed channel marks each floor slab level as a string course. Further enlivening the facades are the yellow awning blinds which shade each apartment window. Below these facades is another quintessential urban element

4

1

Potsdamer Platz

1 Like the roof of the Debis headquarters, the arcade roof is transparent when looking north.

2 Detail section of first floor bridge where arcade crosses narrow side street. Because this is an emergency route for fire engines, the ground floor doors open up to allow them through. In the executed version these pivot horizontally.

3 Axonometric projection showing details of balustrades and fascias to slabs.

4 Below the upper, ground floor arcade with its first floor galleries is another basement arcade.

5 Plan: **a** Alte Potsdamerstrasse; **b** Eichornstrasse; **c** narrow side streets.

too little used today: the recessed, colonnaded arcades that shelter pavements and shade the windows of shops and restaurants.

In this cluster is another facade that will only be recognized as a Building Workshop scheme because it is raised on a similar arcade. Connecting the rear of the Winehaus Huth to the entrance of the arcade, this is faced in the same grey stone as the old building, with its tall conventional windows set back behind stone-lined reveals.

This elevation is a gem of sober proportioning and detail, that impresses not least because conventional windows have never been Piano's forte. Instead, he has always excelled at refined glazing systems such as those which form the roof and end walls of the shopping arcade.

The arcade is an entirely commercial entity, with none of the larger civic dimensions of an Italian galleria. But it is also devoid of the kitsch, glitz or fantasy elements typical of the American-type shopping mall that Piano was determined to avoid. Instead it is treated as a semi-outdoor space, with floors paved in grey granite and ficus benjamina trees planted on the ground floor, all enclosed between terracotta-clad facades by the glazed roof and end walls. The mall itself is 180 metres long, 13 metres wide and extends between, and is set slightly back from, Alte Potsdamerstrasse and Eichornstrasse. It has three levels: a ground floor, first floor which consists of galleries on either side of open wells and a basement that connects to Potsdamer Platz station with its various rail services. The shops extend under the buildings to either side.

Where it crosses two side streets, the first-floor galleries in the glass-enclosed links widen into seating areas for fast food outlets. Particularly after dark, and even more so on cold evenings, the people visible sitting here, as well as the passersby, provide strong enticement to enter the arcade. However, the authorities insisted that fire engines must be able to pass through at these points so a pair of huge doors have been incorporated into the design of the ground-floor glazing. At the end of the arcade it is not just the doors, but the whole tall glass wall which opens up as its door-width panes pivot outwards. Along with the roof, these open up on hot days when sensors activate their electrically driven mechanisms. End glazing and roof, along with the steel structures that support and stabilize them, are further exercises, typical of the Building

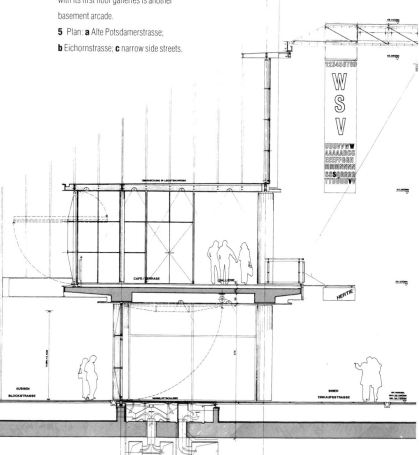

2

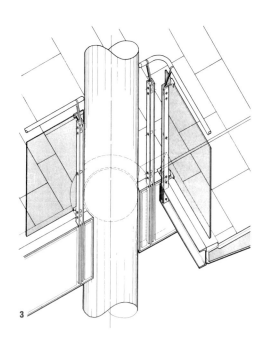

3

4

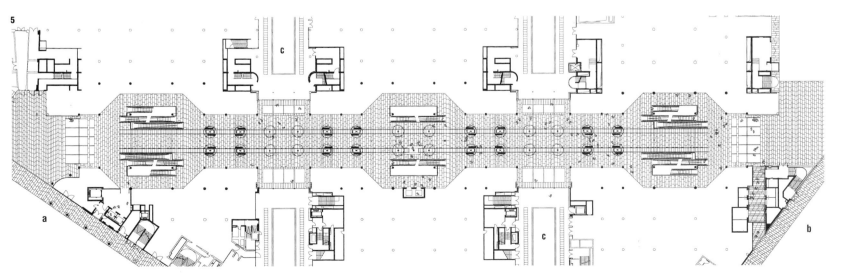

5

1

Details of glazed walls that close each end.
1 Close-up view of a portion of the glass wall, the whole of which (the doors below and the glazing above), is motorized to open automatically and stay open in hot weather.
2 Plan detail of entrance doors.
3 Sectional details of the system of structural ties which stiffens the glazing frames, showing also the mechanism which opens the glass panes.

Details of glass roof.
4 Looking across the top of the roof. Here the top of the south facing fritted glass oversails the north-facing clear glass, which opens automatically in hot weather, to shade it from direct sunlight.
5 Portion of the roof when open.
6 Detail section through roof: **a** south-facing fritted glass; **b** clear opening section; **c** opening mechanism; **d** gutter; **e** service catwalk; **f** opening section when fully open.

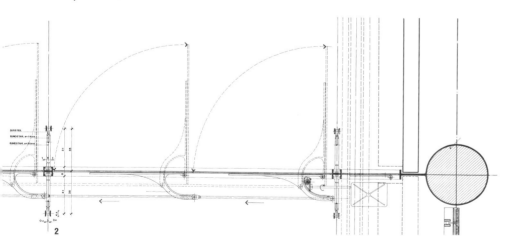

2

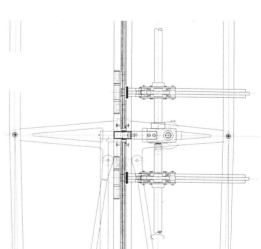

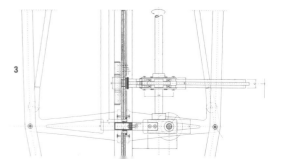

3

4

5

6

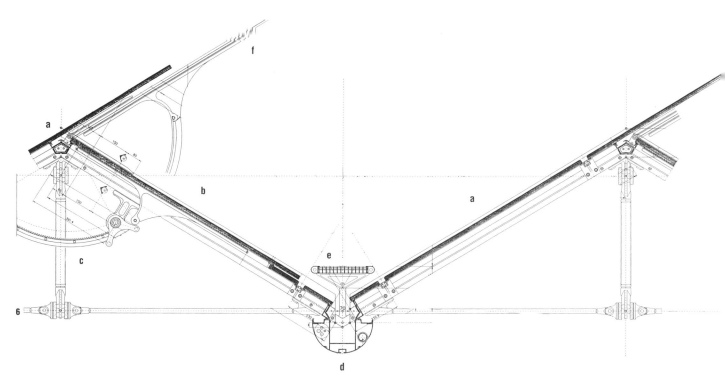

1

Potsdamer Platz
IMAX theatre

1, 3 Cladding the sphere of the auditorium
with double-curved glazed ceramic tiles.
2 View from tower of Debis building across
the roof of its atrium to the IMAX theatre under
construction, with sides of sphere not yet
enclosed in bulging glass wall.
4 Eichornstrasse elevation facing
Debis headquarters.

2

3

Workshop, in virtuoso yet
restrained and immensely elegant
engineering (detailed by Antoine
Chaaya). The roof bears some
familial resemblance to that over
the Debis atrium, especially as both
use sloping fritted glass to shade
direct sun and reflect artificial light.
Here though, this glass is part of the
main roof and extends up and
oversails the supporting beam to
shade the north-facing opening
sections. The cast-steel curved and
toothed arms that are part of the
opening mechanisms of roof and
end wall are becoming a familiar
part of Piano's vocabulary of detail,
resembling those that open also the
external louvres of his double
facades.

The southern-most of Piano's
buildings in this block was
originally designed to include a
prominent domed rotunda
reminiscent of the famous
Kempinski Haus that once stood
nearby (Volume two pp218–19).
This has now become an IMAX
theatre. The rotunda has shrunk
into a corner drum overlooking
Marlene Dietrich Platz, the upper
three floors of which now house a
restaurant; and the dome has been
replaced by the spherical
auditorium. The sphere is both
buried into, and projects above, the
roof and street facade, as if, in
Piano's words, 'the moon had
plunged into the building'. This
analogy is made more vivid by the
way a huge curving bay of glazing
bulges out from the terracotta
facade, as if registering this impact
or belatedly accommodating it. The
same narrative is made more literal
by the images projected on the
sphere from the Debis building, so
that some nights it is made to look
like the moon, and on others might
look like one of the planets.

The dome was built using a new
technique whereby concrete was
sprayed on a huge balloon that was
later deflated and removed. The
exterior is clad in large ceramic tiles
that curve in two directions and are
glazed a pale turquoise.

The auditorium foyer is in the
southeast corner of the building, on
the second floor. It is reached from
the ground floor entrance in the
base of the drum by escalators that
rise past the lower parts of the
sphere in the well behind the
bulging bay of glazing. This glazing
gives a sliver view of Marlene
Dietrich Platz and the new lake
over the tunnel entrance, thus
maintaining a connection with key
parts of the scheme until swallowed
by the foyer with its firmament of
tiny fibre-optic stars cast into the
black terrazzo floor. Off the foyer,
and tucked under the raised main
auditorium, is a tiered waiting
area where those waiting for the
next showing view trailers of
coming attractions.

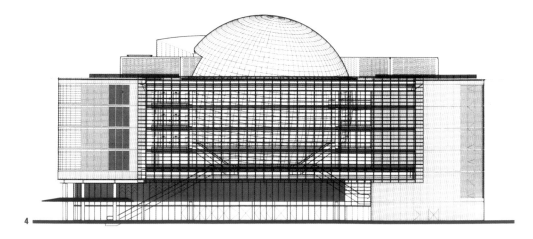

4

5

6

7

Potsdamer Platz
IMAX theatre

5 As seen from the Debis heaquarters, with terracotta drum overlooking Marlene Dietrich Platz and curved wall of glass bulging into Eichornstrasse.

6 Drum and bulging glass wall seen from Marlene Dietrich Platz.

7 Looking down Eichornstrasse past bulging glass wall. To right is entrance to shopping arcade.

8 West elevation.

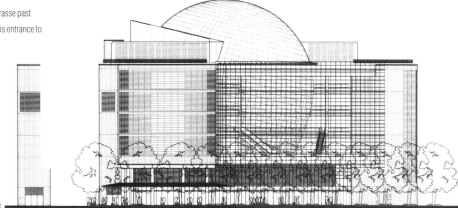

8

190 **1**

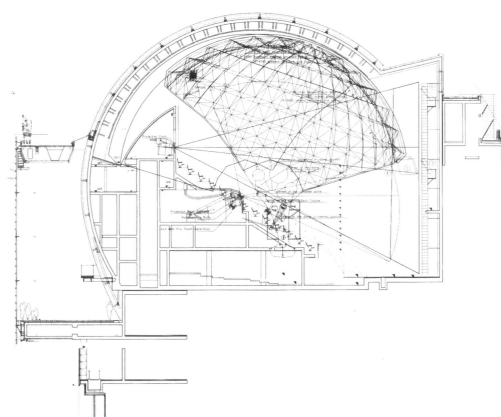

2

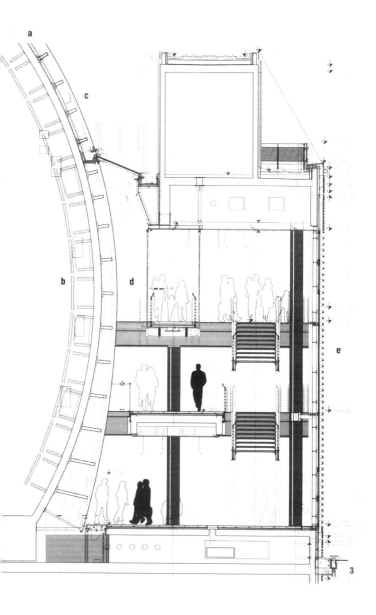

a

c

b

d

e

3

4

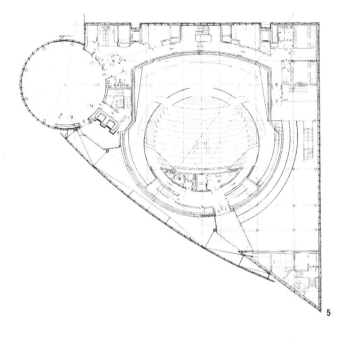

5

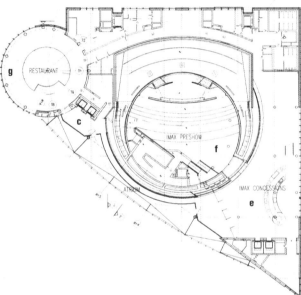

6

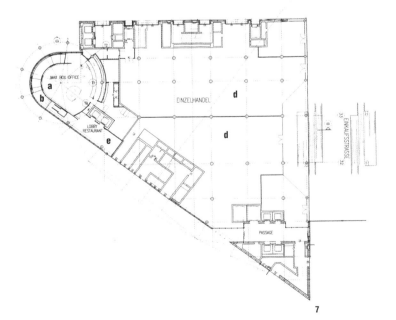

7

8

Potsdamer Platz
IMAX theatre

1 Atrium behind bulging glass wall that provides escalator access to IMAX theatre and restaurant. Walkway curving around sphere of auditorium connects restaurant and IMAX foyer.

2 Section through atrium and auditorium showing structure of spherical screen that can tilt back to allow vertical screen projection.

3 West-east section of IMAX foyer: **a** concrete shell; **b** acoustic absorbency; **c** glazed ceramic tiles; **d** bottom of curving ramp from exit at top of auditorium; **e** terracotta cladding outside entrance to shopping arcade.

4 The bulge of the atrium glazing brings views of the music theatre and Marlene Dietrich Platz, thus connecting it with the heart of the Potsdamer Platz scheme.

5 Auditorium level plan.

6 Foyer level (third floor) plan.

7 Ground floor plan: **a** entrance and box office; **b** bottom of escalator up to IMAX auditorium; **c** lift lobby for restaurant; **d** shop; **e** IMAX foyer; **f** waiting and pre-show; **g** restaurant.

8 Night view from roof of debis headquarters with the surface of the moon projected on the sphere of the auditorium.

1

2

Potsdamer Platz
Residential Blocks B3 and B5
Two residential blocks are by the Building
Workshop: the smaller, B3, is on Alte
Potsdamerstrasse and edges an entrance to
the shopping arcade; the larger, B5, is at the
end of Alte Potsdamerstrasse and curves to
also overlook Marlene Dietrich Platz.
1 View over trees at the south-western end of
Alte Potsdamerstrasse with a corner of B3 on
the left and beyond that is B5, the two visible
wings of which are split by a gap for the
smaller of two staircases giving access to
its courtyard.
2 Facade of B3 overlooking Alte
Potsdamerstrasse.

3

Potsdamer Platz
Residential Blocks B3 and B5

3 Corner where pavement of Alte Potsdamerstrasse on left curves to edge Marlene Dietrich Platz, and where the broader of the two stairs leads up to the courtyard of B5. Note that the treatment of the pavement follows the traditional Berlin pattern, combining rough cobbles and smooth granite flags.

4 Part of Alte Potsdammerstrasse elevation of B3.

5 Close-up view of corner between the end of Alte Potsdamerstrasse and Marlene Dietrich Platz.

6, **7** Close-up views of typical portions of elevations facing narrow streets leading up to shopping arcade.

5

4

6

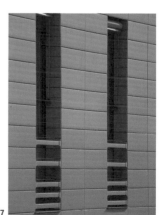

7

Complete works Volume four

Potsdamer Platz
Residential Block B5

Courtyard and plans.

1 View from apartment balcony across courtyard towards gap for entrance stair, and to theatre beyond.

2 Courtyard mixes paving and play areas with trees and flowering shrubs. Facades of the apartments immediately edging it are stuccoed.

3 Stair up to courtyard.

1

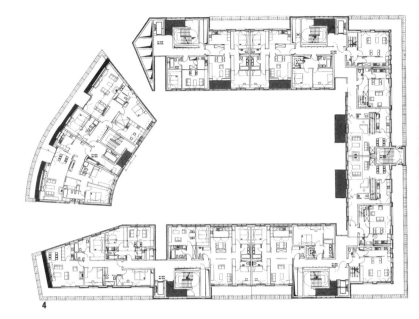

2

3

Potsdamer Platz
Residential Block B5

4 Typical floor plan

5 Courtyard level plan

6 Ground floor plan: **a** shop; **b** hamburger bar; **c** café; **d** storerooms for apartments.

7 View of stair which climbs up from a smaller paved court behind the terracotta-clad block that lies between the two stairs leading up from the street and the larger planted courtyard edged by stucco facades.

Overleaf View out from under covered porch across Marlene Dietrich Platz to the Building Workshop buildings with the B1 office block on the extreme left, the B3 block just visible over the trees and the B5 split by the stair up to its courtyard. On the extreme right is the corner of the Lauber & Wöhr residential block.

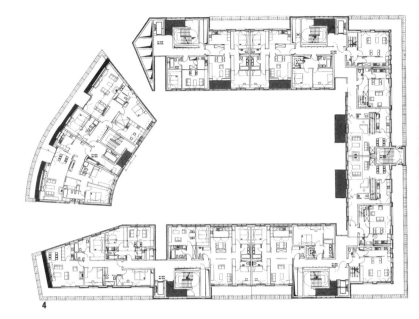

4

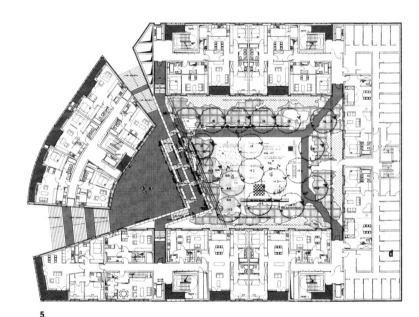

5

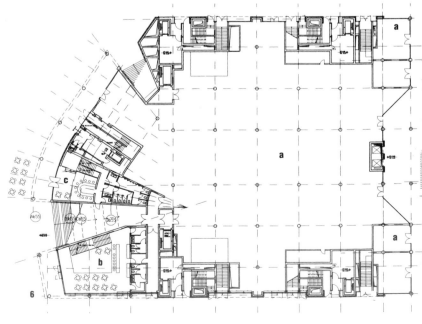

6

Renzo Piano Building Workshop

Potsdamer Platz
Residential block B3

1 Looking along Alte Potsdamerstrasse, past the Winehaus Huth to the corner tower that marks the entrance to the shopping arcade.
2 The stone facade linking the stuccoed side of the Winehaus Huth with the entrance to the shopping arcade behind corner tower is also by the Building Workshop.
3 Section looking towards Alte Potsdamerstrasse.
4 Alte Potsdamerstrasse elevation.
5 Eighth (top) floor plan.
6 Fifth (courtyard level) floor plan.
7 Ground floor plan: shopping arcade; shops; Alte Potsdamerstrasse.
8 The corner tower articulates a major junction between the shopping arcade and the Alte Potsdamerstrasse leading to the porch between the theatre and casino on the right.

1

2

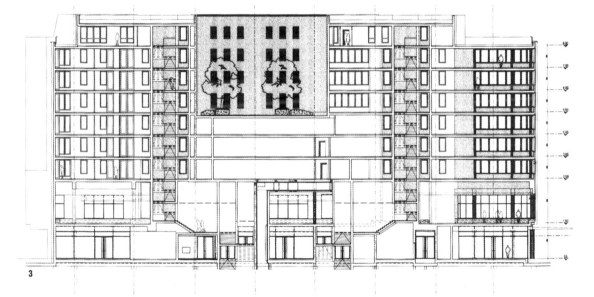

3

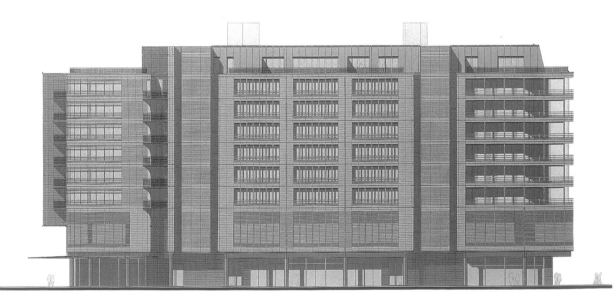

4

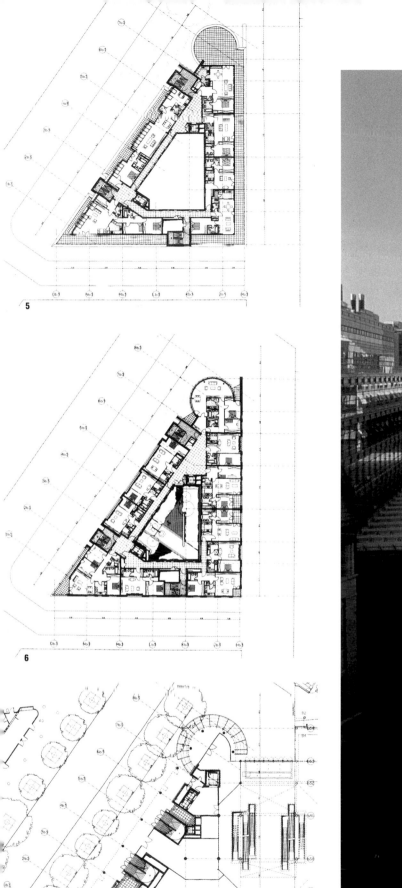

5

6

7 **8**

1

Potsdamer Platz
Office block B1

1 Pointed prow and canopy facing the original Potsdamer Platz. On the right, facing the Alte Potsdamerstrasse, is the office tower by Hans Kollhoff, and beyond it the residential block by Lauber & Wöhr.

2 View along Alte Potsdamerstrasse to where it is terminated by the B1 tower.

3 Oostpromenade elevation.

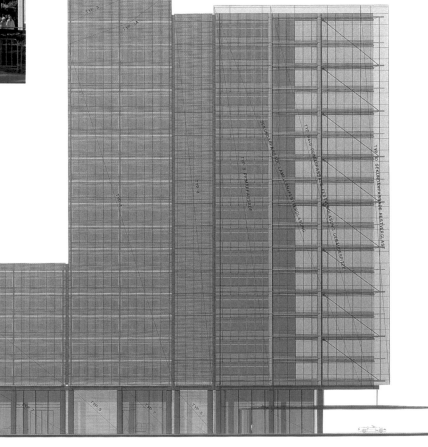

2

3

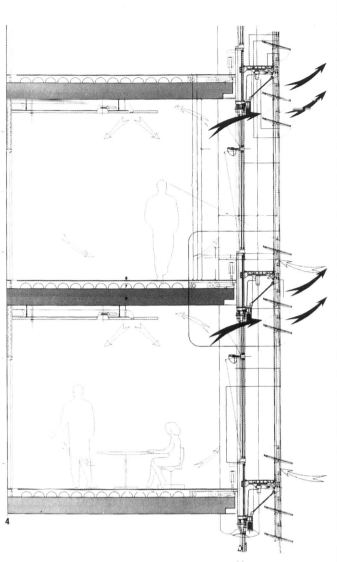

4

5

6

Potsdamer Platz
Office block B1

4 Detail section through edge of office and external wall where outer glass layer combines both opening louvres and fixed glass. Black arrows mark stale warm air and the white arrows mark cool fresh air, or that cooled by the water-chilled ceiling panels.

5 Away from the prow point, the fixed outer layer of glass gives way progressively to the pivoting louvres.

6 View from across the original Potsdamer Platz with Oostpromenade on left, with buildings by Richard Rogers Partnership beyond B1.

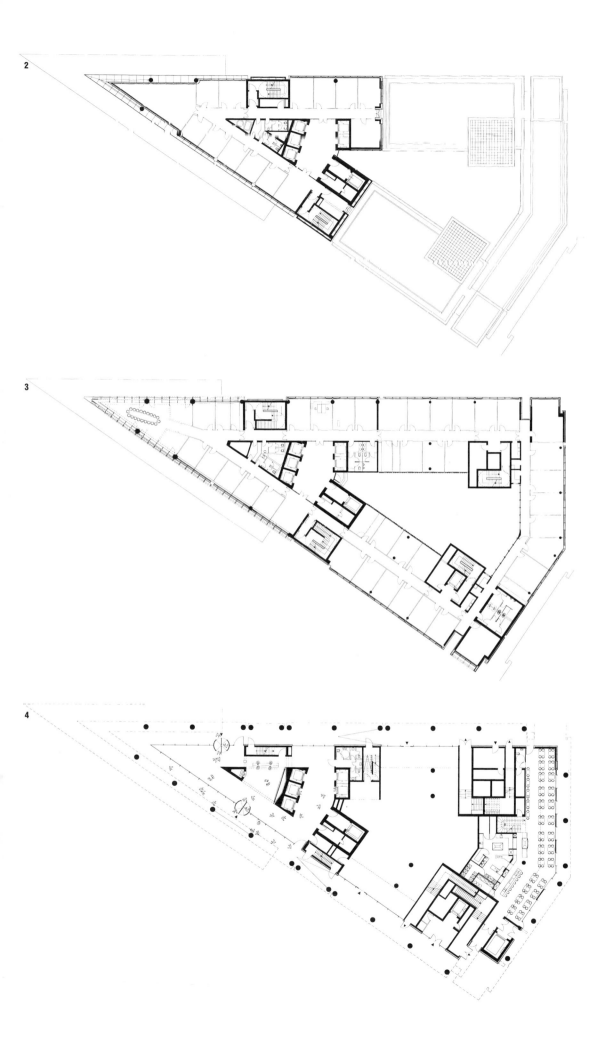

Office block B1

1 Portion of the prow with its outer layer of fixed glass that admits air through its joints.

2 Typical floor plan of tower.

3 First floor plan.

4 Ground floor plan.

5 Interior of board room in prow of tower.

5

1

Potsdamer Platz
Music Theatre and Casino

1 View down Alte Potsdamerstrasse to the theatre and casino with National Library behind.
2 Marlene Dietrich Platz at dusk with inviting views through covered porch and glass wall of music theatre foyer on right. On left is the debis headquarters.
3 Ground floor plan and immediate context:
a Marlene Dietrich Platz; **b** covered porch; **c** lake; **d** water cascade; **e** water channel; **f** hotel by Rafael Moneo; **g** bar-café and entrance to casino; **h** foyer of music theatre.
4 Foyer of music theatre at dusk, with its balconies and suspended stair animated by the audience at interval. The glass wall is stiffened by tapering horizontal trusses.

Marlene Dietrich Platz,
Music Theatre and Casino
The music theatre and casino, together with the porch between them and the Marlene Dietrich Platz form a single set piece. These elements tightly interlock with each other, to create the focal and compositional climax of the whole Daimler-Benz site (it is visible from all the main public spaces, except the arcade, and closes the views from the main routes into the site), and also to be the formal and functional hinge between the site and the National Library

and Kulturforum. Besides having to design a complex that satisfies these roles, the other major challenge for Piano and his team was to remain true to their own design ethos while also providing the sense of glitz and plushness appropriate to a glamorous night out at a musical or in the casino.

The massing responds to both these contextual pressures and the shape of the plot; and though often a very tight squeeze, the functions fit into the resulting volume fairly 'naturally'. The cladding also reponds to context, the bottom part of the building being faced in the same terracotta system as the others by the Building Workshop while the upper parts are clad in a toned-down (both in colour and pattern) version of the gold aluminium panels on Scharoun's Kulturforum buildings. These panels form a loose-fitting coat whose angled and angular planes emphasize the wedge-like massing and the penetration by, and interlocking with, the broad wedge of the Marlene Dietrich Platz. (Some might find the way this is done to be too gesturally scenographic. Others, like Plattner, might applaud Piano for daring to transgress limiting modernist dogmas in the search for a formally legible solution.)

Together the theatre and casino form a single huge volume. Under roofs sloping down from a tall back wall along the road separating it from the National Library, this tapers in plan and section from a tall flytower at the southern end of the theatre to plant rooms and a service area in the tail at the north of the casino. This volume is fractured, however, in the middle where the two elements are slightly slewed in relation to each other. Between them – under an extension of the sloping casino roof, but supported by its own independent structure – is a huge porch. This inward extension of the Marlene Dietrich Platz tapers to a tall slit in the dominant back wall, through which is the rear of the National Library. The floor of this porch is set below the level of the nearby streets, and the piazza (from which the porch is separated by a water channel that helps define the angled sides of the piazza), descends to this level in a series of shallow steps. This dishing gives a sense of containment and depth to the otherwise too-shallow piazza and focuses more attention on the porch as the stage of this outdoor ampitheatre.

The roof of the porch is supported by elegant trusses of thin compression members and even thinner tie rods that radiate to support its triangular form, but seem bafflingly unsupported themselves. Further inspection outside reveals them to be supported by trusses above the roof which also support a secondary roof of aluminium grillage. This shades the circular roof lights, graded in rows from small to large and back again, through which the porch is also artificially lit at night – and

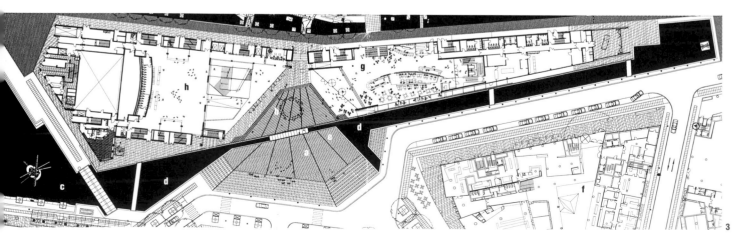

3

1

2

which are a reference to the similarly-shaped roof lights in the reading room of the National Library.

This creates yet another connection between these buildings, beyond those implied by similarity of form and cladding. At the back of the porch, a tall opening cements a yet more direct connection to the library. Piano's intention has always been that a secondary entrance to the library be created at this point, thus ending its lonely isolation and allowing library staff and users to slip out

and into the new scheme for coffee, meals, or whatever. Although the library has yet to agree to this, it seems unthinkable that it will not do so sometime in the near future. Until such time, the view through the slot is partially closed by two trees whose branches invade from the sides and a pair of boulders. The latter will be removed to celebrate the eventual creation of the new entrance.

Although this tall slot focuses the porch and piazza, and indeed the whole scheme beyond towards the library, it is less effective in creating a reciprocal relationship towards the library and welcoming it to feel part of the scheme. The back (east) wall of the theatre and casino (along which escape stairs and services are stacked) rises sheer and rather forbiddingly from the landscaped road between it and the library; and the slot is too narrow and unarticulated to offer much in the way of views through from the rooms on this side of the library. Even if the slot were the same size as it is now, but the walls leading to it were splayed rather than at right angles to the back wall, the effect would be a much more welcoming gesture. Similarly, there is a large window in the back wall that could have

offered enticing views into the theatre foyer, but this is too similar in treatment to the other windows in this facade to draw the eye towards and through it. These would be only minor failings, if they did not compromise the compositional climax and key generating concept of the scheme.

The splayed sides of the porch that narrow to this slot are huge walls of glass. Through these are visible, particularly at night, the foyers of the music theatre on one side and the casino and a restaurant on the ground floor below it on the other. This gives a lively after-dark animation and focus to the whole scheme.

Partly because of the constrained budget, and partly following his own predilections, Piano has chosen to treat the music theatre as some fusion of the industrial and the theatrical – as a workshop-theatre or theatre-factory. This theme is introduced immediately in the foyer. The tall triangular space with terracotta coloured walls is overlooked on its unglazed sides by stacks of galleries, and in the corner between these is a suspended stair whose flights narrow as they climb upwards around its widening central well. Exposed under the ceiling are the roof trusses which, like the similarly exposed horizontal trusses bracing the porch glazing, bear a familial resemblance to those supporting the porch roof outside. These, along with the straight edges of the narrow galleries and the spindly balustrades that front them and edge the stair, evoke the intended industrial image that will be brought alive by the people moving and standing upon them.

This aesthetic works well when converting old buildings where the spindly, austere new

Potsdamer Platz
Music Theatre and Casino

1 Looking between top of porch roof and an upper roof of aluminium grille. Under this shade roof lights shine through the circular roof lights.
2 High-level view of roof and aluminium-clad front of music theatre, with roofs of porch and casino beyond. The covered porch is the focus of the whole masterplan area.
3 Looking north along western facade of Debis headquarters to end of theatre and Marlene Dietrich Platz. Beyond is the hotel by Rafael Moneo.

3

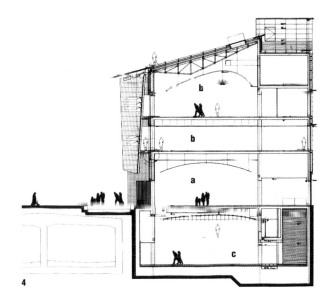

4

Potsdamer Platz
Music Theatre and Casino

Casino.

4 Cross section: **a** restaurant-bar; **b** gaming rooms; **c** gaming machines.

5 Gaming room on second floor with curved ceiling leaf finished with brass and light fittings by the Building Workshop.

6 Second floor plan.

7 Ground floor plan: **a** restaurant; **b** bar; **c** entrance to casino; **d** stairs down to gambling machines.

5

insertions (such as stairs and galleries) play against the rough and substantial old fabric. But when the background walls are smoothly lined in plasterboard, there is nothing for the 'industrial' elements to interact with. In the absence of such dialogue, the foyer lacks, somewhat, in animation and movement. The stair is too stiff and does not flow properly and the galleries are almost prison-like and do nothing to play with the space and offer views between them (as they would if parts projected and receded).

Standing in the foyer imparts a strong sense that a gallery along the back/east wall should have swollen into a bar where prominently visible from the piazza and beyond, preferably in front of a large window offering views in from the National Library.

The expressed industrial elements continue into the auditorium, here in the exposed steel structure that supports the upper and lower circle seating, as well as the narrow balconies that edge the side walls. The result is much more satisfactory than in the foyer as the plush velour of walls and seats (which sit on a cylindrical pedestal through which conditioned air is admitted from the plenum below them) provides a foil with sufficient contrast and presence for interesting interplay. Their orangey-red colour also gives a suitably festive warmth to the space, which is enhanced by the way it is lit. The stage and proscenium are designed to give considerable flexibility to the companies which each occupy the theatre for long runs.

Backstage facilities are squeezed between the tall volume of the stage and flytower and the angular outer envelope of the building. The windows of these rooms are screened and shaded by large horizontally pivoting panels within the

aluminium cladding. The various adjustments of these panels bring life to the bulky southern end of the building that interacts in a fine balance of contrast and harmony with adjacent parts of the National Library.

Across the porch, Piano has made a spirited attempt at the glitz and plush associated with a casino. This combines high-stake gambling on the first and second floors with low-stake fruit machines in the basement. Both are reached through the ground floor in which there is also a bar and restaurant. This level has been cleverly contrived to give a sense of differing degrees of insideness, the unpolished floor of the porch continuing in as polished granite before giving way to carpet.

In the restaurant and in the top floor of the casino, curved elements are suspended below the ceiling to give a feeling of intimacy and containment. Those in the restaurant are arched symmetrically and finished in a wood veneer; those in the casino curve asymmetrically in sympathy with the sloping ceiling above them, and appear to be covered in gold leaf. It is in fact brass leaf, and on it sparkle the reflections of the many small bulbs of gold-painted light fittings. Designed by the Building Workshop these, which are set off by the deep scarlet stucco-lustro walls, deliberately flirt with kitsch in a way that few might imagine Piano would dare. The effect is rather 1950s, but not yet Carlo Mollino. All this is visible from the porch and the piazza, so that together with the adjacent hotel there is sense of life on the piazza until the early hours of the morning. Something of the spirit of prewar Potsdamer Platz lives on.

207

6

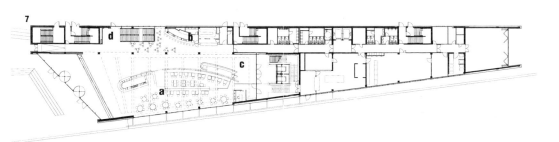

7

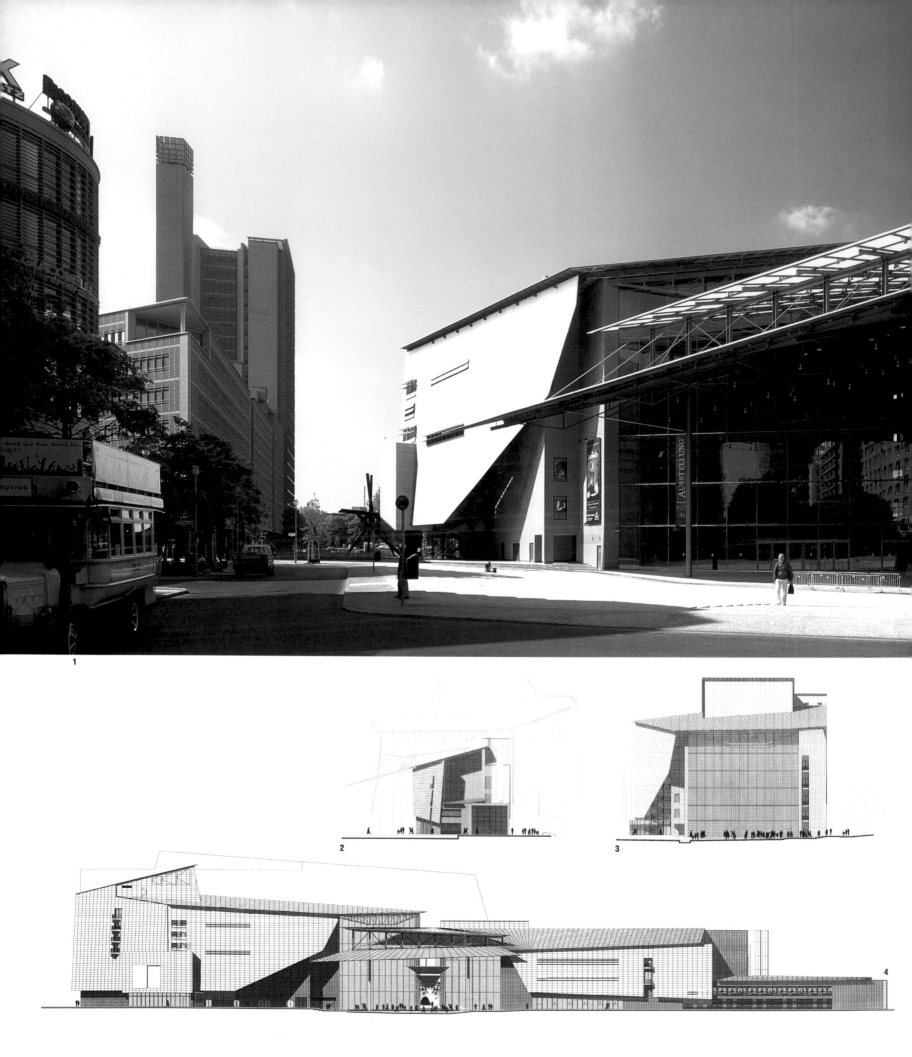

1

2

3

4

Potsdamer Platz
Music Theatre and Casino

1 The covered porch is like a huge stage towards which Marlene Dietrich Platz is dished like an ampitheatre. To the sides, the loose-fitting jacket of aluminium cladding is cut away at an angle, like the parting of theatrical curtains, and above the dramatically angled roofs reach out in an operatic gesture.

2 North elevation.

3 Section through covered porch looking towards music theatre.

4 East elevation to Marlene Dietrich Platz.

5 South elevation.

6 West elevation to National Library.

5

6

1

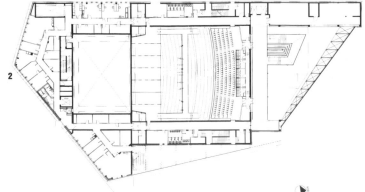

2

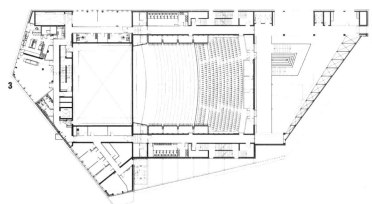

3

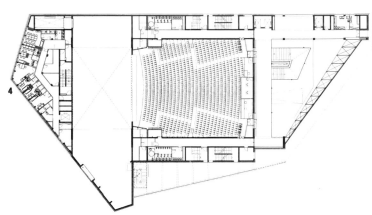

4

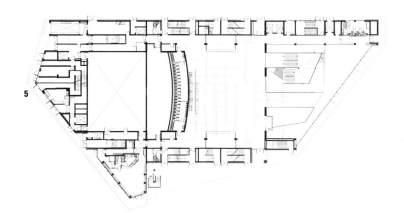

5

Potsdamer Platz

Music Theatre and Casino

1 Night view of covered porch with the interval crowds and the balconies of the foyer of the music theatre visible through the glass side of the porch. In the foreground is the water channel that separates the porch from the Marlene Dietrich Platz.

2 Second circle plan.

3 First circle plan.

4 Stalls level plan.

5 Ground level plan.

6 View of auditorium from stage.

7 Cross section through foyer and pit giving access to auditorium for dining and cinema.

8 Long section through theatre, porch and casino.

Overleaf Night view of Marlene Dietrich Platz from roof of hotel.

6

7

8

Potsdamer Platz

Client Daimler-Chrysler AG

Architect Renzo Piano Building Workshop in association with C Kohlbecker

Competition, 1992

Design team R Piano, B Plattner (senior partner in charge), R Baumgarten, A Chaaya, P Charles, J Moolhuijzen

Assisted by E Belik, J Berger, M Kohlbecker, A Schmid, U Knapp, P Helppi

Modelmaker P Darmer

Masterplan, 1993

Design team R Piano, B Plattner (senior partner in charge), R Baumgarten, G Bianchi, P Charles, J Moolhuijzen

Assisted by E Belik, J Berger, A Chaaya, W Grasmug, C Hight, N Miegeville, G Carreira, E del Moral , H Nagel, F Pagliani, L Penisson, R Phelan, J Ruoff, B Tonfoni

Modelmaker P Darmer

Kohlbecker's office M Kohlbecker, K Franke, A Schmid with L Ambra, C Lehmann, B Siggeman, O Skjerve, W Marsching, M Wiess

212

Design development and construction phase, 1993–

Design team R Piano, B Plattner (senior partner in charge), J Moolhuijzen, A Chaaya, R Baumgarten, M v der Staay , P Charles, G Bianchi, C Brammen, G Ducci, M Hartmann, O Hempel, M Howard, S Ishida (senior partner), M Kramer, Ph v Matt, W Matthews, N Mecattaf, D Miccolis, M Busk-Petersen, M Pimmel, J Ruoff, M Veltcheva, E Volz

Assisted by E Audoye, S Baggs, E Baglietto, M Bartylla, S Camenzind, M Carroll (partner), L Couton, R Coy, A Degn, B Eistert, J Florin, J Fujita, A Gallissian, C Maxwell-Mahon, GM Maurizio, J Moser, JB Mothes, O de Nooyer, F Pagliani, L Penisson, M Piano, D Putz, P Reignier, R Sala, M Salerno, C Sapper, S Schaefer, D Seibold, K Shannon, K Siepmann, S Stacher, RV Truffelli (partner), L Viti, T Volz, F Wenz, H Yamaguchi, S Abbado, F Albini, G Borden, B Bowin, T Chee, S Drouin, D Drouin, J Evans, T Fischer, C Hight, J Krolicki, C Lee, K Meyer, G Ong, R Panduro, E Stotts

CAD operators I Corte, D Guerrisi, G Langasco

Model makers JP Allain, D Cavagna, C Colson, O Doizy, P Furnemont

Kohlbecker's office M Kohlbecker, J Barnbrook, KH Etzel, H Falk, T Fikuart, H Gruber, A Hocher, R Jatzke, M Lindner, J Müller, N Nocke, A Rahm, B Roth, M Strauss, A Schmid, W Spreng

Interior design for Debis tower and casino PL Copat

Structure and services engineers Boll & Partners, Ove Arup & Partner, IBF Dr Falkner, GmbH/Weiske & Partner

HVAC IGH/Ove Arup & Partners, Schmidt-Reuter & Partner

Acoustics Müller Bbm

Transportation Hundt & Partner

Electrical engineering IBB Burrer, Ove Arup & Partners

Traffic engineers ITF Intertraffic

Landscaping and water basins Atelier Dreiseitl

Planting Krüger & Möhrle

Site supervision Drees & Sommer/Kohlbecker

214

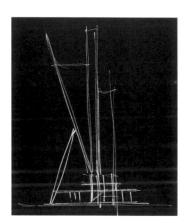

KPN-Telecom Tower Rotterdam, The Netherlands **1997–9**

On the edge of the River Maas, beside where the tall two-legged mast of Rotterdam's Erasmus Bridge leans back like a tug-of-war competitor to take the strain of the suspension cables, the KPN-Telecom Tower will lean forward on a single column, as if on a crutch, so that its front facade slopes at the same angle as the cables. As befits the headquarters of a telecommunications corporation, the facade will be a vast electronic billboard. It will be conspicuous from the bridge and the large square in front of the tower that marks the bridge's landing on the river's south bank, as well as visible from other bridges and a busy motorway on the north bank of the Maas.

An electronic billboard facade was part of the original concept for the Pompidou Centre (Volume one pp52–63). Yet apart from this precedent, the only things that might suggest that this tower is a Building Workshop project are that it not only responds to its immediate context and the nature of the client, whose business is communication, but that the design also so vividly evokes the spirit of the local architecture. Indeed, most informed architects seeing this project would guess it to be by a local Rotterdam architect, possibly one who had worked for OMA.

The design's unstable, leaning and fractured forms recall those of an early Koolhaas scheme for a site along the Maas. This project, like the bridge and now the KPN-Telecom Tower, recognized that any construction on this bank of the Maas had to be able to hold its own against the vast scale of the river and its constant traffic of huge barges and other vessels of various sorts. Moreover the new tower will have the thin and flashy quality that has become a distinctive feature of Dutch architecture, and which is apt enough for Rotterdam. Devastated during the War, this is not a city of genteel historic architecture like

Amsterdam, but a gritty city with a very North American fabric and feeling.

The Erasmus Bridge is a single-masted suspension structure designed by Ben van Berkel. It was built to improve access to, and signify the rebirth of, a vast and disused dockland area south of the Maas. The mast's very distinct form is visible from much of the city as its pale blue colour changes with the play of the light, and with the sky behind it to vary all the way from bright white to dark grey, sometimes merging with the sky and sometimes standing in bold contrast to it. Now the most familiar images of Rotterdam, the bridge and mast have become its prime symbols.

The bridge connects the centre of Rotterdam to the riverside square that forms a gateway to the urban development area of the Kop van Zuid which stretches away

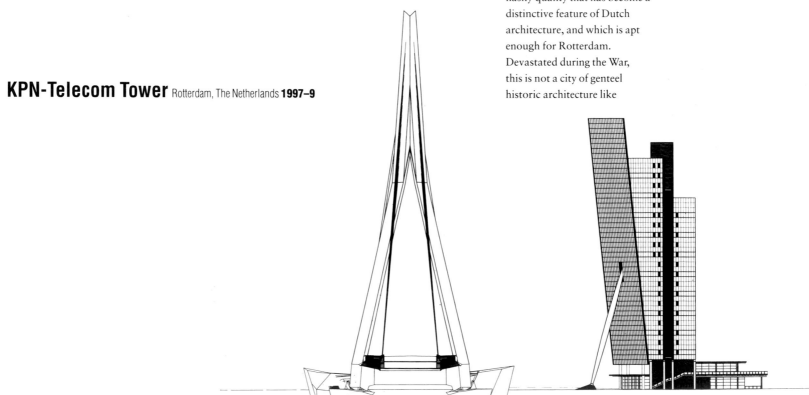

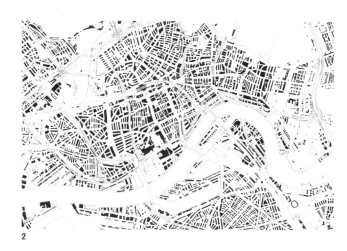

1

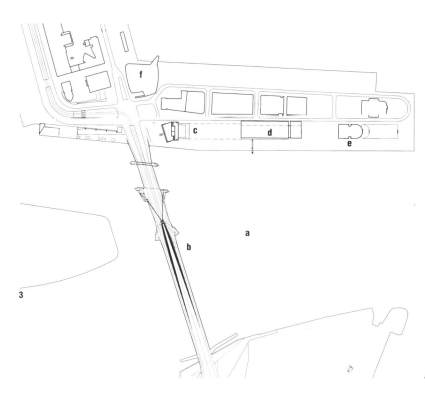

216

2

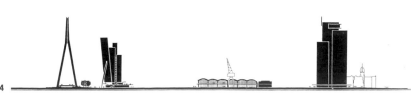

3

to the east and south. Extending westwards, downstream along the riverfront, is what was the terminal for passenger liners, mainly those on the North Atlantic run. The main passenger terminal of the Holland America Line – a concrete structure of two lofty floors below vaulted roofs built by Brinkman and van den Broek in 1937 – has been kept as a monument partially occupied by such public uses as restaurants. But to either side of this, new buildings will fill this riverside block. Each end of the block will

KPN-Telecom Tower
Previous pages Section through Erasmus Bridge and elevation of tower from the River Maas, as seen enlarged in the view of the model, shows how the front façade leans against a gigantic propping column to suggest a visual relationship with the splayed legs of the mast of the bridge.

be terminated with office towers. In acknowledgement of their roles as urban 'book ends', both will be directional in form and face away from each other.

Facing downriver at the western end is to be a 40,000 square metre tower by Foster & Partners, its massing evoking nautical themes and the Art Deco of the heyday of the cruise liners. At the eastern end, and with its main elevation facing obliquely up and across the river, will be the 20,000 square metre KPN-Telecom Tower which is currently under construction. This will eschew nautical themes and nostalgia to engage with the electronic age and, as we have seen, contemporary Rotterdam architecture. Though unintentional, the latter proves once again Piano's uncanny ability to pick up on and reflect aspects of local culture, thus, paradoxically, making him the most global of architects.

The KPN-Telecom Tower will, however, differ from the 'object' buildings typical of Dutch architecture, which tend to keep formally aloof from context (thus in the eyes of some Dutch critics making them prime examples of an emerging global architecture). By contrast, the KPN tower will imply visual connections with the bridge and square in front of it and create physical continuities with the buildings yet to come on the riverside adjacent to it. Taking cues from the old terminal building, the new tower will rise from a podium of the same height as the terminal. Indeed, the local planners have endorsed Piano's suggestion that all other new buildings in the riverside block must extend this podium

as two floors of publicly-oriented uses with a continuous balcony/walkway at first-floor level. From this plinth will rise various other towers and taller buildings, while the composition of the whole block is unified by the common podium and book-end towers. Piano's other contribution to the urban design of the area was to insist on pushing the tower 25 metres westwards and ceding the eastern portion of the site as an extension of the square. This will open the square to the river on this side of the bridge and allow a view of the water to a new theatre being built on the square.

As usual in The Netherlands, design has been constrained by a very tight budget (51.6 million guilders). So the building will be largely mundane in organization, construction and materials, thus conserving the available budget for the dominant billboard facade. The tower will have a central circulation and services core with offices on either side. The offices behind the billboard facade will follow its slewed angle to the rest of the building and extend up to the double-height boardrooms on the twenty-second floor. The escape stair shafts will extend from the core to separate these offices from the lower arm of offices at the back of the building. The external parts of these shafts, like the external faces of the core where it extends above and

4

5

KPN-Telecom Tower

1 Aerial view of wharf in its heyday.

2 Plan of central Rotterdam showing location of new office tower and the points from where it will be prominently visible.

3 Location plan: **a** river Maas; **b** Erasmus Bridge; **c** KPN-Telecom Tower; **d** preserved passenger terminal; **e** new office tower by Foster & Partners; **f** new theatre.

4, **8**, **9** Elevations from river Maas showing:
4 Completion of Piano and Foster towers on

either side of preserved passenger terminal; **8** extension of terminal into a continuous podium; **9** more towers added above the podium.

5 Sketch showing relationship between KPN-tower, Erasmus Bridge and river Maas.

6 Model showing completion of Piano and Foster towers and extension of podium, as in **8** below.

7 Model showing addition of more towers as in **9** below.

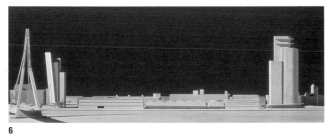

6

7

below the offices, will be faced in brick giving a visually weighty centre to seemingly stabilize a building comprising thin and shiny surfaces.

The core will be the only part of the tower to reach the ground, as the perimeter of the offices are supported on tall cylindrical pilotis. The roof of the ground-floor lobby will project out beyond both these pilotis, and the bottom of the billboard facade above, to form a welcoming canopy. Extending behind the core will be the two-storeyed podium with a broad

balcony, publicly accessible by external stairs from the ground, around the set-back first floor. On the ground floor will be a restaurant for public use, as now demanded by the City of Rotterdam. Until then both levels will be used as showrooms for the sale of telephonic equipment. Extending under the whole site, including that which will be an extension of the square, will be two levels of underground parking. At night this will serve the adjacent theatre.

From the paved roof of this parking (and above piled footings which extend down through it) will lean the 45m tall cigar-shaped steel prop. This will be necessary for lateral stability and wind loads rather than vertical loads. Also providing stability will be the in situ concrete core. The rest of the building will have a concrete frame (that meets the pilotis via cast steel column heads) infilled with pre-cast hollow core slabs. The offices will have conventional punched windows, apart from those behind the billboard facade. But their high-reflective glazing will be set flush with the pale grey pvf2-coated aluminium cladding of the rest of the facades to give as smooth and homogenous an effect as possible during daylight hours.

The billboard facade will be made up of double-glazed units of glass set in a light grey pvf2-coated aluminium frame (which includes the vertical tracks for the cleaning and servicing cradle). This facade will extend 15 metres above the top of the building and one metre past its sides, where the rear of the glass will be fritted in a pattern that will give 70 per cent opacity.

The glazing frames will divide the whole facade into a grid of 1.8 metre squares. At the mid-points of the horizontals bounding each square will be mounted a lamp with a flat 380 mm square Perspex front in the vivid green that is the KPN's corporate colour. Inside these will be lamp elements that have a long life even when switched constantly on and off. The lamps will be individually controlled by a computer which can be programmed to create graphic and animated effects. These are being designed in collaboration with the Dutch graphic designers, Studio Dumbar. Even though the lamps are only a single colour, and are small and widely spaced on the whole facade, computer simulations show the results to be very effective.

With this electronic billboard screen, the KPN-Telecom Tower is bound to become another Rotterdam landmark. But instead of being one that stands out by itself, it will help integrate the surrounding area into a coherent urban ensemble. Just as it sets a precedent, aiming to link the whole block between it and the Foster tower into a single composition, so it will also link the whole block with the Erasmus Bridge, to which it will itself be indelibly attached, as well as perhaps to the square behind.

217

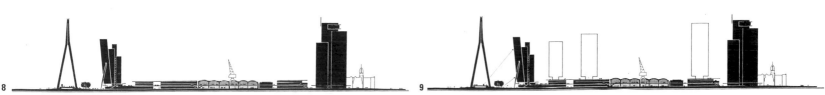

8   9

Renzo Piano Building Workshop

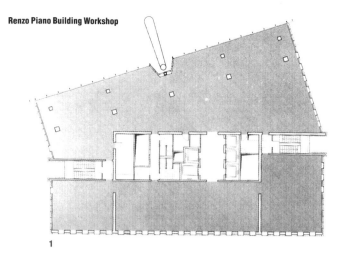

1

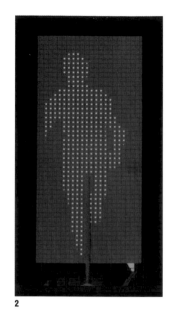

2

3

218 **KPN-Telecom Tower**

1 Twelfth-floor plan.

2, 3 Examples of animation of billboard facade with small, widely spaced lights.

4 Site and ground floor plan.

5 Main billboard elevation.

6, 7 Sections.

8, 9, 10 Detail sections of billboard facade and edge of offices at: 8 roof, beyond which facade extends upwards; 9 junction with cigar column; 10 lowest office level on third floor.

11, 12, 13, 14 Lifting and fixing the steel cigar column into position.

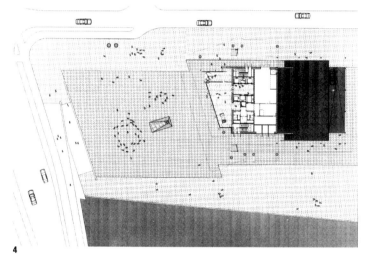

4

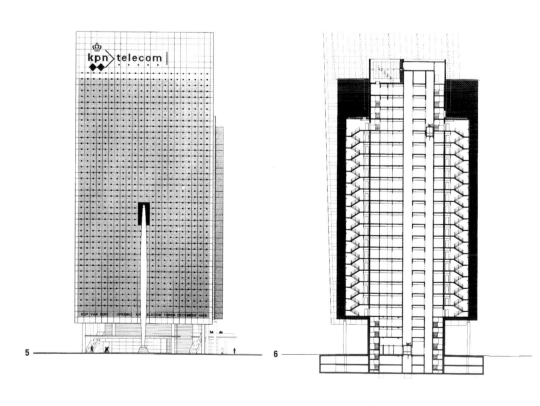

5

6

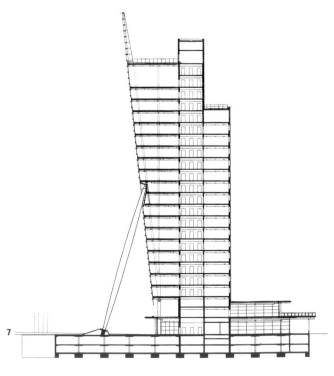

7

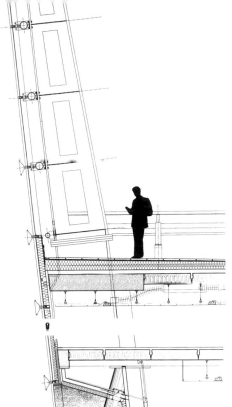

9

12

11

KPN-Telecom Tower

Client William Properties, KPN Telecom

Preliminary Design, 1997
Design team R Piano, O de Nooyer,
J Moolhuijzen (partners in charge), S Ishida
(senior partner)
Assisted by H van der Meijs, M Uber,
C Grant, C Tiberti
CAD operator L Massone
Modelmakers S Rossi, D Cavagna
Cost control Brink Groep Tiel
Structure and services engineers
Corsmit Consulting Engineering,
H Hoogendoorn Raadgevend Ing. Buro
Graphic design Studio Dumbar

**Design Development and Construction
phase, 1997–9**
Design Team R Piano, O de Nooyer,
J Moolhuijzen (partners in charge), D Rat,
H van der Meijs, H van Heugten, O Aubert
Assisted by C Brammen, A Johnson, C Lee
Modelmaker P Furnemont
Cost control and specifications Brink
Groep Tiel
Structure and services engineers
Corsmit Consulting Engineering,
H Hoogendoorn Raadgevend Ing. Buro
Graphic design Studio Dumbar
Acoustics Advies Buro Peutz et Associés Bv
Fire regulation Advies Buro van Hooft
Interiors Architekten Cooperatie Balans

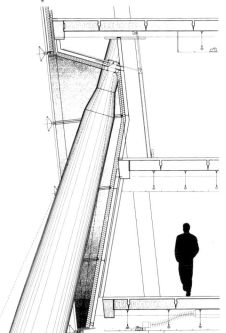

13

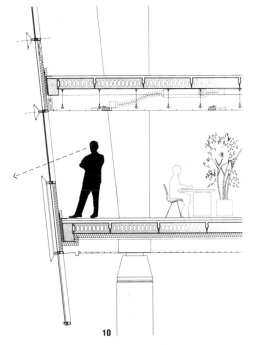

10

14

220

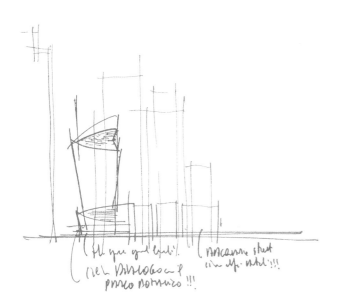

Aurora Place Sydney, Australia **1996–2000**

If the white shell roofs of the Sydney Opera House resemble gigantic spinnakers billowing above the waters of the harbour, then the tall and curving, creamy white facades of Aurora Place, now under construction 700 metres inland and to the south, might soon resemble the missing mainsails. However, the thin translucency of the glass curtain walls floating free from the ground and extending into the sky will contrast with the Opera House's weighty, facetted concrete shells, and will also deflect rather than catch the wind. Thus a contextual dialogue will be set up between these two complexes, the Opera House jutting into the harbour, and the new office tower rising from the edge of a cluster of undistinguished towers where it, and the smaller residential building will enjoy good views over the Royal Botanic Gardens. But, although the design of the new buildings is obviously a response to context, it is also a selective one. Indeed it could be seen as elitist and snobbish, as the new buildings will dissociate themselves from their immediate neighbours to gesture their allegiance to, and claim affinity with, the other exotically classy European down the road.

On the other hand, architects and critics might applaud such discernment whereby the influence of Sydney's world-renowned building is extended into its hinterland and interwoven deeper into the fabric of the city. Indeed, this might in part compensate for a disastrous new building that now obliterates key views of the Opera House. But nevertheless those who endorse that aspect of the design might also feel uneasy about others. In particular, they might wonder if it is shaped too much by such gesturing to context, and if it verges on being overly sculptural at the expense of architectural disciplines like maximizing the use of repetitive components, such as for cladding and partitioning. In short, it lacks that brilliant balance found in the Passenger Terminal of the Kansai International Airport (Volume three pp128–229) where the whole building, including the complex two-directional curves of the boarding wing, are clad with only a single repetitive rectangular panel. Or is such criticism too conventionally modernist and utilitarian to apply to this new phase in Piano's work?

The office and residential buildings are being built on either side of the narrow Phillip

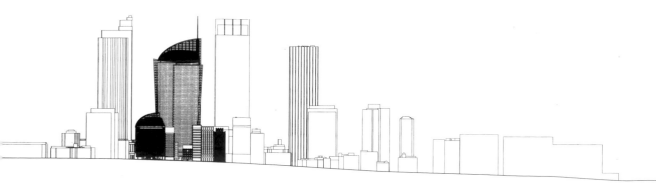

1

222   **Aurora Place**

Previous page Study model of
apartment block and office tower in
immediate context.

1 Aerial view of Sydney.

2, **3**, **4** Studies of the geometric
forms from which parts of the facades
are excised.

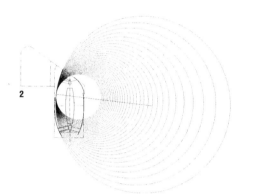

2

3

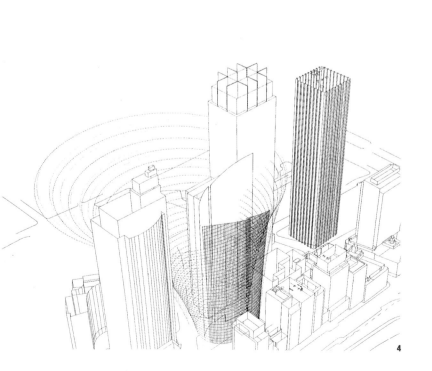

4

Lane, just where it terminates
at Bent Street. This meets at
an angle with Macquarie Street
which edges the Botanic
Gardens park and extends
down to the Opera House.
The complex was commissioned
as part of a boom occasioned
by Sydney hosting the 2000
Olympics, and will be
completed in the same year. The
sites were cleared by demolition
of the existing smaller buildings
(that of the office tower having
been occupied by a 28-storey
tower) and are being
redeveloped to the maximum

permissible plot ratio and
height, the latter determined by
a 'light angle' from the park to
prevent it being unduly
overshadowed.

Apart from cold-shouldering
the neighbours, the two
buildings are conceived of as
together forming a microcosm
of urbanity. The rear, western
facade of the residential block is
clad in a similar curving, creamy
white curtain wall as the office
tower it faces. At the foot of the
two buildings, Phillip Lane will
be closed to traffic and paved as
a mini piazza that widens
towards Bent Street. This piazza
will be partially sheltered by a
canopy suspended between the
two buildings, the bottom floors
of which will be set back in
places behind cylindrical pilotis,
thus providing further shelter.
The finishing touch will be a
sculpture by Japanese artist Kan
Yasuda under the canopy, a pair
of white marble forms, like
gigantic river pebbles, which are
vaguely kidney shaped in plan.
The cold smooth white curves of
the sculpture and the interplay
between its two elements will
echo in miniature key themes of
the architectural composition,
emphasizing the sense of
compression between the
curving facades of the
residential building and tower.

The office tower will be
200 metres tall with 44 storeys
below the roof that slopes with
the 43 degree 'light angle' from
the park. However, a waiver has
been obtained for the fully-
glazed curtain walls of the
curving longitudinal facades
to extend above this line to
terminate in evocative, spinning
curves. From the top of the roof
a mast will rise 200 mm higher
than Sydney's tallest building.

This mast supports a micro-
weather station whose
instruments will relay their
readings to the automatic
controls (which it will be
possible to override) that adjust
the natural ventilation in the
winter gardens that are a feature
of both buildings.

The winter gardens in the
office tower, as well as its
sculptural form and the curtain
walls extending above and
beyond the building, are all
part of the original design
conception. Piano had wanted
to design a tower that was more
than merely a stack of identical
floors: a tower in which there
might be interaction between
floors that would be somehow
differentiated. He also intended
a low energy building making
maximum use of natural light
and perhaps catching and
guiding breezes through it as
natural ventilation. These ideas
will be only partially realized.

The tower will have a central
core with perimetrical columns
against the curtain wall and is
being built as a post-tensioned
concrete structure rising by a
new floor level every six days. It
will be more or less boat-shaped
in plan with the prow at the
southern end where the
projecting curtain walls of the
long facades come closest
together. The projections of the
curtain wall are the legacy of an
early conceptual idea that this
be another application of a

WIND LOAD

5

Aurora Place

5, **6**, **7** Computer studies of predicted performance of structural frame.
8 Study models of different solutions of the tower and the facades that extend beyond its sides and roof.

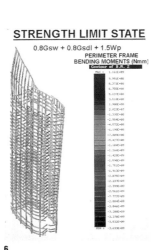

STRENGTH LIMIT STATE
0.8Gsw + 0.8Gsdl + 1.5Wp
PERIMETER FRAME
BENDING MOMENTS (Nmm)

6

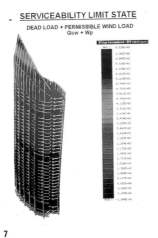

SERVICEABILITY LIMIT STATE
DEAD LOAD + PERMISSIBLE WIND LOAD
Gsw + Wp

7

8

secondary outer glass skin, detached from the building, as used at the Lyon Cité Internationale (Volume three pp74–97) and the Debis tower at Potsdamer Platz (pp156–213), to allow natural ventilation through most of the year and at all heights of the tower. Now only the winter gardens at the end of each floor will be naturally ventilated through banks of top-hung windows. Treated as semi-outdoor spaces (with terracotta tiles on the walls), and roughly 4 metres by 10 metres in plan,

these will serve as 'break out' spaces for smoking, coffees and other forms of socializing, as well as for meetings. And, if their windows and the doors into them are left open, they will allow cool night air to pass through the building and help purge it of excess heat. Piano sees these spaces as social foci, playing a role in relation to the offices analogous to that of piazzas in the city.

The number of lifts and size of the columns will decrease with height. Otherwise, the offices and curtain wall west of the core will remain identical throughout most of the height of the tower, except where grilles in the facades mark the location of air-conditioning plant rooms towards the top, bottom and middle of the building. But east of the core, the office floor will extend slightly further south and north with each level up the building, and the tightness of the curve at its southern end will decrease. The floors therefore will increase in area and length with height and even more so, in lettable floor area and sense of openness. This will result in the floors being ever so slightly differentiated from each other and, more significantly, in the tower's elegant sculptural form that will still capture the suggestive image if not the reality of catching the winds.

As a consequence of these changes in the plan of each floor, the curtain wall system will have to accommodate changes of angle in plan, section and elevation. On the exterior, the curtain wall consists of only frame-less sheets of glass with recessed joints between them. The mullions supporting the glass will be concealed on the

inside by splayed reveals, both mullions and reveals being extruded aluminium. Though the glass will be secured only by silicone sealant, provision is being made to add fixing clips should a five-yearly inspection prove this to be necessary.

To cope with the splayed edges of the facades, as well as with the two-directional curves in the south-east facade, the glass sheets will not all be of the same size and shape. Many appear rectangular and identical in dimension but will, in fact, be neither. Not only are these 'specials' a relatively small portion of the total number of glass sheets, their manufacture presents no problems to contemporary computer-controlled production techniques. Indeed, Piano claims the required numbering in the factory, so as to match the specials with their specific locations, merely constitutes a logical extension of his 'piece by piece' constructional approach and philosophy. (See the introductory essay in Volume one for further explanation of this approach.)

The glass will be 'low iron' and without a greenish tint. The spandrel panels facing slabs and upstands will be single glazed and entirely fritted an opaque creamy white. The 'window', or viewing panels, will be double glazed and treated with a high-performance 'low-emissivity'

223

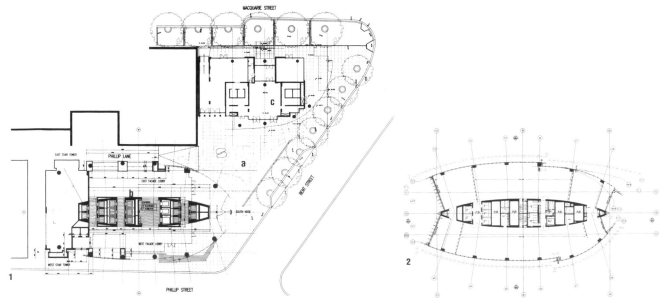

224

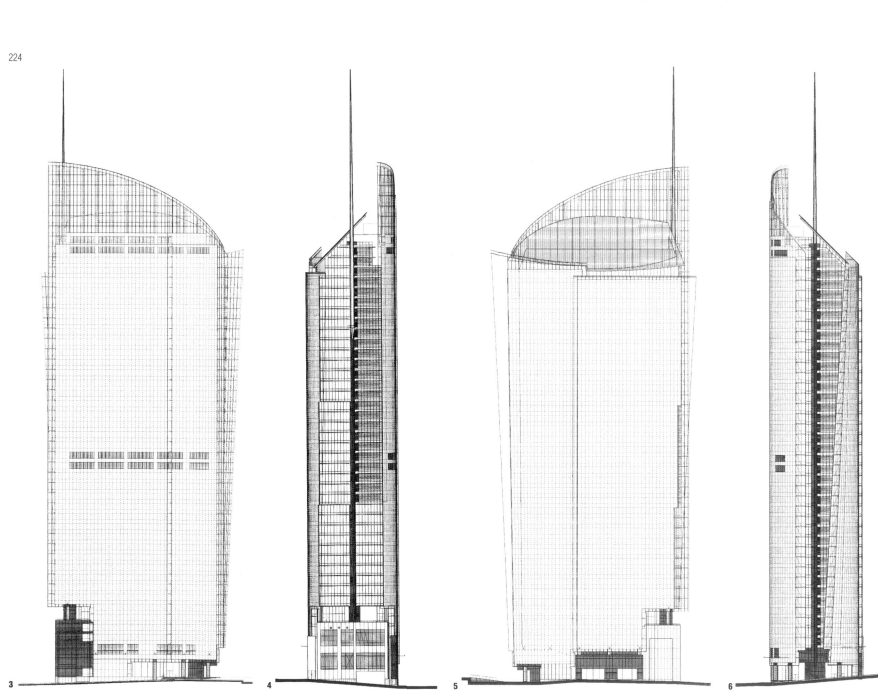

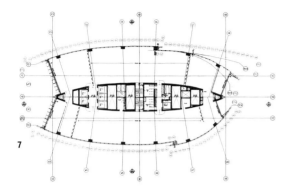

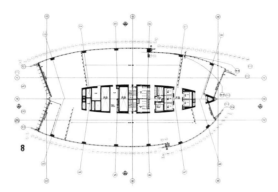

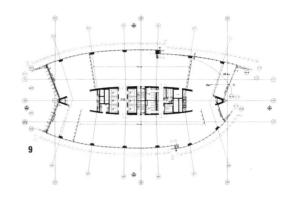

7   8   9

Aurora Place

1 Site and ground floor plan: **a** Aurora Place; **b** base of office tower; **c** base of apartment block.

2 Level 6 floor plan of office tower.

3 East (Phillip Street) elevation of tower.

4 South elevation.

5 West elevation.

6 North elevation.

7–9 Floor plans.

10 West (Macquerie Street) elevation of apartment block.

11 North elevation.

12 West elevation.

13 Model of Aurora Place (in white) in its larger context that includes the Royal Botanic Gardens in front of it and the Sydney Opera House to the right.

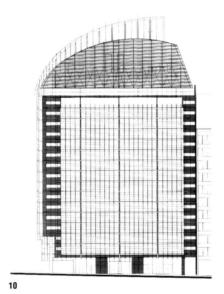

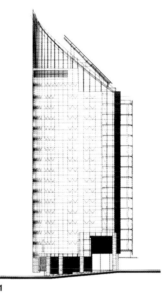

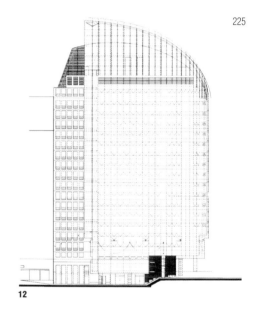

10   11   12

13

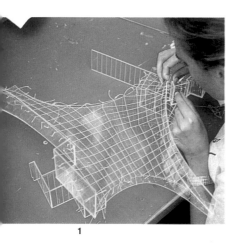

1

226 **Aurora Place**

The glass canopy suspended between
the blocks.

1 Model of network of supporting cables.
2 Detail of element securing two panes of
glass and its junction to suspension rod
and stabilizing cable.
3 Section through canopy with bottom of
apartment building in elevation behind.

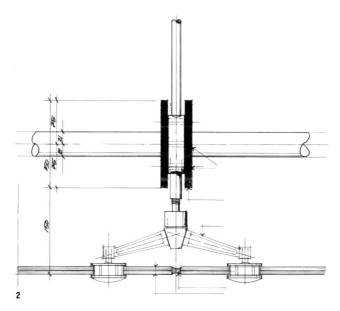

2

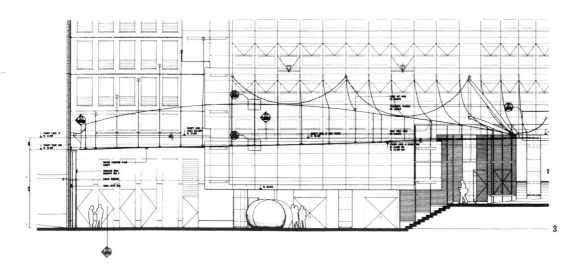

3

coating that admits a high
degree of natural light while
controlling solar heat gain. They
will also be fritted along their
edges with the same colour as
the spandrels to conceal the
mullions and reveals inside,
with the frit pattern forming
a graded transition between
80 per cent opacity and
transparency. The result will
appear a paradoxical
combination of sleek
continuous skin and punched
window. With the changing
curves and play of light, this
should produce many varying
optical effects: at times the
'window' will appear darker,
and at others lighter, than the
fritted edge; and from some
angles the windows might have
a more reflective sheen, and so
seem to stand forward from the
surrounding fritting. Moreover,
because the glazing extends
beyond them, the edges and
top of the tower will seem to
dematerialize, especially at night
when lit from below. (These are
some of the visual effects that
Piano anticipates. But despite
full-size mock-ups – of which
there have been five to date –
and on-site testing in Sydney's
specific light conditions, it is
impossible to predict exactly the
visual outcome of such
innovative solutions. But this is
part of the thrill, and the risk, of
Piano's creative credo of always
stepping into the dark to extend
the boundaries of architecture.)

Where the curtain wall
extends above the roof, the
upper parts of the top-most
sheets will be unframed, to aid
the illusion of dematerializing
into the sky. The unglazed parts
of the north and southern ends
of the tower and the base will be
faced in terracotta. To suit the
bright Sydney sun, these will be
burnt to a darker colour than
those used at Potsdamer Platz.
The windows on the short
north facade will be shaded
by horizontal sunshades as
well as automated, motorized
sun blinds.

The apartments will be a
seventeen-storey building with
four large (160-square-metre)
and luxurious apartments on
each floor, except on the two
penthouse levels set back from
the mandatory cornice line.
(To bring a sense of light into the
middle of the very deep and low-
ceilinged apartments, the plan
of each offers somewhere a clear
view between front and back
windows.) The top of the
curtain wall will end in a similar
fashion to that of the office
tower, and its base will also
be terracotta-clad. But the
equivalent to the contrast
between the long and short
elevations of the tower will be
found between the west and east
facades. The former will be
curved and clad in a glass
curtain wall system similar to
that of the offices, although here
single-glazed throughout with
a less vertical proportion to the
glazing units and with top-hung
windows set into the curtain
wall. The eastern facade,
which fronts winter gardens
overlooking the park, will
consist of banks of horizontal
louvres of frameless glass
pivoting between projecting
glass mullions.

Again, although it will look
similar, this will not be a double
facade as Piano used in Lyon
and Berlin. But its detailing is
an evolution of these earlier
schemes, not least in now
mounting the louvres on
tempered glass mullions.
(This solution has now been
experimentally tested by being
opened and closed 41,000
times, the anticipated equivalent
to fifty years of heavy use, in a

4

Aurora Place

4 Test mock up of terracotta cladding units in white steel frame.

5 Test made up of fritted glazing stabilized with mullions perforated with circular holes.

6 Close-up view of the junction of four panes with deep gap between them and graduated pattern of fritting.

7 Plan detail of window junction with splayed reveals concealing mullion and glass secured by adhesive with deep gap between panes.

5

6

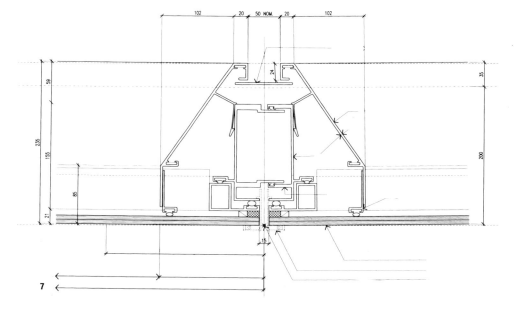

7

200 kilometre per hour wind.) Again the louvres will be motor operated via an elegant cast steel mechanism. But only the upper two louvres will pivot upwards, while the lower three (which are protected from inside by a cast-steel balustrade) will pivot downwards. This will create an unobstructed eye-level opening almost one metre high. Because the winter gardens are nearly 3.5 metres deep, with terracotta-tiled walls and stone paved floors, it does not matter if rain enters when the louvres are not closed. Nevertheless, the Building Management System will automatically close these in intemperate weather, as well as lower sun blinds when required. Set back from both west and east elevations will be vertical strips of facade. These are to be faced in terracotta, with parts of their windows screened by grilles of terracotta elements; the kit of parts and their application will be similar to that used on the Potsdamer Platz.

As at the Banca Popolare di Lodi, there will also be a glass canopy suspended from ties between the buildings. Here the canopy will protect people on the piazza from the downdraft caused by the tall buildings as much as from rain. But at Lodi the glass is held stable against up and side drafts by radial cables below it, as well as those above. Here all the cables will be above the glass. Stability will be achieved by having ties in two directions: those sagging in catenaries between the buildings; and those that hold these catenary ties down by arching over them in a lateral direction between cables curving horizontally inwards to edge the two ends of this network. The glass will be suspended from this network on stiff rods.

All in all, this is a striking scheme that will be a memorable addition to Sydney; it will also no doubt become intrinsic to the city's identity, not least because of its visual association with the Opera House. Much of the poetic beauty of the tower will come from the laudable intentions still legible in its final form. But its suggestive forms will promise more than they will deliver in terms of the original goals of being a naturally-ventilated, low-energy building that is also a vibrant social mechanism. Probably the plot is too small to allow such ambitious goals to be fulfilled to the same degree as achieved by, say, Foster and Partners' nominal Commerzbank tower in Frankfurt. (There, the large and lushly planted sky gardens are overlooked by the offices that draw their natural ventilation from them, and so better fulfill Piano's analogy of serving as a piazza for the offices than the winter gardens stuck in a corner, as here.) Also, some modernist sensibilities are bound to be disturbed by the way the primary curtain wall extends beyond the offices as if it were a secondary, independent glass skin. But if the building will only be poetically suggestive of some of its topical, if compromised, ambitions, it and the apartments will still be landmarks in terms of technique (many of their elements could not have been built a couple of years ago) as well as townscape, and supremely refined in their forms and detail.

227

1

2

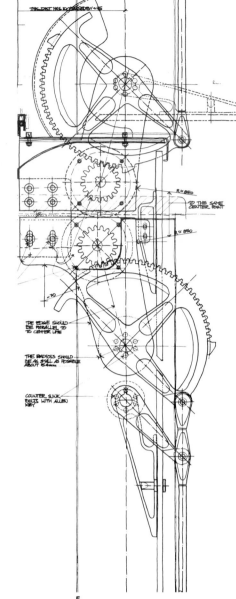

228

3

Aurora Place

Prototype of opening facade of apartment block winter garden, as assembled below the laboratory-workshop at Punta Nave.

1 Opening and pivoting mechanism secured to tempered glass mullions.
2 Steel and wood balustrade set inside opening glass facade.
3 Cast-steel components of the opening mechanism.
4 Prototype facade being studied by Renzo Piano and colleagues

4

5

6

7

Acknowledgements

The development of the Building Workshop since its birth over 30 years ago is due to the efforts of those listed below; a list that includes those who have either worked with us or with whom we have had a close association. The list does not include the many more people who have contributed in some other way to our efforts over the years. We take this opportunity to express our gratitude to all.

Renzo Piano

Camilla Aasgard
Sebastien Abbado
Laurie Abbot
Peter Ackermann
Naderi Kamran Afshar
Emilia Agazzi
Bart Akkerhuis
Francesco Albini
Alessandra Alborghetti
Jean Philippe Allain
Michele Allevi
Michel Alluyn
Massimo Alvisi
Marco Amosso
Arianna Andidero
Sally Appleby
Andrea Aranclo
Catherine Ardilley
Magda Arduino
Stefano Arecco
Eric Audoye
P Audran
Véronique Auger
Frank August
Alexandre Autin
Carmela Avagliano
Patrizio Avellino
Rita Avvenente

Carlo Bachschmidt
Jack Backus
Alessandro Badi
Susan Baggs
Emanuela Baglietto
Antonella Balassone
Nicolo Baldassini
François Barat
Henry Bardsley
Giulia Barone
Sonia Barone
Laura Bartolomei
Fabrizio Bartolomeo
Mario Bartylla
Christopher Bartz
Bruna Bassetti
Katy Bassière
Mario Bassignani
Sandro Battini
Roger Baumgarten
Paolo Beccio
Eva Belik
Antonio Belvedere
Annie Benzeno
Jan Berger
François Bertolero
Alessandro Bianchi
Giorgio Bianchi
Patrizia Bianchini
Gianfranco Biggi

Grégoire Bignier
Germana Binelli
Judy Bing
Rosella Biondo
Jean François Blassel
A Blassone
Paolo Bodega
Marko Bojovic
Willaim Boley
Sara Bonati
Manuela Bonino
Gilles Bontemps
Jeremy Boon
Gail Borden
Antonella Bordoni
Andrea Daaah
Pierre Botbeni
Isabelle Boudet
Mariolijne Boudry
Sandrine Boulay
Bret Bowin
Carola Brammen
Ross Brennan
Paolo Brescia
John Breshears
Gaëlle Breton
Flore Bringanid
Cristina Brizzolara
Cuno Brullmann
Giuseppe Bruzzone
Maurizio Bruzzone
Michael Burckhardt
Christiane Bürklein
Mary Byrne
Hans-Peter Bysaeth

Federica Caccavale
Alessandro Calafati
Chrystel Calafell
Benedetto Calcagno
Patrick Calleya
Maurizio Calosso
Michele Calvi
Stefan Camenzid
Nunzio Camerada
Daniele Campo
Florence Canal
Andrea Canepa
Stefania Canta
Vittorio Caponetto
Daniela Capuzzo
Alessandro Carisetto
Monica Carletti
Elena Carmignani
Isabella Carpiceci
Ibert Carreiragi
Emanuele Carreri
Mark Carroll

Elena Casali
Chiara Casazza
Marta Castagna
Cristina Catino
Maria Cattaneo
Enrica Causa
Dante Cavagna
Simone Cecchi
Giorgio Celadon
Ottaviano Celadon
Massimo Cella
Alessandro Cereda
Antoine Chaaya
Patricia Chappell
Patrick Charles
Jean Luc Chassais
Pierre Chatelain
Hubert Chataney
Ariel Chavela
Tina Chee
Laura Cherchi
Raimondo Chessa
Christopher Chevalier
Catherine Clarisse
Geoffrey Cohen
Franc Collet
Daniel Collin
Christophe Colson
Shelly Comer
Philippe Convercey
Pier Luigi Copat
Michel Corajoud
Colman Corish
Monica Corsilia
Ivan Corte
Giacomo Costa
Leopoldo Costa
Raffaella Costa
Loïc Couton
Rosa Coy
Paolo Crema
Maddalena Daimondi Croo
A Croxato
Mario Cucinella
Irene Cuppone
Catherine Cussoneau
Lorenzo Custer

Stefano D'Atri
Catherine D'Ovidio
Isabelle Da Costa
Thomas Damisch
Michel Dananco
Paul Darmer
Lorenzo Dasso
K Matthew Daubman
Mike Davies
Daniela Defilla
S Degli Innocenti

Andreas Degn
Silvia De Leo
Alessandro De Luca
Dahlia De Macina
Simona De Mattei
Alessio Demontis
Evelyne Delmoral
Michel Denancé
Olaf de Nooyer
Julien Descombes
Michel Desvigne
Laura Diaichelburg
Carmelo Di Bartolo
Ottavio Di Blasi
Hélène Diebold
Maddalena Di Sopra
Brian Ditchburn
Vittorio Di Turi
John Doggart
Olivier Doizy
Eugenio Donato
François Doria
Michael Dowd
Mike Downs
Klaus Dreissigacker
Delphine Drouin
Serge Drouin
Frank Dubbers
Giorgio Ducci
Paul Du Mesnil Du Buisson
Jean Luc Dupanloup
Philippe Dupont
Susanne Durr
John Dutton

Mick Eekhout
Craig Eigenberg
Stacy Eisenberg
Birgit Eistert
Ahmed El Jerari
Antonio Fammi Fammi
Lukas Epprecht
James Evans
Allison Ewing

Roberta Fambri
Roberto Faravelli
Giorgio Fascioli
Maxwell Fawcett
Monica Fea
David Felice
Alfonso Femia
Jacques Fendard
Ruben Prado Fernandez
Agostino Ferrari
Orietta Ferrero
Maurizio Filocca
Laurent Marc Fischer

Eileen Fitzgerald
Richard Fitgerald
Peter Flack
Johannes Florin
Renato Foni
M Fordam
Gilles Fourel
Sylvie Fradin
Gianfranco Franchini
Kenneth Fraser
Nina Freedman
Marian Frezza
Claudia Friederichs
Enrico Frigerio
Junya Fujita
Pierre Furnemont

Rinaldo Gaggero
Sergio Gaggero
Alain Gallissian
Andrea Gallo
Antonio Gallo
Carla Garbato
Robert Garlipp
Maurizio Garrasi
G Gasbarri
Angelo Ghiotto
M Giacomelli
Davide Gibelli
Alain Gillette
Sonia Giordani
Alberto Giordano
Roberto Giordano
Antonella Giovannoni
Giovanna Giusto
Marion Goerdt
Marco Goldschmied
Enrico Gollo
Anahita Golzari
Alessandro Gortan
Philippe Goubet
Emanuele Aroobummal
Robert Grace
Giorgio Grandi
Cecil Granger
Walter Grasmug
Vittorio Grassi
Don Gray
Nigel Greenhill
Magali Grenier
Daniele Grieco
Emilio Guazzone
Giovanni Guerrieri
Paolo Guerrini
Domenico Guerrisi
Alain Guèze
Barnaby Gunning
Ranjit Gupta

Antoine Hahne
Greg Hall
Donald L Hart
Thomas Hartman
Margrith Hartmann
Gunther Hastrich
Ulrike Hautsch
Adam Hayes
Christopher Hays
Eva Hegerl
Oliver Hempel
Pascal Hendier
Pierre Henneguier
Marie Henry
Gabriel Hernandez
Caroline Herrin
Christopher Hight
Kohji Hirano
Harry Hirsch
Andrew Holmes
Eric Holt
Abigal Hopkins
Masahiro Horie
Hélène Houizot
Michelle Howard
Bruno Hubert
Jean Huc
Ed Huckabi
Frank Hughes
Charles Hussey

Filippo Icardi
Frediano Iezzi
Akira Ikegami
Djénina Illoul
Luca Imberti
Paolo Insogna
Shunji Ishida

Charlotte Jackman
Angela Jackson
Tobias Jaklin
Robert Jan van Santen
Amanda Johnson
Andy Jonic
Luis Jose
Frédéric Joubert

Shin Kanoo
Jan Kaplicky
Elena Karitakis
Robert Keiser
Christopher Kelly
Paul Kelly
Werner Kestel
Irini Kilaiditi
Tetsuya Kimura
Laurent Koenig
Tomoko Komatsubara

Akira Komiyama
Misha Kramer
Jeff Krolicki
Eva Kruse
Betina Kurtz

Jean Baptiste Lacoudre
Antonio Lagorio
Simone Lampredi
Giovanna Langasco
Frank La Riviere
Stig Larsen
Denis La Ville
François La Ville
Christina Lee
Sojin Lee
Jean Lelay
Renata Lello
Claudia Leoncini
Laurent Le Voyer
Riccardo Librizzi
Olivier Lidon
Lorraine Lin
Bill Logan
Johanna Lohse
Federica Lombardo
François Lombardo
Steve Lopez
Riccardo Luccardini
Simonetta Lucci
Rolf Robert Ludwig
Claudine Luneberg
Massimiliano Lusetti

Paola Maggiora
Domenico Magnano
Nicholas Malby
Milena Mallamaci
Natalie Mallat
Claudio Manfreddo
Ester Manitto
Roberta Mantelli
Paolo Mantero
Flavio Marano
Andrea Marasso
Francesco Marconi
Massimo Mariani
Stefano Marrano
Alberto Marre Brunenghi
Cristina Martinelli
Luca Massone
Daniela Mastragostino
Manuela Mattei
William Matthews
Marie Hélène Maurette
Gian Mauro Maurizio
Caroline Mahon Maxwell
Kathrin Mayer
Ken McBryde

Katherine McLone
Grainne McMahon
Jonathan McNeal
Nayla Mecattaf
Simone Medio
Barbara Mehren
Roberto Melai
Mario Menzio
Eveline Mercier
Benny Merello
Gabriella Merlo
Peter Metz
Jean C M'Fouara
Daniela Miccolis
Marcella Michelotti
Paolo Migone
Edward Mijic
Sylvie Milanesi
Emanuela Minetti
Takeshi Miyazaki
Gianni Modolo
Sandro Montaldo
Elisa Monti
Julia Moser
Joost Moolhuijzen
Denise Morando
Nascimento
Gérard Mormina
Ingrid Morris
Jean Bernard Mothes
Farshid Moussavi
Mariette Müller
Philip Murphy
Andrea Musso

Hanne Nagel
Shinichi Nakaya
Hiroshi Naruse
Roberto Navarra
Pascale Nègre
Chi-Tam Nguyen
Andrew Nichols
Hiroko Nishikama
Susanne Lore Nobis
David Nock
Elizabeth Nodinot
Mojan Nouban
Marco Nouvion
Eric Novel
Koung Nyunt

Alphons Oberhoffer
Anna O'Carrol
Stefan Oehler
Noriaki Okabe
Antonella Oldani
Sonia Oldani
Grace Ong
Patrizia Orcamo

Stefania Orcamo
Roy Orengo
Carlos Osrej
Tim O'Sullivan
Piero Ottaggio
Mara Ottonello
Nedo Ottonello

Antonella Paci
Nicola Pacini
Carmelo Pafumi
Filippo Pagliani
Paik Joon
Michael Palmore
Roger Panduro
Giorgia Paraluppi
Chandra Patel
Pietro Pedrini
Roberto Pelagatti
Luigi Pellini
Danilo Peluffo
Gianluca Peluffo
Hembert Peñaranda
Lionel Pénisson
Mauro Penna
Patrizia Persia
Morten Busk Petersen
Claire Petetin
Gil Petit
Ronan Phelan
Paul Phillips
Alberto Piancastelli
Carlo Piano
Daniele Piano
Lia Piano
Matteo Piano
Mario Piazza
Enrico Piazze
Gennaro Picardi
Alessandro Pierandrei
Fabrizio Pierandrei
M Pietrasanta
Claudia Pigionanti
Marie Pimmel
Alessandro Pisacane
Sandra Planchez
Bernard Plattner
Monica Poggi
Jean Alexandre Polette
Andrea Polleri
Antonio Porcile
Roberta Possanzini
Fabio Postani
Tommaso Principi
Nicolas Prouvé
Costanza Puglisi
Sophie Purnama

Gianfranco QueiroloCristianna Raber
Michele Ras
Maria Cristina Rasero
Roberto Rasore
Dominique Rat
Neil Rawson
Judith Raymond
Antonella Recagno
Olaf Recktenwald
Philippe Reigner
Daniele Reimondo
Luis Renau
Bryan Reynolds
Tom Reynolds
Elena Ricciardi
Kieran Rice
Nemone Rice
Peter Rice
Marco Riceputi
Jean Yves Richard
Ophelia Richter
Christopher Robertson
Giuseppe Rocco
Richard Rogers
Renaud Rolland
Emilia Rossato
Paola Rossato
Stefano Rossi
Caroline Roux
Bernard Rouyer
Tammy Roy
Lucio Ruocco
Joachim Ruoff
Ken Rupard

Antonella Sacchi
Angela Sacco
Jean Gérard Saint
Riccardo Sala
Maria Salerno
Maurizio Santini
Francesca Santolini
Paulo Sanza
Carola Sapper
Paul Satchell
Alessandro Savioli
Susanna Scarabicchi
Maria Grazia Scavo
Stefan Schäfer
Helga Schlegel
Giuseppina Schmid
Caspar Schmidt-Morkramer
Jean François Schmit
Maren Schuessler
Andrea Schultz
C Segantini
Daniel Seibold

Ronnie Self
Barbara-Petra Sellwig
Patrik Senné
Giuseppe Senofonte
Anna Serra
Kelly Shannon
Randy Shields
Aki Shimizu
Madoka Shimuzu
Kirsten Siepmann
Alexander Simittchiev
Cécile Simon
David Simonetti
Thibaud Simonin
Alessandro Sinagra
Luca Siracusa
Jan Sircus
Alan Smith
Stephanie Smith
Franc Somner
Richard Soundy
Enrico Spicuglia
Claudette Spielmann
Susanne Stacher
Adrian Stadlmayer
Alan Stanton
Graham Stirk
Eric Stotts
David Summerfield
Jasmin Surti
Christian Susstrunk
Andreas Symietz

José Luis Taborda Barrientos
Stefano Tagliacarne
Hiroyuki Takahashi
Norio Takata
Noriko Takiguchi
Hélène Teboul
Anne Hélène Téménides
Carlo Teoldi
Peter Terbuchte
Brett Terperluk
G L Terragna
David Thom
John Thornhill
Cinzia Tiberti
Luigi Tirelli
Elisabeth Tisseur
Vittorio Tolu
Taichi Tomuro
Bruno Tonfoni
Graciella Torre
Laura Torre
Olivier Touraine
Franco Trad
Alessandro Traldi
Renata Trapani

Elisabetta Trezzani
Renzo Venanzio Truffelli
Maria Cristina Turco
Leland Turner
Mark Turpin

Yoshiko Ueno
Kiyomi Uezono
Paolo Ugona
Joong-Yeun Uhr Sim
Troy Uleman
Peter Ullathorne

Colette Valensi
Maurizio Vallino\
Ruddy Valverde
Kees Van Casteren
Harrie Van der Meijs
Mauritz Van der Staay
Michael Vaniscott
Antonia Van Oosten
Robert Jan Van Stanten
Arijan Van Timmeren
Boris Vapné
Maurizio Varratta
Paolo Varratta
Claudio Vaselli
William Vassal
Francesca Vattuone
Bernard Vaudeville
Martin Veith
Maria Veltcheva
Reiner Verbizh
Laura Vercelli
Maria Carla Verdona
Eric Verstrepen
Silvia Vignale
Antonella Vignoli
Mark Viktov
Alain Vincent
Paul Vincent
Patrick Virly
Marco Visconti
Lorenzo Viti
Bettina Volz
Erik Volz
Philippe Von Matt

Louis Waddell
Jean Marc Weill
Florian Wenz
Nicole Westermann
Nicolas Westphal
Frank Wiemann
Chris Wilkinson
Neil Winder
Martin Wollensak
Jacob Woltjer
Sarah Wong

George Xydis

Masami Yamada
Sugako Yamada
Hiroshi Yamaguchi
Tatsuya Yamaguchi
Emi Yoshimura
John Young

Gianpaolo Zaccaria
Kenneth Endrich Zammit
Lorenzo Zamperetti
Antonio Zanuso
Martina Zappettini
Walter Zbinden
Maurizio Zepponi
Massimo Zero
Alessandro Zoppini
Ivana Zunino

Bibliography

Complete bibliographies of books and monographic issues of journals are listed below. The articles list dates from the beginning of 1997 – for a more complete articles bibliography it should be read in conjunction with volumes one, two and three.

Books

Piano, R, Arduino, M, Fazio, M *Antico è Bello*, Rome/Bari, Laterza, 1980

Donin, G *Renzo Piano, Piece by Piece*, Rome, Casa del Libro Editrice, 1982

Dini, M *Renzo Piano, Projects and Buildings 1964–1983*, London, Electa/Architectural Press, 1984

Nono, L *Verso Prometeo*, Venice, La Biennale/Ricordi Editori, 1984

Piano, R *Chantier Ouvert au Public*, Paris, Arthaud Editeur, 1985

Piano, R *Dialoghi di Cantiere*, Bari, Laterza Editrice, 1986

Piano, R and Rogers, R *Du Plateau Beaubourg au Centre Georges Pompidou*, Paris, Editions du Centre Georges Pompidou, 1987

Renzo Piano, Il Nuovo Stadio di Bari Milan, Edizione l'Archivolto, 1990

Renzo Piano, Buildings and Projects 1971–89 New York, Rizzoli, 1990

Exhibit Design: Renzo Piano Building Workshop Milan, Libra Immagine, 1992

Renzo Piano, progetti e architetture, Vol 3, 1987–94 Milan, Electa, 1994 (English edition by Birkhäuser, Basel, 1994; German edition by D V A, Stuttgart, 1994)

The Making of Kansai International Airport, Osaka, Japan: Renzo Piano Building Workshop Tokyo, Kodansha, 1994, by Renzo Piano Building Workshop

Gardin, G B *Foto Piano*, Peliti Associati, Roma 1996

Piano, R *Giornale di bordo*, Passigli ed., Firenze, 1997 (German edition, *Logbuch*, by Hatje Cantz Verlag, 1997; English edition, *The Renzo Piano Logbook*, by Thames and Hudson, London, 1997; French edition, *Carnet de travail*, by Le Seuil, Paris, 1997; American edition, *The Renzo Piano Logbook*, by Monacelli Press, New York, 1997; Japanese edition by Toto, Tokyo, 1998)

Bordaz, R *Entretiens avec Renzo Piano*, Paris, Cercle d'art, 1997

Renzo Piano – Fondation Beyeler: Une maison de l'art Birkhaüser, Basel, 1998

Blaser, W *Renzo Piano Building Workshop – Museum Beyeler*, Benteli Verlag, Bern, 1998 (French/English edition)

Monographic issues of journals

Japan Architect No 15, Autumn 1994: *Kansai International Airport Passenger Terminal Building*

Architectural Review November 1994: *Kansai* (Special issue edited and written by P Buchanan)

Process Architecture December 1994: *Kansai International Airport Passenger Terminal Building*

Articles

1997

GA Document International 97 No 51 1997, pp82–3: 'Renzo Piano, Beyeler Foundation Museum' by R Piano

Arrivederci January 1997, pp74–8: 'Gli architetti della cultura globale' by V Cappelli

Carnet January 1997, pp142–9: 'Un piano per la musica' by F Sironi

Casabella February 1997, pp34–7: 'Renzo Piano: Vent'anni di progetti e realizzazioni di architettura' by S Polano

Architectural Record March 1997, pp42–53: 'Project Diary: Lingotto Factory Rehabilitation, Turin, Italy by C Pearson

Bauwelt March 1997, pp530–3: 'Das andere Atelier Brancusi'

Design Report March 1997, pp46–53: 'Piazza mit Rennbahn und Heliport' by J Goetz

World Architecture March 1997, pp66–71: 'Building Blocks' by S Brandolini

Architecture April 1997, pp77–9: 'Brancusi's new studio' by P Buchanan

Domus Dossier April 1997, pp34–5: 'Renzo Piano, Alexander Calder, una retrospettiva' by R Piano

De Architect May 1997, pp56–9: 'Formele aanzet conflicteert met contextuele uitwerking Science and Technology Center New Metropolis in Amsterdam van Renzo Piano' by D Wondt

Modulo May 1997, pp400–402: 'Suono e rumore del lamellare' by F Laner

Journal de la Construction de la Suisse Romande June 1997, pp36–8: 'Le Lingotto: Pionnier dans la Ville'

Techniques & Architecture June 1997, pp48–52: 'Renaissance Transformation du Lingotto, Turin, Italien' by JFP

Archis July 1997, pp8–17: 'Renzo Piano, New Metropolis in Amsterdam' by A Wortmann

233

Architecture August 1997, pp49–53: 'Modern-Day Medici'

Building August 1997, pp36–40: 'Buoy wonder. Renzo Piano' ship-shaped museum' by M Spring

Mercedes August 1997, pp16–21: 'New Metropolis: la scienza esplode nel buio' by C Garbato

RIBA Journal August 1997, pp18–9: 'Jolly green giant' by J Welsh

Terasrakenne August 1997, pp26–7: 'Kansain kansainvalisen lentokentan matkustajaterminaali, Osaka, Japan'

Aquapolis September 1997, pp 6–13: 'Kansai International Airport. Creation of an Airport on the sea' by K Mikanagi

Architecture September 1997, pp128–35: 'Ship Shape' by P Buchanan

Architecture Interieure Crée September 1997, pp78–81: 'Piano se fait une toile, avec fluos' by G Ehret

Bell'Europa September 1997, pp120–7: 'Amsterdam vista da un altro Piano' by G Mariotti

DBZ September 1997, pp24: 'Was Zukunft ist'

ADA (Associate Danske Arkitecter) October 1997, pp14–8: 'Drommen om skonhed by F I H Nielsen

Architectural Digest October 1997, pp91–106: 'Renzo Piano's Fondation Beyeler' by M F Schmertz

Bauwelt October 1997, pp272–9: 'Museum vor Parklandschaft' by A Compagno

De Architect October 1997, pp30–3: 'San Nicola Stadion van Renzo Piano in Bari' by P Buchanan

Fassade October 1997, pp15–20: 'Potsdamer Berlin-Fassadenkonstruktionen zwischen Histoire, Begegnung und Energetic' by T Lodel

Fassade October 1997, pp5–11: 'Renzo Piano Building Workshop' by A Compagno; pp90–101: 'New Metropolis Science and Technology Centre, Amsterdam' by R Ingersoll

Korean Architects October 1997, pp150–5: 'Auditorium, Rome'; pp76–89: 'Beyeler Foundation, Basel'; pp102–7: 'Brancusi Atelier, Pompidou Center, Paris'; pp138–41: 'Lodi Bank'; pp108–19: 'Lyon International Center'; pp132–7: 'Jean-Marie Tjibaou Center, New Caledonia'; pp142–9: 'Padre Pio Church, Foggia'; pp120–31: 'Renzo Piano Building Workshop and Unesco Laboratory, Vesima' by R Ingersoll

Ottagono October 1997, pp110–3: 'Atelier Brancusi a Parigi' by R Piano

Space Design October 1997, pp73–7: 'Laboratory Unesco & Workshop'

VFA Profil October 1997, pp 22–6: 'NewMetropolis' by R Uhde

Architecture Intérieur Crée November 1997, pp114–5: 'La Fondation Beyeler à Basle'; pp120–1: 'Chronique d'une révolution annoncée' by J P Ménard

Architektur Aktuell November 1997, pp58–71: 'Kein Museum wie andere' by S Loffler

Beaux Arts Magazine November 1997, pp94–100: 'Ernst Beyeler-Suisse et Discret' by I Wavrin

Connaissance des Arts November 1997, pp55–9: 'Beyeler – Luxe, calme et volupté' by P J

De Architect November 1997, pp26–9: 'Ushibuka Brug in Kumamoto' by P Buchanan

Domus November 1997, pp54–60: 'Museo della fondazione Beyeler, Riehen, Basilea' by M Bruderlin

Finestra November 1997, pp135–7: 'Il nuovo Lingotto: un progetto solare'

Il Giornale Dell'Arte Vernissage Suppl. November 1997: 'Gil straordinari "invenduti" di Ernst Beyeler'

Moebel Interior Design November 1997, pp51–4: 'Hochleistung und Understatement' by U Buttner

Nikkei Architecture November 1997, pp56–61: 'Ushibuka Haiya Bridge'

ARCA December 1997, pp48–53: 'Un cuneo nel cielo' by E Ossino

Architektura & Biznes December 1997, pp12–7: 'Druga fala rewolucji' by M M Kolakowski

Detail December 1997, pp1383–9: 'Stahlbetonkonstruktionen im erneuerten Reichstagsgebäude in Berlin' by R Fink

Ottagono December 1997, pp42–4: 'Renzo Piano, Auditorium, Roma' by R Piano

Architectural Review December 1997, pp54–8: 'Titanic Triumph' by P Buchanan; pp59–62: 'Pastoral Pavilion' by R Ryan

Ufficio Stile January–December 1997, pp34–7: 'Alta tecnologia e flessibilità spaziale' by S Falcieri

GQ February–March 1997, pp110–5: 'Aeropuerto 2001' by D Cohn

Techniques & Architecture April–May 1997, pp80–3: 'Beaubourg a 20 ans' by C Sabbah

Abitare July–August 1997, pp107–17: 'Renzo Piano and Amsterdam New Metropolis' by F Irace

Architectura Viva July–August 1997, pp86–91: 'Una proa encallada' by R Piano

Architectural Digest October–November 1997, pp54–8: 'Nobles Geschenk in uraltem Stein' by A Gonzales

Detail October–November 1997, pp1100–1: 'Metropolis Museum Amsterdam'

Arquitectura Viva November–December 1997, pp23: 'Los grandes proyectos' and 'Roma, entre el passado y el futuro' by A Munoz; p7: 'Renzo Piano en Suiza: la Fundacion Beyeler'; pp42–5: 'Discreta vitrina' by R Piano

1998

Architectural Review January 1998, pp34–43: 'Potsdamer Preview' by P Davey

Artnews January 1998, pp108–11: 'Ernst Beyeler's Dream Museum' by M Krienke

Lotus January 1998, pp6–21: 'Surrealismo urbano: una scatola verde nella baia di Amsterdam' by A Rocca

DBZ January 1998, pp43–8: 'Kunst im Park' by C Froschi

Bauwelt January 1998, pp164–5: 'Nur ein gruner Hungel' by K G

Architectural Review September 1998, pp79–81: 'Solid and void' by P McGuire

A+U February 1998, pp76–91: 'Science and Technology Museum "newMetropolis"' by N Yamamoto; pp92–103: 'Beyeler Foundation Museum'; pp104–25: 'Debis Building – Potsdamer Platz Reconstruction' by R Piano

Bouw Detail No1 1998, pp30–7: 'Complexe geometrie bepaalt detaillering'

GA Document No55 1998, pp50–9: 'Beyeler Foundation Museum'

Arquitectura Viva September 1998, pp46–57: 'Un invernadero para el arte: Coleccion Beyeler, Basilea' by R Ingersoll

Artnews January 1998, pp108–11: 'Ernst Beyeler's Dream Museum' by M Krienke

Bauwelt January 1998, pp164–5: 'Nur ein gruner Hungel' by K G

DBZ January 1998, pp43–8: 'Kunst im Park' by C Froschl

L'Industria Delle Costruzioni January 1998, pp4–13: 'Il Museo NewMetropolis ad Amsterdam' by M Galletta

Lotus January 1998, pp6–21: 'Surrealismo urbano: una scatola verde nella baia di Amsterdam' by A Rocca

Architectural Review January 1998, pp34–43: 'Potsdamer Preview' by P Davey

AMC le Moniteur Architecture February 1998, pp21–7: 'Musée de la Foundation Beyeler' by G Davoine

Archis February 1998, pp59–61: 'Prestige & diversion, grands projets in Japan' by C Hein

AMC le Moniteur Architecture March 1998, pp84–5: 'Basle, Musée Beyeler'; pp82–3: 'Houston, Musée de Menil'

Architettura Svizzera March 1998, pp27–30: 'Museum Fondation Beyeler 4125 Riehen'

Arquitectura Viva March 1998, pp69–71: 'Ars longa, vita brevis Dominique de Menil, 1908–17' by S Fox; pp69–71: 'La oreja alada Renzo Piano, premio Pritzker' by R Ingersoll

Bauwelt March 1998, pp536–41: 'Debis-Zentrale am Potsdamer Platz' by N Hirsch

Werk, Bauen + Wohnen March 1998, pp26–9: 'Umbau von "Lingotto" in ein Kulturund Geschäftszentrum' by P Fumagalli

ARCA April 1998, pp46–51: 'Contnitore e contenuto Cy Twombly Annex to the Menil Collection' by M A Arnaboldi

Architectural Review Australia April 1998, pp60–7: 'Phoenix' by S Smith

Detail April 1998, pp381–97: 'Museum of Art in Basel'

Techiques & Arquitecture April 1998, pp10–13: 'Infrasculpture Musée national de la science et de la technologie, Amsterdam' by MCL

Abitare May 1998, pp155–61: 'Centro Culturale Jean-Marie Tjibaou' by F Irace

Architectural Record May 1998, pp160–9: 'Beyeler Museum, Basel, Switzerland' by J Russell

Bauwelt May 1998, pp964–9: 'Streng Heheim, viel Licht'

234

Casabella May 1998, pp74–81: 'Ricostruzione della Potsdamer Platz, Berlino'; pp66–71: 'Museo della Fondazione Beyeler, Riehen, Basilea'; pp72–3: 'Padiglione Cy Twombly, Menil Collection, Houston'; pp82–3: 'Galleria del vento Ferrari, Maranello Moderna'; pp62–5: 'Lovigato artificiosità'; pp82–3: 'Torre per uffici e residenze, Sydney' by C Conforti

RIBA Journal International May 1998, pp4–5: 'Building of the month: Renzo Piano's Tjibaou Cultural Centre in New Caledonia' by J Welsh

Alluminio E Architettura June 1998, pp32–51: 'Genova: il porto antico-L'acquario-La città dei bambini-La scatola cinematografica' by Santolini

Architectural Record June 1998, pp31–4: 'An ambitious mayor and major plans for the Millennium are making the Eternal City a hotbed of design' by I Steingut

DBZ June 1998, pp39–46: 'Auf die Fein Linie Gebracht' by R Kohler

Bauwelt July 1998, pp1556–3: 'Gepentisches Gebalk' by E Roux

Formes et Structures July 1998, pp32–8: 'Centre culturel Jean-Marie Tjibaou'

A+U August 1998, pp80–111: 'Renzo Piano Building Workshop Cultural Centre Jean-Marie Tjibaou' by R Miyake

AIT August 1998, pp38–43: 'Natur-parcours Kuturzentrum Jean-Marie Tjibaou in Neukaledonien' by D I

Approach August 1998, pp3–19: 'Link between Nature and Culture Tjibaou Cultural Centre in New Caledonia' by R Miyake

Arquitectura y Ambiente August 1998, pp21–9: 'Renzo Piano en Nueva Caledonia' by A Zabalbeascoa

Il Nuovo Cantiere August 1998, pp42–53: 'La ricostruzione del settore Daimler-Benz a Berlino' by M Nastri

Abitare September 1998, pp151–9: 'Renzo Piano presso Basilea Fondation Beyeler' by M G Zunino; pp151–9: 'Renzo Piano' by R Piano

Der Architekt September 1998, pp498–501: 'Einheit und Variation' by M Remmile

Domus September 1998, pp52–3: 'Prouvé inventore: 32 brevetti' by F Picchi

Il Nuovo Cantiere September 1998, pp54–7: 'Il laterizio nei sistemi di facciata' by I Oberti

L'Empreinte September 1998, pp29–34: 'Grandeure et Urbanite' by F Accorsi

Tegl September 1998, pp8–12: 'Sprodt som kiks – stort som et hus' by S Ulrik

The Architectural Review September 1998, pp79–81: 'Solid and void' by P McGuire

AMC le Moniteur Architecture October 1998, pp86–7: 'Berlin Siège de Daimler Benz'

Architecture October 1998, pp96–105, 152–6: 'Piano nobile' by L R Finfley

Art – Das Kunstmagazin October 1998, pp40–3: 'Was fehlt, sind zeit und phantasie'; by P M Bode

El Croquis October 1998, pp48–59: 'Museo de la fundacion Beyeler'; pp60–83: 'Centro Cultural Jean-Marie Tjibaou'

Finestra October 1998, pp109–12: 'Ragnatela Ecologica' by M Giabardo

L'Architetto October 1998, pp13–15: 'Renzo Piano a Washington. Architettua Mestiere di Frontiera'

Ambiente November 1998, pp66–7: 'Un premio para Renzo Piano'

Building Design November 1998, pp10–15: 'Goodbye to Berlin?'

De Architect Dossier 7 November 1998, pp30–3: 'Kansai International Airport, Renzo Piano Building Workshop'

Häuser November 1998, pp51–62: 'Wo der Wind sein lied singt' by I Maisch

Les Cahiers Techniques du Bâtiment November 1998: 'Dix coques mixtes resistant a V P des vents de 250 KM/H'

AIT January–December 1998, pp21: '110 Meter Kunst am Stuck'

Architecture Australia January–December 1998, pp42–7: 'Piano forte'

Architettura del Paesaggio December 1998, pp23–7: 'Paesaggio e architettura – Il Centro Culturale Jean-Marie Tjibaou, Nouméa, Nouva Caledonia' by O Gambardella

Arquitectura Viva January–December 1998, pp56–9: 'La Espiral de Piedra'

Art – Das Kunstmagazin December 1998, pp12–23: 'High-tech und die Liebe zu wind und wellen' by P M Bode

Baumeister December 1998, pp41–57: 'Potsdamer Platz'

Domus December 1998, pp44–9: 'Strumenti per la tavola e per cuocere' by M C Tommasini

Licht & Architektur (DBZ) December 1998, pp33–7: 'Ein Mercedes unter den Events' by K M Rosansky

Nikkei Architecture December 1998, pp72–105: 'Potsdamer Platz'

Projekt December 1998, pp5, 79–80: 'Prestiznu – Pritzkerovu Cenu Za Architekturu' by S Moody

Schweizer Ingenieur und Architekt December 1998, pp27–33: 'Piano/Kohlbecker in Berlin' by J Tietz

Architecture Review December 1998, pp30–6: 'Sea and sky' by S McInstry

Japan Architect December 1998, pp100: 'Ushibuka Haiya-Bridge'

Werk Bauen + Wohnen December 1998, pp16–23: 'Die Veranstaltung von Stadt' by D Hoffmann-Axthelm

Detail April–May 1998, pp434: 'Patina ab Werk'; pp381–6: 'Kunstmuseum in Basel'; pp378–80: 'Bankgebäude in Lodi, Italien'

Système Solaires May–June 1998, pp3–5: 'Renzo Piano, un architecte sous l'influence des climats' by J P Menard

Costruzioni July–August 1998, pp92–4: 'Puntelli per archi'

Domus July–August 1998, pp7: 'Renzo Piano il Pritzker Architecture Prize 1998' by G Macchi

Finestra July–August 1998, pp142–6: 'La Bolla trasparente' by M Giabardo

L'Architettura July–August 1998, pp414–26: 'Centro Culturale Jean-Marie Tjibaou, Nouméa, Nouva Caledonia' by R Piano

Presenza Tecnica July–August 1998, pp19–32: 'La Banca di Renzo Piano'; pp74–81: 'Pritzker Architecture Prize 1998: Renzo Piano reinventa l'architettura'

Techniques & Architecture August–September 1998, pp438–9: 'Modestie et ambition' by J P Dantec

Inarcassa July–September 1998, pp63–7: 'Renzo Piano non sono Brunelleschi, ma Robinson Crusoe' by C Corradi

Arquitectura Viva September–October 1998, pp44–51: 'La catedral fragil' by F Chaslin

Costruire in Laterizio September–October 1998, pp352–60: 'Permanenza e temporaneità del costruire in una prospettiva sostenibile' by R Bologna

OFX September–October 1998, pp46–61: 'Pots-Daimler (Benz) Platz' by C Gavinelli

Architektur Freizeit October–November 1998, pp24–9: 'Baustelle zwischen zwei Kulturen'

Arquitectura Viva November–December 1998, pp70–1: 'Vuelta all'orden – Renovacion del Centro Pompidou de Paris' by J C Garcias

Arte y Cemento November–December 1998, pp86–93: 'Renzo Piano Premio Pritzker Prize do Architectura '98'

Industrie Bau November–December 1998, pp76–9: 'Eine Ideen-Fabrik fur die Autos der Zukunft' by J Horschig

L'Architettura November–December 1998, pp625–41: 'Potsdamer Platz, Berlin' by R Piano

Leonardo November–December 1998, pp14–9: 'Kulturzentrum J M Tjibaou poesie des pazifiks' by R Uhde

1999

Arquitectura Viva No75–6 1999, pp200–201: 'Anuario ESPANA 1999 Pianoforte'

Contact 1999, pp4–8: 'Le nouveau centre se trouve à Berlin'

Finestra Brasil No16 1999, pp65–71: 'Em simbiose com a natureza' by M B de Castro

GA Document No58 1999, pp84–7: 'Renzo Piano – 88 Phillip St Office Tower & 155 Macquarie St Residential building'

UME University of Melbourne 9 No 9 1999, pp36–49: 'Concert halls Flaminio District, Rome Contextual Piano' by P Tombesi

Arkinka January 1999, pp42–7: 'La arquitectura se hace imperfecta permanentemente'; pp16–27: 'La arquitectura se hace imperfecta permanentemente'; pp48–59: 'La arquitectura se hace imperfecta permanentemente'; pp60–9: 'La arquitectura se hace imperfecta permanentemente'; pp16–27: 'La arquitectura se hace imperfecta permanentemente'; pp30–8: 'La arquitectura se hace imperfecta permanentemente' by F C LLosa

Intelligente Architektur January 1999, pp24–9: 'Ideenwerkstatt Daimler-Ben-Design-Center in Sindelfingen' by van J R Krause

Lotus January 1999, pp32–51: 'Oltre la tecnica' by A Rocca

Architectural Review January 1999, pp28–42: 'Building Berlino' by P Davey

Architektur Intelligente Hullen March 1999, pp62–7: 'Zwischen irdischer Keramik, spharischen Geometrien und filigranen Fischbauchen'

De Architect March 1999, pp57–61: 'Architectionische interpretatie van een culturele verbintenis' by S McInstry

Harvard Design Magazine March 1999, pp22–5: 'Toward an Architecture of Humility' by J Pallasmaa

235

L'Arca April 1999, pp4–11: 'Cognitivo e conoscitivo Debis Haus, Berlin' by M A Arnaboldi

Techniques & Architecture La Pierre April 1999, pp90–3: 'La lumière du porphyre'

Architektura Murator May 1999, pp14–21: 'Museum ogrodzie'

Arte y Cemento May 1999, pp100–7: 'Centro Cultural Tjibaou, la ultima gran obra de Renzo Piano'

Domus May 1999, pp20–35: 'La ricostruzione di Potsdamer Platz, Berlino' by G Zohlen

L'Arca (+L'Arca International) May 1999, pp40–7: 'Il vecchio, il nuovo e la memoria. La Banca Popolare di Lodi (passé, présent et memoire. Banca Popolare di Lodi)' by M B Giordano

Monument – Architecture/Design May 1999, pp59–63: 'Tradition and Modernity' by P McGillick

Structural Engineering International May 1999, pp86–7: 'Glass Roof for a bank in Lodi, Italy' by G Corvaja

Aquapolis June 1999, pp22–31: 'Supporting Actions. The case of new Metropolis in Amsterdam' by J M Bradburne

Costruire June 1999, pp124–7: 'Archi di fede' by V Travi

The ARUP Journal June 1999, pp26–9: 'Kanak Cultural Centre, Nouméa, New Caledonia' by M Banfi, A Guthrie

Ambiente September 1999: 'Amsterdam desde otro Piano'

Arredamento – Mimarlik September 1999, pp124–6: 'Rivista turca, in turco …' by N Sonmez

Fassade September1999, pp27–31: 'La bolla – Konferenz-raum aus glas' by A Compagno

L'Arcaplus September 1999, pp34–9: 'Nuove stazzioni urbane' by G Muratore

Casabella October 1999: 'Concorso di architettura "Nuovi segni"'

DB Deustche Beseitung October 1999, pp22–3: 'Fast so gross wie Sankt Peter' by C Haberlik

Architecture Intérieure Crée November 1999, pp78–83: 'Le chemin ténu de l'architecture: Hotel Hilton' by G Ehret

Architektura Murator November 1999, pp35–41: 'Architecktura jako ewolucja' by P Buchanan

L'Architecture D'Aujourd'Hui December 1999, pp56: 'Expressionistes. Renzo Piano Building Workshop. Centre Culturel J M Tjibaou'; pp56: 'Eclairaged de liex publics. Luminaires suspendus de Renzo Piano et Alvaro Siza'

Telema December 1999, pp27–32: 'La tecnologia è un grande aiuto ma io progetto sempre con le idee' by D Seta

International Multisala February–March 1999, pp35–51: 'Berlino – Potsdamer Platz l'Imax di Renzo Piano' by M Daro and E Wegerhoff; pp36–8: 'Due piazze di fine millennio' by M Darò; pp43–51: 'Recent Revival' by E Wegerhoff

Area March–April 1999, pp24–37: 'Centro Culturale Tjibaou, Nouméa, Nouva Celdonia' by N Flora

Architectural Digest April–May 1999, pp33: '"Ein Haus soll singen" Ansichten eines Poeten der Architektur: Renzo Piano über die Gebäude der Zukunft'

Presenza Tecnica May–June 1999, pp6–12: 'L'eterno qui e' di casa' by S Bigliardi

AMC Le Moniteur Architecture June–July 1999, pp152: 'Berlin Imax, Renzo Piano'

Monument Architecture & Design July–August 1999, pp34–9: 'Renzo Piano' by H Dokulil

World Architecture July–August 1999, pp91–3: 'Spirit of the age'

AR – Bimestrale Dell'Ordine Degli Architetti September–October 1999, pp10–24: 'V Congresso Nazionale degli Architetti a Torino'

Costruire in Laterizio September–October 1999: 'Progetto e costruzione' by M C Torricelli

Techniques et Architecture Technical Thinking October–November 1999, pp69–75: 'Construire une émotion' by JFP

Chiesa Oggi No39 2000, pp42–5: 'L'arcata del 2000' by G Grasso

Archis January 2000, p33: 'Power and Powerlessness – The plans to redevelop the Renault grounds in Paris' by P Uyttenhove

Bauwelt January 2000, pp26–31: 'Pompidou 2000' by F Chaslin

Connaissance des Arts January 2000, pp46–7: 'Piano, fortissimo'

Quaderni di Arts January 2000, pp76–90: 'Musei e città Museo' by P Ciorra

Architectural Review January 2000, pp56–9: 'Toroid affair' by V Gore

Bauwelt February 2000, pp2–3: 'Piano entrift Paul-Klee-Zentrum' by Hubertus Adam

World Architecture February 2000, p64: 'The second coming' by A Mornement

236

238

Photographic credits

All line drawings of projects are the copyright of the Renzo Piano Building Workshop.

(Page references are followed by figure numbers)

Aerophoto-Schipol B.V/©RPBW: p37; p39, 6; p38, 2.

Ove Arup & Partners: p127, 6.

©Sylvio Borcout C.N.A.C: p32, 2; p33, 6, 7.

©Gianni Berengo Gardin: p14, 1; p40, 1, 3, 5; p66, 1, 2, 3, 4, 5, 7, 8; p129, 11, 12, 13, 14, 15; p130, 1, 2; p135, 6; p141, 9, 10; p164, 1, 2, 3; p178, 1, 3; p188, 1; p192, 2.

Niggi Bräuning:p10, 2; p58, 2; p60/1; p68, 1; p75, 4; p58, 1.

Fondation Beyeler: p64, 1.

©RPBW/Enrico Cano: p13, 4, 5, 6; p14, 2; p137; p138, 1, 2; p140, 2, 4; p141, 5, 11; p142; p143, 4; p144, 5, 6; p145; p147, 4; pp148/149; p151, 3; p152, 1, 3; p153, 5; p161, 1, 2; p166, 6, 7, 0; p167; p168; p170, 2; p171, 5; p172, 3; p189, 6; p200, 1; p201, 5; p202; p211, 7; p150, 1.

©S Conta: p80, 1, 2.

©RPBW/Loïc Couton: p59, 4.

©RPBW/Michel Denancé: p4; p8, 2, 3; p10, 1; p25; p27, 4, 5, 6, 7, 8; p28; p30, 1, 2, 4, 5, 6; p31, 7, 8, 9, 10; p32, 1; p33, 4, 5; p34, 1, 4, 5; p35, 6; p39, 7; pp42/3; p44, 1; p45, 6; p46, 1; p48, 2; p49, 6; p51, 4; p55, 1, 2; p57; p59, 6; p62, 1, 2, 3; p63, 4, 5, 6; p65, 5, 6; p67; p68, 2, 3; p69, 5, 6, 7; p73; p74; p75, 3; p76, 1; p77, 3, 4; p80, 3; p81, 4; p82; p93, 4; 170, 1, 2; p178, 4; p188, 2; p215.

Thomas Dix: p72, 2; pp78/9.

© Edition du Pacifique: M Follo/C. Rives: p89, 10.

M Follo/C Rives; p89, 7, 10.

G Giansanti©Centro Documentae Ferrari: p121, 7, 8, 9, 10.

©RPBW/S Goldberg/Publifoto: p12, 1, 2; p120, 1; p122, 1, 2, 3, 4, 7; p123, 8.

©RPBW/John Gollings: p7; p10, 3; p11, 4; p92, 1; p94, 1, 2, 3, 4; p95; p97, 4; p99, 8; p105, 4, 5, 6; p106, 4; p111; p114, 1, 3, 5; p115, 4; pp116/117.

©Tim Griffith/ESTO: pp102/103.

©RPBW/Peter Horn: p125; p126, 1; p131, 10; p132, 1, 2, 6; p133, 8, 10, 11, 12; p134, 3; p135, 5.

©RPBWShunji Ushida: p88, 5; p127, 5; p130, 4, 5; p139, 4; p140, 1; p141, 6, 7; p144, 1; p222, 1; p226, 1; p227, 4, 6; p228, 3, 4, 7; p229, 10, 11.

©Yuki Kameda: p20, 1.

©RPBW/C Kelly: p228, 1, 2

Teo Krijgsman: p48, 5.

Maeda: p22, 1, 2, 4, 5, 6; p23, 7, 9.

W Matheus: p66, 9.

H Van Der Meijs: p41, 6, 9, 10; p44, 2, 3, 4.

©Mercedes Bema: p132, 5.

Joost Moohluijzen: p219, 11, 12, 13, 14.

Shigeyuki Morishita: p92, 2; p114, 4.

©Vincent Mosch: p14, 3; p15, 4, 5, 6, 7; p165, 5, 6; pp166/167; p169, 2, 3; p171, 4, 10; p172, 1, 2; p173, 4; p174, 2; p175; p176, 3; p177, 4, 5; p179; pp180/181; p182, 1, 2, 3; p183; p184, 1; p185, 4; p186, 1; p187, 4, 5; p189, 5, 7; p190, 1, 4; p191, 8; p192, 1; p193, 3, 4, 5, 6, 7; p194, 1, 2, 3; p195; pp196/197; p198, 1, 2; p199; p200, 2; p201, 6; p203, 5; p204, 1, 2; p205; p206, 1, 2, 3; p207, 5; pp208/209; p210, 1; pp212–213.

©newMetropolis Museum: p52, 1, 2, 3, 4, 5; p53, 6.

©O De Nooyer: p53, 7, 8, 9.

©RPBW/Noriaki Okabe: p21, 5, 6, 7, 8.

©RPBW Archive: p38, 1.

©RPBW/P A Pantz: p11, 7; p87; p90/1; p98, 2, 3, 4, 5; p99, 6, 7, 9; p100, 1.

©RPBW/H Peñaranda: p40, 2.

©RPBW: p89, 9; p166, 3.

©RPBW/Bernard Plattner: p188, 3.

©Centre Pompidou: p26, 2; p29, 3, 4, 5.

©RPBW/Publifoto: p128, 2, 3, 4; p221; p223, 8; p225, 13.

©Publifoto/S Goldberg: p119, 2.

©Christian Richters: pp70/1; pp84/5; p92, 3.

©RPBW/L Ross: p227, 5.

©Hans Schlaupp/Architekturphoto: p112, 1; pp108/109

©Lu Seeber: p9, 4, 5, 6.

©Shinkenchiku-sha: p8, 1; p11, 5; p19.

Tanaka: p20.

©Unifor Foto/Mario Carrieri: p126, 4; p130, 9; p134, 1.

©Unifor Foto/G Basilico: p 154, 4; p155, 8.

©RPBW/William Vassal: p88, 1, 2, 3; p89, 6, 8; p97, 6, 7; p98, 1; p99, 10; p100, 2, 3, 4, 5, 6, 7; p101, 8, 9; p105, 3; p106, 2, 6; p107, 9, 11, 12, 13, 14.

239

Renzo Piano Building Workshop